Karen Anderson • Peter Blundell
Lynda Fitzmaurice • Richard McGill

Edexcel Diploma

Information Technology

Level 2 Higher Diploma

A PEARSON COMPANY

Heinemann is an imprint of Pearson Education Limited, a company incorporated in England and Wales, having its registered office at Edinburgh Gate, Harlow, Essex, CM20 2JE. Registered company number: 872828

www.heinemann.co.uk

Heinemann is a registered trademark of Pearson Education Limited

Text © Pearson Education Limited 2008

First published 2008

12 11 10 09 08
10 9 8 7 6 5 4 3 2 1

British Library Cataloguing in Publication Data is available from the British Library on request.

ISBN 978 0 435471 64 4

Edited by Alex Sharpe

Typeset by Tek-Art, Croydon, Surrey

Original illustrations © Pearson Education Ltd 2008

Illustrated by Zooid

Cover design by Siu Hang Wong

Cover photo/illustration © iStockPhotos

Printed in the UK by Scotprint

Websites
There are links to relevant websites in this book. In order to ensure that the links are up to date, that the links work, and that the sites are not inadvertently linked to sites that could be considered offensive, we have made the links available on the Heinemann website at www.heinemann.co.uk/hotlinks. When you access the site, the express code is 1644P.

Contents

Credits

Acknowledgements

Screenshots
The author and publisher would like to thank the following individuals and organisations for permission to reproduce screenshots:

Adobe product screen shots reprinted with permission from Adobe Systems Incorporated.
Apple product screen shots reprinted with permission from Apple.
Crown copyright material reproduced with permission of the Controller of Her Majesty's Stationery Office and the Queen's Printer for Scotland.
Microsoft product screenshots reprinted with permission from Microsoft Corporation.
SkySports screenshot reprinted with permission from BSkyB.

Photographs
The author and publisher would like to thank the following individuals and organisations for permission to reproduce photographs:

istockPhoto/Konstantin Inozemtsev p 112
istockPhoto/Thaddeus Robertson p 127
Andy Spain/Alamy p 127
Richard Cooke/Alamy p 127
Benetton p 133
Blutgruppe/Zefa/Corbis UK Ltd. p 2
Amazon p 18
Bruno Vincent/Getty Images p 19
Cristina Lombardo p 20, 179
Apple Computer Inc. p 22
Pearson Education Ltd/Debbie Rowe p 32
Benn Blankenburg/iStockphoto p 66

AA hotel booking p 28
Hewlett Packard p 6
Digital Vision/Alamy p 7
The Savoy, A Fairmont Hotel p 7
TV Licensing p 26
Richard Freeda/Aurora/Getty Images p 174
INTERFOTO Pressebildagentur/Alamy p 178
Pearson Education Ltd. Naki Photography. 2007 p 178
Jeff Greenberg/Alamy p 179
Mihai Simonia/Shutterstock p 140
Nikon p 191
Digital Vision/Alamy p 204

Every effort has been made to contact copyright holders of material reproduced in this book. Any omissions will be rectified in subsequent printings if notice is given to the publishers.

Welcome to the IT Diploma

The IT Diploma is a ground-breaking qualification created by employers, the Government and the leading education bodies. The Diploma will give you skills and experience that employers value and will provide you with opportunities to progress on to Level 3 studies.

Get stuck in!

The Higher Diploma is about the same size as 5–6 GCSEs, but carries the equivalent points value of 7 GCSEs at grades A*–C. The Higher Diploma includes the following elements:

Principal learning The knowledge, understanding and skills essential to working in the IT sector, covered by this book.

Generic learning Functional skills in IT, English and Maths, and personal learning and thinking skills have been embedded in this book to give you opportunities to develop and practise your skills.

The project You will plan, develop, deliver and review a technology-related project. In Unit 7 of this book you will learn project management skills that will help you achieve this.

Additional/specialist learning You can choose from more than 800 different qualifications to support your IT principal learning.

Getting involved

As part of your Diploma, you will also need to take at least 10 days' work experience, ideally relevant to your subject. In fact, employer engagement and applied learning are such key parts of the Diploma that you should consider which local companies may be willing to offer you work experience as early as possible.

Going further

The Diploma is available at Foundation (Level 1, equivalent to 5 GCSEs at grades D–G), Higher (Level 2) and Advanced (Level 3, equivalent to 3.5 A Levels at grades A*–E). The Advanced Diploma is recognised by universities and you could achieve up to 420 UCAS points.

From the Higher Diploma, you can progress to:

* Advanced Diploma
* A Levels
* BTEC National or other Level 3 vocational courses
* Work

We hope you enjoy your studies on this cutting-edge course and that you feel inspired by the real-life scenarios to follow your own interests in the project. Good luck!

BUT WHICH EMPLOYERS?

Vodafone, BT, Cisco, Fujitsu, Microsoft, Oracle, IBM, John Lewis, LogicaCMG and somewhere in the region of 600 other employers have all contributed to the development of this qualification.

How to use this book

This book has been divided into seven units to match the Higher Diploma in IT qualification structure. Each unit follows the Edexcel learning outcomes and each double-page spread covers an individual theme or topic.

Features of the book

Throughout the book you will find the following features:

Functional skills
Functional skills have been built into many of the activities in this book. These features highlight opportunities to develop and practise your functional skills in English, IT or Maths. Remember, you will need a Pass in all three functional skills to achieve the full Diploma.

Starter stimulus
A discussion point or short activity that will introduce the key concepts of the double-page spread.

COMPETITIVE BUSINESS
Discuss how technology can save money for an organisation. What can IT do to improve competitiveness?

Efficiency and competitiveness

Technology can make an organisation very successful or may cause it to fail if it is inefficient and uncompetitive.

Efficiency

Efficiency keeps costs low by reducing wasted time or effort, for example when taking and processing orders. Technology can help by quickly and accurately taking an order from a web page and instantly printing despatch details in a warehouse.

Online payments can be secure and quick, eliminating problems caused by inefficient retyping of details.

Customer feedback identifies where systems need improving. Technology can instantly copy feedback from web pages back into the organisation.

Case study: Games Workshop

Games Workshop, a successful table-top fantasy and futuristic battle-games company, dramatically reduced the time taken to manufacture new models using a new **CAD/CAM** system linked to £1.2 million **CNC** machines. CAD/CAM reduced tool set-up times from around 400 hours to 80 hours. With more than 60 new tools set up each year and improved quality control, the savings are massive.

CAD/CAM
Computer-aided design/Computer-aided manufacture. When a product is designed using a computer (CAD) then the design is used to manufacture the product (CAM).

CNC
Computer numerically controlled (CNC) machines can manufacture CAD designs.

Tyranid Carnifex model from Games Workshop

Activity 1.12

1 Describe how Games Workshop uses technology to improve its business competitiveness. You may visit the Delcam website to help you answer.

2 Compare ways the Amazon and Dell websites offer choice to customers.

3 Analyse how Dell website technology might make the company more competitive when a customer wants to specify components for a new system.

To help you complete this exercise links to some useful websites have been provided. Go to www.heinemann.co.uk/hotlinks. When you access the site, the express code is 1644P.

Mobile technology allows businesspeople more time to visit customers. A laptop used during the visit can save time later with no need to retype paper notes into IT systems.

Competitiveness

Competitiveness spurs organisations to perform better than rivals by producing more attractive products, quicker services or similar improvements. A strong web presence advertises to new markets where potential customers can find information about products and the organisation.

Online businesses are very competitive and work hard to ensure that anyone searching websites for goods they provide finds their companies.

Buying online is becoming more popular. A booking website that sells tickets online can attract more customers than a telephone number where customers might wait in a queue for a sales assistant to become available.

Manufacturers using automation technology can find real competitive advantages with quick production of low-cost products.

Functional Skills – ICT
The activity tasks can show how you entered, developed and formatted your information using text, tables and images to suit its meaning and purpose.

Personal Learning and Thinking Skills
Your independent enquiry skills can be demonstrated when you use websites to analyse and evaluate information

Summary
* Efficiency makes an organisation cheaper to run
* Competitiveness allows an organisation to be more attractive than its rivals by producing better and cheaper goods, and improved services such as quicker deliveries.

Key words
Key concepts and new words are explained clearly and simply to make sure you don't miss anything important.

Case study
Case studies show the concepts covered in this book applied to the real world through real-life scenarios. Questions and activities will encourage you to push your understanding further.

Personal learning and thinking skills
Elements of the generic learning are embedded in the principal learning. These features highlight opportunities to develop and demonstrate your personal learning and thinking skills.

Want to achieve more?

Each unit ends with advice on getting the best from the assessment. This tells you how you will be assessed and how your work will be marked and gives you useful reminders for key unit themes. Hints and tips give you guidance on how to aim for the higher mark band so you use your new skills and knowledge to best effect.

Personal learning and thinking skills

Elements of the generic learning are embedded in the princicpal learning. These features highlight opportunities to develop and demonstrate your personal learning and thinking skills.

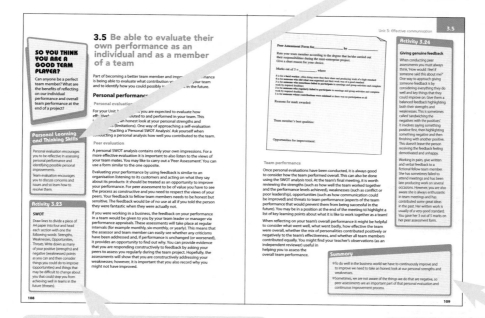

Activity

Each double-page spread contains an activity or a short sequence of questions to test your understanding and give you opportunities to apply your knowledge and skills.

Summary

The most important points to understand, summarised so you can quickly refresh your knowledge.

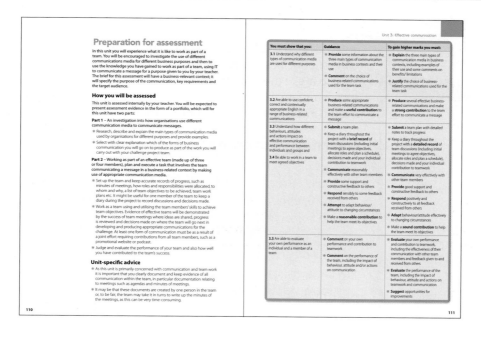

Introduction

This unit will help you understand the technology used by organisations. One day you may become part of a team of IT professionals that develops and improves systems like these.

LET'S MAKE IT BETTER!

Think about your favourite websites and software, and how you use them. Do you wish computer technology worked better? If so, list how you think IT could be improved.

Functional Skills – English

Activity tasks 1 and 2 can show you are able to present information in ways that are fit for purpose and audience.

Activity 1.1

1 Think of a shop/leisure centre/business (for example a newsagent) that you use frequently. What technology do they use and how does it help them?

2 What other technology could they use? What benefits would it bring to them?

3 Why might they not want to add any new technology?

The potential of technology to change business and people's lives is still huge. In the last 20 years computers have changed the world in many ways and this is still happening.

This unit looks at the role of technology in organisations and how it helps them to be successful by reducing costs and producing faster services and better goods than the competition. Organisations that use technology include retail and online businesses, local government, manufacturing and sport and leisure.

As technology is still changing the way many organisations, individuals and society operate, you will be shown how change is happening. You will investigate the effects of new technology by looking at issues such as different working patterns and the skill requirements modern workers need to work with these technologies.

You will need to be able to identify components of technology systems in different business scenarios and to explain what each component does to help make the systems communicate and work together. Then, when you complete this unit, you should be able to explain why organisations should implement new, or improve their existing, technology systems.

Learning outcomes

Be able to identify the key components of technology systems, explaining their function in different business scenarios

Know why example organisations should implement or improve a technology system

Understand the role and contribution of technology to the success of a range of organisations, including impact on efficiency and competitiveness

Know how technology is changing the way organisations, individuals and society operate

This unit is externally assessed through a one-hour computer-based test.

1.1 Key components of technology systems

You need to know about IT technology components and what they are used for. Components include servers, operating systems software and some of the many types of network.

Computers

Modern technology systems have computers communicating over networks inside and outside an organisation. The network often allows access to the Internet. Network software runs on each computer, allowing the computers to communicate while users work on tasks such as word-processing. A network allows email and video conferencing which are important to a modern business.

Networks

Networks connect computers within an organisation's site, site to site, and organisation to organisation. There could be **LAN**s in Bristol, London and Newcastle with a **WAN** connecting them all together. Businesses and organisations often run client–server networks. Clients are the workstations. Servers control the network.

Software

There are many types of software used on computer systems:

* the operating system, for example Microsoft Windows
* network software, for example Novell GroupWise
* application software, for example Microsoft Word
* wireless software, for example Hotspotter
* bespoke software, written especially for the organisation

Linked components

Computers on a network use a network card (sometimes integral to the **motherboard**) to connect to the network using cable or WiFi. Network cables, usually Category 5 (shortened to Cat 5) have RJ45 connectors which plug into a box called a switch. If the network is wireless, the WiFi transceiver will connect to the servers using Cat 5 cables. A network will use a DSL (digital subscriber line) modem router to connect to the Internet.

TALK, TALK, TALK!

List different types of server, identifying their differences and their uses.

Make a list of all the equipment needed to make a network operate.

LAN
A Local Area Network connects computers on a single site.

WAN
A Wide Area Network connects an organisation's LANs.

Motherboard
The main circuit board inside a computer.

Personal Learning and Thinking Skills

You will be able to show skill as a team worker if you cooperate with others and reach agreements to create a technology system.

Activity 1.2

1 Create a presentation describing the roles of servers and clients on a network.

2 Evaluate the choice of operating systems currently available.

Summary

* Local Area Networks can be connected using a WAN.
* Servers control a network. Clients log on to the network.
* Connections can be cable or wireless.

A typical technology system

Computers can connect via a local area network (LAN). The LAN can have Internet access.

ALL TOGETHER NOW!

List some of the advantages that a network can bring to an organisation. What disadvantages might there be?

This diagram shows how computers can connect inside a typical technology system to provide a local area network (LAN) with Internet access.

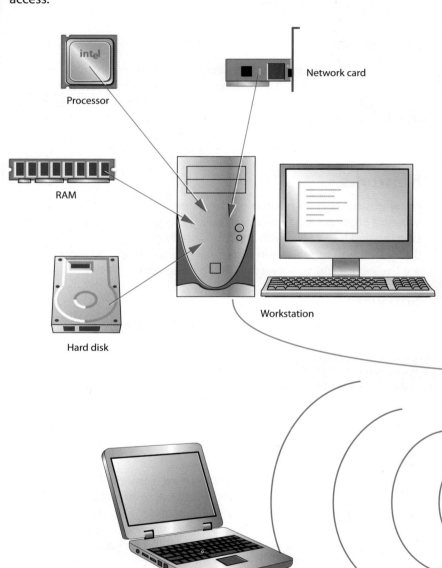

Processor

Network card

RAM

Hard disk

Workstation

Laptop

Network card
Normally has an RJ45 socket accepting a Cat 5 cable to connect to a network switch or Internet router.

Processor
The heart of a computer. This is the component that runs software code.

RAM
Electronic random access memory used to temporarily hold software and documents the user has opened.

Hard disk
Used to store software and documents when the computer is switched off.

Workstation
A computer used by an employee connected to the company network.

Laptop
A portable computer, especially useful for visiting clients, giving presentations and taking work home.

WiFi transceiver
Used to broadcast and receive 802.11 transmissions between a computer and the network.

Switch
Normally uses RJ45 sockets accepting Cat 5 cable to connect networked computers or other devices.

UPS
An uninterruptible power supply which stores enough electricity to let a server save work before switching off if there is a power cut.

Servers
Large corporate networks have servers to control them. Servers can each have different functions such as controlling the email system or Internet connections.

DSL modem router
Hardware used to connect a computer system to the Internet.

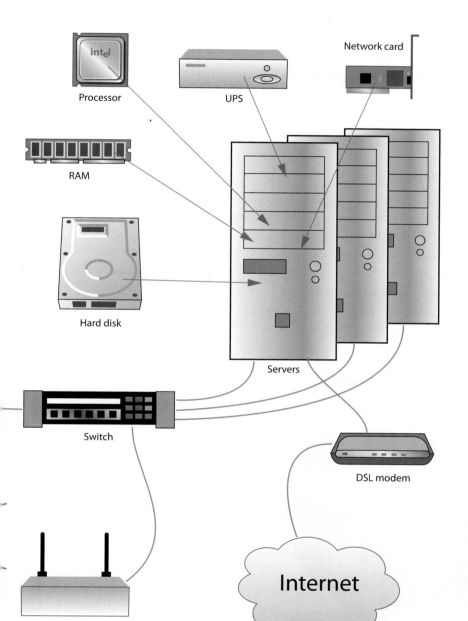

Processor

UPS

Network card

RAM

Hard disk

Servers

Switch

DSL modem

WiFi tranceiver

Internet

Activity 1.3

1 Identify the components needed to connect a workstation to a network and explain their roles.

2 Create a specification for the system shown in the diagram. This will have named components, found from online retailers, with their prices (make sure you include VAT and carriage).

3 Justify your choice of components by stating why you believe they are totally fit for their purposes.

You may look at the PC World website or other online retailers' websites to help with this activity. (Go to www.heinemann. co.uk/hotlinks. When you access the site, the express code is 1644P.)

802.11 WiFi
Radio transmission standard for computers and other devices connecting to a network.

Summary

* A network is made from many components.
* A LAN can connect to a WAN and/or the Internet.
* Servers usually have dedicated roles on a network.

Computers and communications

Computers usually have one of two roles in a network, either as a **server** (which controls the network) or as a workstation (which is used by a person to log on to the network).

Networks enable many forms of communication including emails and video conferencing.

A network can be wired or wireless, the latter making it easier for mobile devices to connect.

Servers

Networks used by larger organisations can be complex with several servers. Each server has control over part of the network. These are some types of server:

* application server to control programs used on the network
* file server holding user files used by people on the network
* mail server controlling the email system
* proxy server to filter data, controlling which websites can be accessed from the network

Server
A powerful computer controlling all or part of a network.

Workstations

A workstation is any computer connected to the network, including desktop PCs and portable computers.

A docking station may be used to connect a laptop to a network, but a direct cable connection or WiFi are often used. Docking stations can have their own screen, keyboard and mouse.

Network connections

Wired connections use Cat 5 cables with RJ45 plugs to connect each workstation to a switch which in turn connects to the servers.

Wireless WiFi connects laptops and desktops to a network using a transceiver (hotspot), which has a maximum range of 100m (but this is often halved due to walls and other obstructions blocking the signal path).

Dial-up lets a user connect a computer into a standard telephone socket to connect from almost anywhere that has a phone line.

Communications

Networks offer many types of communication including emails and video conferencing.

Video conferencing has reduced the need for people to travel to meetings, locally and worldwide, thereby saving time and expense whilst helping the environment.

Video conferencing

Case study: The Savoy, a Fairmont Hotel

The Savoy is a well-known hotel targeting the top end of the market offering £1,000 per night accommodation and featuring the world famous Savoy Grill, fitness gallery, florist, shop, airport limousine and other services.

SAVOY
A FAIRMONT HOTEL
LONDON

This hotel offers WiFi hotspots so guests with laptops can keep in touch with work or browse the Internet. Printers may be borrowed by guests for their rooms.

Functional Skills – English

You can use the activity to show you have selected and used a variety of sources of information independently for a complex task.

Activity 1.4

1 Use the Web to find a new server for sale and list the specification.

2 Compare the roles of workstations and servers.

3 Research the 820.11b and 802.11g WiFi standards then produce a short report comparing them.

Summary

* Servers control most business networks.

* Workstations are used by people who log onto a network to do their job.

* WiFi hotspots now make it very easy to connect to the Internet from many public places.

Networks and the Internet

Modern technology systems often depend on a network that enables computers to communicate with each other to share information and other resources such as printers.

Local and Wide Area Networks

The different types of network include Local Area Networks (LAN), Wide Area Networks (WAN), the Internet, intranets and extranets.

A business might have client–server LANs at different sites. The diagram shows how these might be connected by a WAN. The Internet is a WAN. Each network has a router to find a path (route) through the Internet for the data when it needs to travel to another site. A WAN like this could be used by an estate agency so information about the properties each branch is selling can be seen by all.

CONNECTING COMPUTERS

Computers can communicate in many ways. What ways can you think of?

Why does a website accepting online payments need good security?

Workstation
A computer attached to the network, used by people to log on and do work.

Server
The network is controlled by one or more servers.

Browser
Browsers, such as Microsoft Internet Explorer or Mozilla Firefox are programs which display web pages.

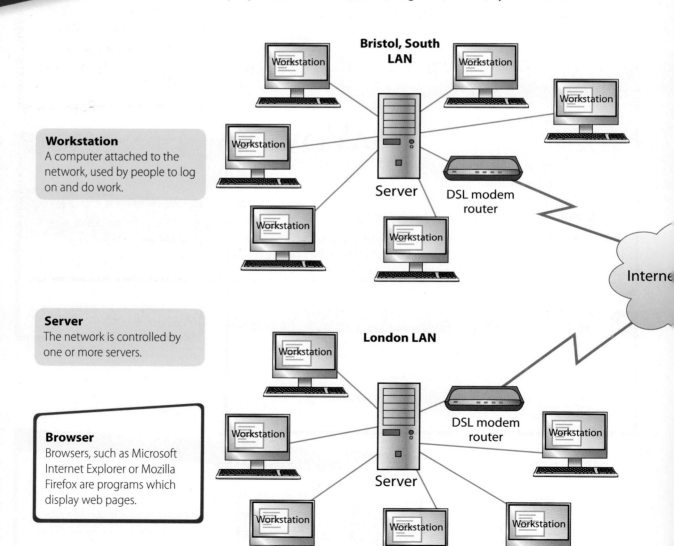

A typical WAN

The Internet

The Internet is a type of WAN and as such can be used to transfer computer data like any other network. Additionally it allows a computer to access data on the World Wide Web using a **browser** to show the web pages.

Internet security

Transactional websites sell products. E-customers can add items to a 'shopping trolley' then pay for them using their credit card or other payment method. A business involved in online trading needs to have good security on any transactional web pages that accept online payments. Skilled hackers search for this payment information so they can transfer money using stolen e-customer banking details.

Intranet

An intranet usually runs on an organisation's network for staff to view Web-like pages that are controlled by the company, such as news sheets, help screens, holiday application forms and similar.

Extranet

An extranet is part of an intranet that can be viewed from outside an organisation's network. Users need to log on from an Internet page of the organisation's website.

Functional Skills – ICT

Your research into transactional websites and their need for security should allow you to understand the need for safety and security practices when setting up and running such a site.

Activity 1.5

1 List the components needed for a simple client–server network.

2 Explain the roles of a DSL modem router in a network.

3 Describe and analyse why transactional websites need good security.

Summary

* Networks are the means by which computer systems communicate.
* There are different networks each providing different distance coverage.
* LANs, WANs, the Internet, intranets and extranets are all types of network.
* Network security is paramount to a company that wants to protect its business and to an individual using a transactional website.

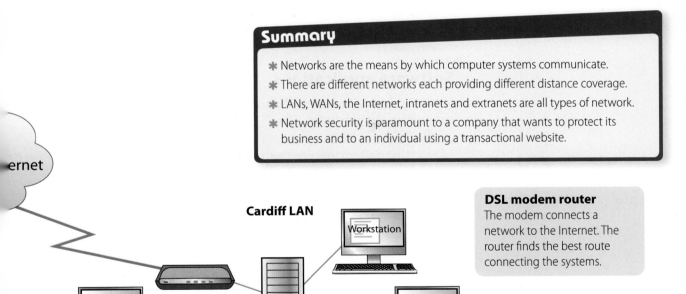

DSL modem router
The modem connects a network to the Internet. The router finds the best route connecting the systems.

Software

Software brings a computer system to life and makes IT workable. There are two main types of software: operating systems and applications.

Operating systems

The first thing a computer does when it is switched on is to load the operating system (usually from its hard disk) and run it. If this is not possible, the computer system cannot start up and is useless! There are many operating systems available. Three popular ones are:

* Microsoft Windows (for PCs)
* Apple Mac OS (for Macs)
* Linux (for most types of computer hardware)

There are many versions of each of these.

Network applications

Network applications are programs used on networks, such as:

* email applications (like Microsoft Outlook), which let users send and receive emails
* network games, which let several people play the same game at the same time
* firewalls, which help to protect computer systems from Internet viruses and attacks

Software applications

Software applications are programs people use to work with computers. They include:

* office applications (word processor, spreadsheet, presentation software and database) such as Microsoft Office
* graphic drawing applications, such as CorelDRAW, to create artwork and diagrams
* music applications, such as Sony ACID Pro, to create new music mixes
* video applications, such as Apple Final Cut Studio, to edit videos

Wireless software

Wireless software products, such as Hotspotter, can detect WiFi hotspots within range of a laptop or another wireless-enabled device. Software is bundled with each WiFi transceiver to configure settings such as whether the station ID is broadcast and which devices have permission to connect.

Bespoke software

Bespoke software is especially written for an organisation because there is nothing else exactly right for the job. Bespoke software is expensive as it takes a lot of time to produce. Development costs are paid by the organisation that commissioned it, whereas commercial software like Microsoft Office has millions of purchasers to spread the cost of development.

Case study: Pace Software Development Ltd.

Pace Software Development is a software house offering bespoke software. Pace also provides computer support and consultancy services.

An example of bespoke software produced by PACE is the VAS Contacts and Training system written for Voluntary Action Sheffield. This is a web-based application managing all the training and events undertaken by VAS.

1 Produce a two-sided flyer advertising the services Pace provides.

Activity 1.6

1 Produce a simple user guide for some of the features you find useful in a version of the Microsoft Windows operating system.

2 Compare Microsoft Windows with another operating system such as Mac OS or Linux.

3 Analyse the success of the Microsoft Windows operating system.

Summary

* Software is the program code that runs on a computer.
* Operating systems and applications are examples of software.

1.2 Why organisations should improve technology

Business requirements and technology change, so systems need to be altered and improved. Identifying what new components should be purchased and when is vital to an organisation.

Introduction

Software and computers have a relatively short life mainly because there are always new and improved developments in the technology. Newer systems can deliver services, such as live TV, which were previously not possible, in order to meet changing needs and expectations of users.

A network may need to be improved to increase **bandwidth** or to introduce mobile communications.

A network may need to be implemented when **stand-alone** systems are no longer viable because there is a need to share work between staff members and improve communications.

Networks may be improved in areas such as:

* faster communications links
* installing new servers
* improving or implementing a Web presence

Technology and competitiveness

Technology can give an organisation a competitive advantage. The hardware and services that can be delivered keep improving, so every organisation with a technology system must keep reviewing what they have and how it delivers to remain competitive.

These systems must be able to deliver:

* cost-effectiveness
* communications within the organisation
* communications with customers
* speedy delivery of services to the customers
* a professional and impressive image to customers

ONWARDS AND UPWARDS!

As a group, discuss how the technology systems where you study could be upgraded and whether the upgrades are worth the cost.

Bandwidth
In computing, the speed that data can travel through the network. High bandwidth is needed for uses such as live video.

Stand-alone
A computer system not connected to a network.

Functional Skills – English

You can give a presentation on areas where technology is changing the way organisations, individuals and society operates.

Activity 1.7

1 Work in a group to produce a presentation explaining how technology systems can be developed to improve cost-effectiveness, communications within the organisation, communications with customers, speedy delivery of services, and a professional and impressive image to customers.

2 List reasons to improve a technology system.

3 Compare what somebody working in an office needs with what a person remote working at home needs.

4 Analyse ways technology can be used today that were not practical five years ago.

Improving computers

Technological developments mean that hardware and software become out of date and are replaced or improved. Computers should regularly be reviewed to ensure they are still providing an effective service.

Improving software

Reasons for using improved software include:

* the users' needs have changed – helping the users to work more effectively is a valid reason for improving the software

* customer expectations – a rival website may offer faster and more attractive pages, so an organisation may improve their website to remain competitive

* increasing productivity – new application software may be used to carry out tasks in a way that saves money because they are completed more quickly or quality is enhanced

* obsolescence or changing technology – a new or improved software product will work better with new hardware, so the organisation should plan for extra hardware costs

Improving hardware

Computers have a relatively short life as new developments in technology are regularly brought to market. New software often means that hardware also needs upgrading by adding more memory or faster components. Before upgrading a computer there are two issues that need to be considered:

* is the upgrade going to be effective? Other parts may not give enough performance for the new component to work properly

* computers quickly **depreciate**, so a system's current value should be considered to make sure any upgrade is cost-effective

Changing the use of a computer, for example from an office tool to a manufacturing control system, would almost certainly mean that hardware changes and upgrades need to be made.

Functional Skills – ICT

Completing the activity tasks can show you have evaluated the effectiveness of the ICT system you have used.

Personal Learning and Thinking Skills

Your outcomes to the activity tasks can show your skills as a reflective learner when reviewing how improvements could be made to these systems.

Activity 1.8

1 Outline ways you would like your computer improved.

2 Outline any risks to an organisation of improving its systems, suggesting how they might be avoided.

3 Research and list the benefits that a DVR system can bring to site security. Describe how live video from DVR cameras can be seen on another computer using broadband.

Depreciate
Losing value as an item gets older.

Summary

* New technological products are always becoming available.
* The needs of an organisation and clients will change.
* Competitor organisations will always improve their technology.
* Hardware and software often needs upgrading or replacing.
* A business needs to analyse the cost-effectiveness of change.
* Risks associated with change need to be considered and minimised.

Improving networks

Network systems need to be regularly examined to make sure they meet users' needs. An organisation's Web presence needs to be compared with its competitors' to check it is still the best.

Improving networks

Providing greater network bandwidth with faster cabling and network cards will mean that workstations can communicate better. There may be reasons for improving communications, for example remote log-on to the network may be made easier, thereby better supporting mobile and home workers.

An organisation may enhance stand-alone computer systems by connecting them to a new network. Staff can then benefit from sharing files and other resources like printers.

Improving servers

A server is a powerful computer controlling all or part of a network. Large networks will have several servers, each controlling part of the system such as email.

If a server does not perform quickly, the network slows down reducing response times. Some servers are slow because the software is poorly set up. This type of problem will need a skilled IT professional to examine the system and reconfigure it.

Often server performance can be dramatically improved by adding more **RAM**. The increased RAM holds more programs and data so the computer does not have to spend time accessing the hard disk.

New Web and mail servers may need to be installed as a company expands, because the current ones become overused and slow down.

RAM
Random-access memory (RAM) is one or more small circuit boards plugged into the motherboard. Electronic memory works much faster than the hard disk where speed depends on how quickly the disk spins and the read/write heads find the data: mechanical movement is many times slower than electricity!

Improving Web presence

A website is very important to many organisations. It 'shows off' an organisation and is where new and existing customers get a feel for how professional and trustworthy the organisation is. An online retailer uses a website as a shop where customers find the product information they need.

Every website should be checked regularly to make sure:

* everything is up to date
* the site works at an acceptable speed
* all links to other sites work
* competitors' websites are not more attractive

Webmaster
The webmaster is responsible for producing and maintaining the website.

The **webmaster** can edit web pages to improve most of these. Speed can be improved by replacing high-quality images with lower-quality ones that look similar but download more quickly.

The speed of a website also depends on web hosting systems that store the web pages and that connect to the Internet. A website that is too slow may need to be upgraded to a different web host with faster hardware.

Activity 1.9

1 List ways an organisation can improve the speed at which users can access their website.

2 Describe the benefits an organisation could obtain from improving their website.

3 Analyse the benefits and any drawbacks to implementing a new server into a network.

Case study: Woolworths

Woolworths is a brick and click business with 820 stores in many towns offering a wide range of products.

In 2007 Woolworths decided to replace all their Office 97 applications software with Office 2007. At the same time they were to replace their Windows NT operating system with Windows XP.

It's unusual for an organisation that has been content with old applications to opt for such a massive technology change, especially on such a scale. 1300 computers were to be replaced. It was a 10 year jump, technology wise, in terms of hardware, software and connection speeds.

The commercial development manager, Gordon Rennie, said at the time, 'In many ways we have gone from being well behind the curve to being ahead of it.'

There is a lot of risk in making such a big leap forward in one go but the changeover had been planned thoroughly to minimise the chances of many errors. SkillSoft, which produced support material for the training project, said: 'Gordon and his team have been waiting for the green light on this for a while and were eager to get it right.'

Training was delivered with some 60 days of trainer time being booked in all. The format was a number of half-day (3.5 hour) training workshops, which gave people the basics. Tuition software is available on their workstations after training time to support them later.

Why this approach? They didn't want a kind of 'Wembley Stadium' mass meeting, unrealistic given nature of their business. A retailer can't take that many people off line at one time and keep open.

Summary

* Poor network performance can adversely affect an organisation's effectiveness.
* A website is a company's shop window where a user can find information and buy products.

1.3 Role and contribution of technology

Technology is used by successful organisations to reduce costs through increased efficiency. This leads to improved competitiveness.

SUCCESSFUL TECHNOLOGY?

How does technology help an organisation become successful? List some online organisations that you've heard of and write down how they use computers and the Internet.

Retailer
A company or individual who sells to the public.

This unit shows how technology is used by society, organisations and individuals to increase market research, improve customer service and save costs. You will investigate new types of business that have been helped by internet growth, such as search engines, music download sites and online auctions.

Online **retailers** sell products using the Internet. Other online businesses provide services such as sending e-cards (for example celebrating a birthday) to an email address.

Technology is used by manufacturers, for example automation to produce products. Websites can advertise and sell products worldwide, or provide sport and leisure services, such as live scores on websites and game highlights that you can view whenever you want.

The Internet provides services, publicity and ways for customers to interact, for example:

* online ticket booking – for quick and easy bookings with no need to travel to a booking office and no need to queue
* social networking sites – to easily and cheaply contact friends wherever they are in the world
* local government – to provide online information

Functional Skills – English

You can select and use a variety of sources of information independently when doing the activity tasks.

Personal Learning and Thinking Skills

Demonstrate your skills by carrying out research to complete the activity tasks.

Technology in business

Computer technology systems are now essential for most businesses and organisations. They should improve efficiency by reducing wasted effort and providing network communication so that work, resources and data can be shared.

A business network usually has one or more servers. These servers control the network, store work, control emails and give users access to services, such as printing.

Technology can contribute to business success by increasing market reach using websites. Customers find a website by using search engines like Google and they can view product information whenever they want. Internet pages can be viewed anywhere in the world.

Customer service can be improved with information provided almost instantly through the Internet; for example, a customer can track a parcel to see where it is or if it has been delivered.

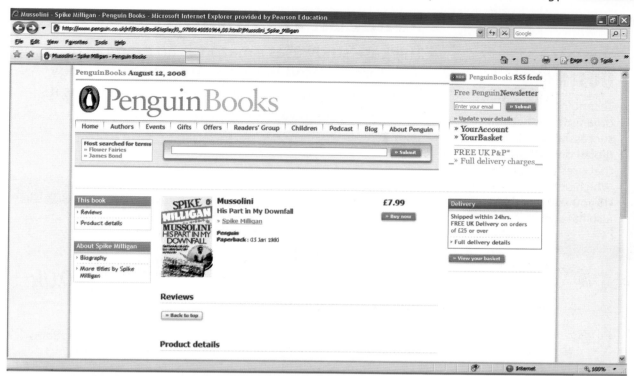

An ecommerce website

Activity 1.10

1 Use the Internet to find two online businesses for which technology has contributed to their success and provided advantages.

2 Compare ways technology has contributed to the success of the two online businesses.

3 Describe and analyse why technology has made the two online businesses more successful.

Summary

✳ Technology can maximise market size.

✳ Websites can present up-to-date information.

✳ Many organisations use technology to reduce costs.

Amazon technology

This case study uses Amazon as an example of an Internet-based business. Amazon technology improves company competitiveness and helps its warehouses operate efficiently.

ONLINE BUSINESS

Technology helps organisations become successful. Amazon is a global online retailer that uses technology. Which online retailers do you know of that also have shops?

Case Study: Amazon

Amazon is an international online Internet retailer whose core business is selling books, but they also offer music, videos, electronic devices, software and games, home and garden goods, toys, gifts, jewellery and online auctions. The Amazon zShop site has pages from other retailers selling goods and services.

Amazon started during 1995 in the USA, launching in the UK in October 1998 with 1.4 million book titles, including all UK titles then on sale with up to 40 per cent off.

This cost a massive amount of money to get started, with expenditure on website technology, advertising and setting up warehouses and buying stock for customers. Amazon always believed they would eventually make a profit, and they achieved this in 2001.

Websites make Amazon very competitive with easy-to-use search and browse features, customer reviews, secure credit card payment, personalised recommendations and direct shipping.

Amazon organise their massive warehouses efficiently using computer technology.

When a delivery is received, it is placed into a plastic crate which travels by conveyor belt to staff who allocate warehouse space to each crate. The staff use portable scanners to read bar-coded labels on items and locations so Amazon's system remembers where each item is located.

This is the only way goods are organised. Technology records where everything is stored. Without a computer printout it would be impossible to find anything again.

Goods for **despatch** are put onto trolleys using pick lists printed by Amazon's system with the shortest route needed to gather orders. There can be items from several orders on a trolley which then need to be sorted again when boxes are packed for despatch.

Despatch
Despatch is when goods are sent from a supplier to the customer.

Amazon warehouse in Milton Keynes

Activity 1.11

1 Produce a flow diagram of the retail process at an online company such as Amazon, from the order being received to the product being sent to the customer, and highlight where technology is used and how it makes the operation more efficient. Work in a group with each member producing a page showing each technology. Act out how the system works.

2 Identify ways that Amazon uses technology to improve efficiency and competitiveness.

3 Describe how Amazon warehousing systems operate.

4 Justify why Amazon find it efficient to use a warehousing system where goods are NOT arranged in a set order on shelving similar to how books are kept in a library.

Use the Kim Gilmour web page or other websites to help with this activity. Go to www.heinemann.co.uk/hotlinks. When you access the site, the express code is 1644P.

Functional Skills – ICT

Your research into Amazon can bring together information to suit content and purpose.

Summary

* Internet-based businesses can easily reach customers anywhere in the world.
* There can be a lot of cost involved in starting an Internet-based business.
* Many organisations would find it impossible to operate without their technology.

Efficiency and competitiveness

Technology can make an organisation very successful or may cause it to fail if it is inefficient and uncompetitive.

Efficiency

Efficiency keeps costs low by reducing wasted time or effort, for example when taking and processing orders. Technology can help by quickly and accurately taking an order from a web page and instantly printing despatch details in a warehouse.

Online payments can be secure and quick, eliminating problems caused by inefficient retyping of details.

Customer feedback identifies where systems need improving. Technology can instantly copy feedback from web pages back into the organisation.

CAD/CAM

Computer-aided design/ Computer-aided manufacture. When a product is designed using a computer (CAD) then the design is used to manufacture the product (CAM).

CNC

Computer numerically controlled (CNC) machines can manufacture CAD designs.

Case study: Games Workshop

Games Workshop, a successful table-top fantasy and futuristic battle-games company, dramatically reduced the time taken to manufacture new models using a new **CAD/CAM** system linked to £1.2 million **CNC** machines. CAD/CAM reduced tool set-up times from around 400 hours to 80 hours. With more than 60 new tools set up each year and improved quality control, the savings are massive.

Tyranid Carnifex model from Games Workshop

Activity 1.12

1 Describe how Games Workshop uses technology to improve its business competitiveness. You may visit the Delcam website to help you answer.

2 Compare ways the Amazon and Dell websites offer choice to customers.

3 Analyse how Dell website technology might make the company more competitive when a customer wants to specify components for a new system.

To help you complete this exercise links to some useful websites have been provided. Go to www.heinemann.co.uk/hotlinks. When you access the site, the express code is 1644P.

Mobile technology allows businesspeople more time to visit customers. A laptop used during the visit can save time later with no need to retype paper notes into IT systems.

Competitiveness

Competitiveness spurs organisations to perform better than rivals by producing more attractive products, quicker services or similar improvements. A strong web presence advertises to new markets where potential customers can find information about products and the organisation.

Online businesses are very competitive and work hard to ensure that anyone searching websites for goods they provide finds their companies.

Buying online is becoming more popular. A booking website that sells tickets online can attract more customers than a telephone number where customers might wait in a queue for a sales assistant to become available.

Manufacturers using automation technology can find real competitive advantages with quick production of low-cost products.

Functional Skills – ICT

The activity tasks can show how you entered, developed and formatted your information using text, tables and images to suit its meaning and purpose.

Personal Learning and Thinking Skills

Your independent enquiry skills can be demonstrated when you use websites to analyse and evaluate information

Summary

* Efficiency makes an organisation cheaper to run.
* Competitiveness allows an organisation to be more attractive than its rivals by producing better and cheaper goods, and improved services such as quicker deliveries.

iTunes technology

This case study uses Apple as an example of an Internet-based business operating a music download site. The iTunes Store is part of the Apple computers website and supports its iPod MP3 player product range.

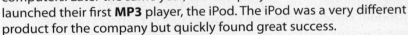

MP3

MP3 (**MP**eg-1 audio layer-**3**) is a file format for digitally compressing audio files for storage on a hard disk or in other electronic memory. Moving Picture Experts Group (MPEG), is part of the International Standards Organisation (ISO). MP3 has been a global success. It offers good sound quality that does not need large amounts of storage space.

Apple is a successful international company producing the Macintosh range of personal computers which includes product names such as iMac, MacBook and Mac. In January 2001, it released iTunes: software for playing and storing music and video for Macintosh computers. Later the same year, the company launched their first **MP3** player, the iPod. The iPod was a very different product for the company but quickly found great success.

The iPod was radically different from other MP3 players available at the time, using a wheel to make it much easier to find any track from the tens of thousands held in memory.

Courtesy of Apple

iTunes Store (courtesy of Apple)

iTunes software, bundled with iPod MP3 players, was first used for loading music with Apple computers. This software was later developed to run on Windows PCs as well. Apple currently offers iTunes software as a free download.

Apple added the iTunes Store to its website in 2003 to allow people to buy and instantly download music, video games and other digital entertainment. Apple claims the site has had over 3 billion downloads.

Functional Skills – ICT

You can use the iTunes case study to show how you researched information for a report on how technology has contributed to the success of online businesses.

Activity 1.13

1 Create a presentation to last about 3 minutes that shows different iPod models, highlighting the features each offers.

2 List the advantages that the Apple family of media technologies (iPod, iTunes and iTunes Store) have over similar products from other sources.

3 Compare a current model of the iPod with a similarly priced rival product.

4 Read the Low End Mac article, then analyse the main reasons for Apple's success with iTunes and their related technologies.

To help you complete this exercise, links to some useful websites have been provided. Go to www.heinemann.co.uk/hotlinks. When you access the site, the express code is 1644P.

Personal Learning and Thinking Skills

Your independent enquiry and self-management skills can be demonstrated by planning and carrying out research about iPods.

Summary

* Websites can improve competitiveness by supporting other products from the same business.
* Integrating products with a website can improve customer satisfaction and loyalty.
* Online ordering can generate more business.

1.4 How technology is changing ways organisations, individuals and society operate

Social websites and instant messaging bring people together. The Web also gives us an enormous amount of information. Technology reduces the need to travel, which can impact on the workforce.

Introduction

Technology changes the ways we interact and operate. Organisations, individuals and society are all affected by technology changing how we work and communicate.

Some organisations now locate call centres and other departments wherever in the UK or the world staff have the skills and the wage levels needed to provide cost-effective services. Having worldwide locations also allows 24/7 customer service without having to worry about time zones.

Wireless and high-speed Internet access mean that you are no longer restricted to just one place to use a computer.

Technology has changed workplace skills and staff have had to be retrained to enable them to use the new systems.

Some workers now benefit from flexible working hours, adjusting time at work to fit with lifestyles, for example to miss rush-hour traffic jams when travelling to work.

Society

Technology has changed the ways that groups of people, of common religious, cultural, scientific, political or other backgrounds, communicate with each other. Instant messaging has brought many people closer together, making it easy to email or exchange messages. E-government keeps people informed about how local and national government is being planned and delivered.

Organisations

Most organisations have made big changes in how they operate as technology has developed and become cheaper. For example teleworking has reduced the need to travel, thereby saving money, reducing pollution and creating fewer traffic jams.

Individuals

Changes in the ways organisations use their technology have also had a big impact on individuals. Some jobs have been lost in the UK following 'off-shoring'. Other roles are becoming more flexible as broadband enables many employees to work from home or remote locations.

Broadband is changing many lives, providing high-speed Internet access that allows TV programmes and music files to be downloaded. Wireless Internet access has enabled people to use the garden and other places to 'surf the Web'.

The advent of more flexible working days has been especially beneficial to parents with school children as they can rearrange their work schedules around the school times.

Personal Learning and Thinking Skills

You can demonstrate your independent enquiry skills by carrying out research and then by judging its relevance and value to the activity tasks.

Activity 1.14

1 Create a short presentation using the Web to find a business that uses technology to run a call centre in India.

2 How has technology made distance less important?

3 Analyse how mobile technology has changed how organisations operate.

Summary

* Technology has changed how many organisations operate.
* Distance is much less important.
* Workers need to adjust to these changes.

Changing types of work

Many businesses use technology to help them work more efficiently and with less cost. It can be more cost-effective to run an organisation with offices and production spread around the world using fast, cheap communications technology.

Off-shore working

For this unit, off-shore working means that an organisation has premises in a different country from the one you are in.

Off-shore working needs quick communications between computer systems, such as **VoIP**, sending scanned documents between sites and video conferencing.

VoIP

VoIP (Voice over Internet Protocol) allows voice phone calls at the same time as computer data is transferred. The data connection is charged for, but the voice call is usually almost free, making VoIP a cost-effective means of communication.

Case Study: Changes at TV Licensing

TV Licensing collects payment for 24.5 million television licences in the UK (2006/7). Capita plc is one of the organisations working under the TV Licensing name and handles most of the administration including its call centres and its enforcement officers. It has an off-shore presence in Mumbai, India, using technology to carry out back office work, helping to reduce costs.

Security is very important for off-shore working. Capita insists that its Mumbai offices meet the requirements of the Data Protection Act and BS7799 to 'continuously ensure high standards for clients when processing their data in a secure manner with adequate protection'.

Organisations use off-shore working to save some major costs on wages. The cost of living is cheaper in some countries and workers are paid lower wages compared with those in the UK. The relative strengths of the respective currencies also affect the cost-effectiveness of basing production facilities and call centres overseas.

Off-site working

Off-site working (teleworking) is working in a different place from the main premises, often at home. Employees can telework and still communicate with their organisation. Teleworking allows an individual to provide a service to, and communicate with, a client without having to visit and work from the client's site.

Off-site working can bring benefits to an organisation because costs can be saved by running smaller premises. Staff often appreciate the flexibility off-site working brings to their lifestyles.

Mobile working

Mobile working is when a laptop or other portable device is used by somebody who travels to clients or other places. A laptop can be used to show clients products and useful information, to produce estimates and quotations, and to enter client information for products such as home insurance.

Information entered into a laptop is transferred to the main system later using a remote connection such as broadband or dial-up if the user is off-site, or by connecting to the company's network directly using a network cable or wireless connection in the office.

Functional Skills – English

Use the activity tasks to describe how technology is changing the way organisations, individuals and society operate.

Personal Learning and Thinking Skills

Your independent enquiry skills can be shown by using the Internet to carry out research, explore issues around changing working practices and draw conclusions.

Activity 1.15

1 Identify why an organisation might implement off-shore working.

2 Compare off-site and mobile work.

3 Analyse why mobile working may impress a client when a rep calls.

Summary

* Technology allows a business to be global.
* Worldwide operations can be cost-effective.
* Computer and communication technology allows workers to be flexible with where and when they work.

YOU AND TECHNOLOGY

As a group, discuss what you think work will be like in 10 years' time. Explore whether or not it is better to go to work in an office or from home. Why? Discuss how video games consoles have changed through the years.

Rep
A rep (representative) is a mobile worker representing an organisation, who visits potential clients to discuss business.

Individuals and technology

Technology alters the ways that organisations do business, changing the expectations of their workforce. The idea of going to a place of work is being modified.

Changing working models

Your parents expected their skills to last for most of their working life; nowadays many staff will be expected to retrain whenever technology changes. Twenty years ago people working with computers went to work and used a workstation. **Reps** used laptops when visiting customers. Data entered into the laptop was transferred later to the main network by floppy disk, by plugging in a network cable or by attaching the laptop to a docking station.

Teleworkers at home use broadband for a fast, reliable connection between home and work. Mobile workers such as reps often transfer work from their laptop back to the main systems using WiFi hotspots in public places such as cafés and hotels.

Flexible working helps people with other responsibilities; for example it allows parents to transport children to and from school.

Case study: The AA

The AA (Automobile Association) is a business operating a fleet of breakdown vehicles and offering services such as route planning through their website.

The AA's technology systems in their control centres recognise the locations of breakdowns and allocate and guide patrol assistance to the client. The systems also use data sent back from AA patrols, National Express coaches, Eddie Stobart lorries and other sources to identify traffic problems and to update SatNav technology systems so motorists are warned of problems as they happen.

Skills

People working with technology often need to learn new skills, such as using a new operating system.

Many people find learning new skills difficult. Some people experience anxiety or stress from changing work requirements because they find it very unsettling to discover their knowledge is no longer correct or wanted.

Activity 1.16

1 As a group, think of, then manually perform, any task that you think has been made more efficient by technology.

2 As a group, demonstrate how the AA's technology systems gather information about traffic conditions used in data received by a vehicle's SatNav device. Each group member represents somewhere information comes from (patrols, coaches, lorries), is stored (AA technology system) or is received (SatNav device in a car). You can find useful information on the ESRIUK website.

3 Produce a presentation that shows the AA website being used to plan a route.

4 Compare the AA route planner with another website offering a similar online service.

5 Describe how the AA's technology systems gather data about traffic jams.

To help you complete this exercise, links to some useful websites have been provided. Go to www.heinemann.co.uk/hotlinks. When you access the site, the express code is 1644P.

Summary

* Technology has changed the ways a company does business.
* Technology is always changing and people need to learn new skills to adapt.

Technology and society

Changes in technology impact on society. We can now communicate using computers, mobile phones and other devices. Many people use instant messaging to chat with friends as they use their computer for other tasks. Many successful websites help bring together people with similar interests, to catch up with the latest news, to post messages to forums or simply to search for friends.

Social websites

There are many social websites on the Internet where people can use **forums** to discuss things that matter to them. These websites bring together people who have similar interests, for example to share photos or music.

Some social websites have got into legal trouble when copyrights were breached, such as sharing music copied from a CD. When you buy music it must be for you – a copy cannot be legally given to another person.

FRIENDS ON THE NET

Do you use MSN instant messaging or have you a presence on MySpace or YouTube? Investigate other ways that technology brings people together.

Forum

Part of a website where people can post questions or comments. Other people who see this can reply with answers or further comments.

Case study: Directgov

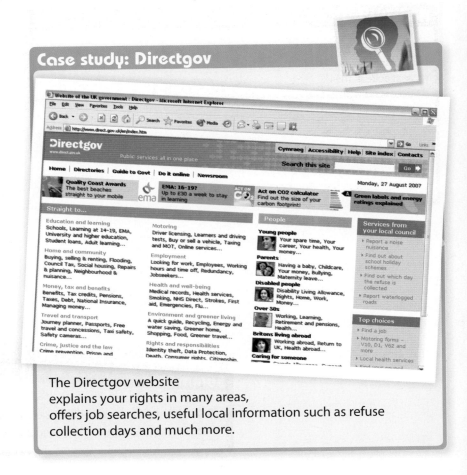

The Directgov website explains your rights in many areas, offers job searches, useful local information such as refuse collection days and much more.

Messenger services

Instant messaging services have brought people together wherever they are in the world with 'conversations' that can be seen almost as soon as they're typed at the computer keyboard.

Government websites

The Government's e-strategy is designed to offer us more knowledge of local and national government workings and provides ways to communicate with them. Every local council now has a website which can be visited by anyone to find out things like who the councillors are, what planning applications are currently being considered, events in the area, rubbish collection days and much more.

The Directgov website gives information about topics such as education, passports, tax, health and many other areas. (Go to www.heinemann.co.uk/hotlinks. When you access the site, the express code is 1644P.)

Organised groups

Technology helps organised groups of people keep in touch and share news through websites. A group may be connected because of religious, cultural, scientific, political or other reasons.

> **Functional Skills – English**
>
> Use the activity to show you can write documents communicating information, ideas and opinions effectively and persuasively.

Activity 1.17

1 Visit the Wikipedia website to search for 'list of social networking websites' to bring up a page showing many of the social websites that are currently available on the Internet. (Go to www.heinemann.co.uk/hotlinks. When you access the site, the express code is 1644P.)

2 Click on the name of any site to link to a Wikipedia page describing the purpose of the site. You can use the external links section at the bottom of the Wikipedia page to visit the site.

3 Create a video or a blog entry for a previous activity. Upload it to one of the social network sites then present it to your group.

Summary

* Technology has altered our society.
* Communication worldwide is easier and quicker.
* Information on almost all topics is freely available.

2 Exploring organisations

Introduction

Why explore organisations? Well, there are many different types of organisation, all with different structures and ways of doing things. Most of us will probably at some time in our lives end up working for a range of different organisations, so developing an understanding now of how businesses vary and why will be useful for the future.

HOW DIFFERENT?

Working for a small family business that supplies and maintains computer systems for local companies will be very different from working for a global organisation like IBM, but in what ways?

Organisation
An organisation is a group of people who work together to achieve shared goals.

Organisational structure
The organisational structure defines the relationships between people and business functions that enable an organisation to produce the goods or the services it supplies in order to achieve its objectives.

Organisational culture
The way things are done and the relationships that develop between people and groups within an organisation over a long period of time are known as the organisational culture.

Business simulation
A business simulation is a game that shows what it is like to operate a real business that is influenced by a variety of factors including competition.

To pass this unit you should investigate and compare at least two different **organisations**. You will identify what business sectors they belong to, how they are **structured** and why, what **culture** exists in each and why, and the duties carried out by members of staff in key positions or roles within each business. You will also consider how different businesses create and maintain good relationships with their customers. Your investigations will provide you with a detailed understanding of what factors contribute to the success of a business. This is where it gets very exciting! You will use this knowledge to work in teams and participate in a **business simulation** game, which is also a part of the assessment for this unit.

Learning outcomes

2.1 Know that organisations have different structures, cultures and roles

2.2 Understand the purpose of key business processes

2.3 Understand how and why technology is used to support business processes

2.4 Understand that a number of factors contribute to the success of a business

Case Study: Just like the real thing!

All over the UK, schools and universities are hosting business enterprise events in which small teams (of about five pupils) get to experience what it is really like to run a business. Using computerised business games, called business simulations, teams get the opportunity to run a 'virtual' business, making a variety of decisions in response to information provided, which will ultimately lead to business success or failure. Some simulations have students running their own ice-cream factory; others are based on a small smoothie business. As you can imagine, the weather and seasons will have a large impact on the demand for these types of product.

Want to have a go? There are a variety of free business simulation games available on the Internet. Sport4Life have developed an educational game where you can run your own football franchise store. Participating in the game will help you develop an understanding of what it is like to manage a small business. You can experiment with all the different decisions a typical owner would have to make and ultimately see the impact of these decisions on the success of the business. There is even a leaderboard and a prize for the best-performing team! You can access it at www.sport4life.biz.

Activity 2.1

Working in pairs or small groups, consider the benefits to you and your fellow students of using business simulations/games in Unit 2 classes. Discuss your opinions with the rest of the class.

Profit

If an organisation's income is more than its costs, the difference is called a profit. If the costs outweigh the income, the organisation will make a loss.

Dividend

A dividend is a share of a company's profits that a shareholder will receive based on how many shares they own.

2.1 Know that organisations have different structures, cultures and roles

To achieve a better understanding of organisations, you will need to investigate the type of organisation they are, the structures they have developed over time and how things are done (the culture that has evolved within each organisation and the roles and responsibilities of key people who carry out the core duties and processes of the business to ensure it is successful).

Organisations

How do we begin to understand what an organisation is if there are so many different types? We can group them according to what sector they belong to, whether or not they aim to make a profit and whether they would be considered a 'brick', 'click' or 'brick and click' type of organisation.

Private-sector organisations

Most organisations in the UK are privately owned. They are said to belong within the **private sector**. Private sector organisations aim to supply goods and services demanded by customers at a price that is higher than it cost to supply them, so that they make a **profit**. They are privately owned and run by people who have invested in them to attract a financial return.

For example, Manchester United, the world-famous football team, has been floated on the stock exchange so that anyone can buy shares in it and be rewarded financially with returns – called **dividends** – each year if the business performs well.

Public-sector organisations

In the UK, a wide variety of services are also offered and operated by the government. These organisations exist to provide services to the public using money raised by taxing the public. They are said to belong within the **public sector**. For example, in some countries schools are publicly run so that every member of the public has the right to access schooling and education services. If *only* private sector enterprises offered education and schooling, they would want to make profit and charge prices that not everyone in the country could afford to pay. But keeping schools and education in the public sector means that governments can use taxes paid by the public to ensure access to education for everyone, not just those who can afford it. Organisations in the public sector share the following features:

* they supply services such as defence or healthcare, which would be difficult to supply profitably by privately run enterprises without having to charge very high prices or collect money from every member of society – a practical impossibility for private-sector organisations

* they provide services that are essential to the well-being of the whole population of a country, such as healthcare, street lighting or defence

Examples of public enterprises include the National Health Service (NHS), which was created to provide a range of free health and medical services for everyone in the UK.

Not-for-profit organisations

There are a number of other organisations that cannot be classified as public or private. Not all enterprises aim to provide a national service or to make a profit; some exist to make the world a better place. These are charities. They are non-profit enterprises that actually aim to raise surplus money that can be used to benefit people, animals or other causes.

Examples of not-for-profit organisations include:

* Oxfam, a well known international charity formed to help people living in poverty
* The Royal Society for the Protection of Animals (RSPCA), a British charity which aims to prevent cruelty, promote kindness to and alleviate the suffering of animals

Organisations: Brick, Click or Brick and Click

We are seeing an increase in large, traditional organisations – sometimes referred to as 'brick and mortar' organisations – developing their own websites. They have learnt that it is possible to expand their operations by taking advantage of the Internet and e-business. In fact, many organisations that make the move from 'brick' to 'click' outperform established dot-com (or click-only) companies within months.

Organisations such as Tesco, Marks & Spencer and many more have used information technology and the Internet to evolve and access markets and customers they have never been able to reach before. Being able to describe organisations as brick (physical high-street presence, but no website), brick and click (physical high-street presence with website) or click (no high-street presence, all business operated via the Web) organisations is just another way of helping us to group diverse organisations and see similarities between them.

Activity 2.2

Investigate businesses in your area

Working in small groups, produce a colourful and eye-catching poster that shows at least ten diverse examples of organisations in your local area. For each organisation illustrated, clearly state their purpose (what they do and why), whether they are public or private, operate for profit or not-for-profit and whether they are a brick, click or brick and click organisation.

Personal Learning and Thinking Skills

Completing this activity will develop your skills of enquiry. You will use sources of information to research a wide variety of business types and categorise them.

Functional Skills – ICT

Using ICT to carry out research and present findings.

Summary

* Different organisations have different objectives. In general, organisations in the private sector wish to maximise their profits and organisations in the public sector wish to provide maximum service value to the public.
* We can also describe organisations in terms of whether their main aim is to make a profit or not. Charities are not profit-orientated but they do aim to raise surpluses of money to spend on helping people, animals and good causes.
* Brick and click is another interesting way of categorising organisations. Most businesses these days have a web presence.

Organisational structure

An organisational structure comprises the relationships between people and functions that enable a business to produce the goods or the services it supplies in order to achieve its objectives.

Business objectives

The specific aims or goals that an organisation seeks to achieve are called business objectives.

Organisational chart

An organisational chart is a diagram illustrating the many aspects of an organisation including job titles of key staff, the departments or teams in which they work and their relationships with each other. Organisational charts are similar to family trees with the most experienced, authoritative and responsible people at the top and the least responsible at the bottom.

Chain of command

The lines of communication that run from the managers at the top of the organisational chart to employees at the bottom are known as the chain of command.

Span of control

The number of employees controlled by a particular person within an organisation is known as that person's span of control.

Organisational Structures and Roles

Some organisational structures can be very complex. The structure of an organisation can be illustrated effectively by using a diagram called an organisational chart.

Organisational structures

An organisation's structure describes how its activities are arranged. In medium to large organisations employees carrying out similar tasks work in teams, for example sales teams. This is called specialisation. If this didn't happen organisations would be unmanageable. A clearly structured organisation may be called **formal** because everyone who works within it has a title and a list of responsibilities. Each group of workers in a formal structure will have a manager who ensures that their work is acceptable and the organisation is operating efficiently.

In smaller organisations you may see a more **informal** structure in which work is shared among a few members of staff. They are likely to carry out a wider range of duties; for example, business managers might be responsible for taking orders and for resolving complaints. As organisations grow they become more formal to keep their overall performance under control.

Although the structures vary, they have one thing in common: they exist to ensure employees carry out their duties efficiently so that customers remain satisfied and organisations achieve their **business objectives**, whatever they may be.

Organisational chart

The **organisational chart** is similar to a family tree and looks very much like a pyramid with the person at the top having the most authority. Each person in the organisation is responsible to the person immediately above them. This is sometimes referred to as the **chain of command**. Managers and supervisors have the authority to pass work to people below them in the chain of command. How much authority a person has in an organisation is sometimes referred to as their **span of control**. The higher up the organisational chart you are the wider your span of control.

Roles

Managing Director (MD)

Managing Directors take responsibility for the day-to-day decisions that need to be made in the running of the company. They are supported by their managers or heads of department.

Managers

Managers are senior members of staff who are often responsible for one department or function within the organisation. Managers are accountable for the daily decision-making in their area of

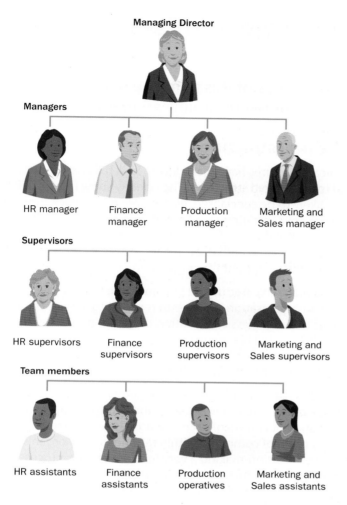

Managing Director

Managers

HR manager | Finance manager | Production manager | Marketing and Sales manager

Supervisors

HR supervisors | Finance supervisors | Production supervisors | Marketing and Sales supervisors

Team members

HR assistants | Finance assistants | Production operatives | Marketing and Sales assistants

Chain of command

responsibility, solving any problems that occur, planning for the future development of their function, ensuring targets for performance are achieved and generally organising staff and resources so that the organisation achieves its objectives.

Supervisors and team leaders

Supervisors and team leaders are staff who are responsible to the managers above them and for the team members below them. They supervise and lead the work of their team.

Team members (operatives)

Team members, or operatives, are staff who carry out the day-to-day tasks essential to the smooth running of a business. In retail organisations they might be the shop assistants. In manufacturing they are the machine operators, production workers and so on. It is common at this level to also see trainees and apprentices learning the skills of certain jobs while still attending college.

Summary

* An organisational chart is an illustration of how people working within an organisation and carrying out certain roles are linked to one another.

Types of organisational structure

For the purpose of this unit, you need to be aware of a variety of different organisational structures.

Hierarchical structures

Hierarchical structures have many levels, look tall and are often referred to as pyramid structures. They clearly show responsibilities. Roles are likely to be specialised, with employees in each function or department concentrating on a limited range of duties. Hierarchical structures are usually very formal and often have clear rules and procedures associated with the roles, for example codes of dress, so that standards throughout the organisation can be maintained.

The taller a hierarchical structure becomes, the less flexible it is. This can mean an organisation is slower to respond to market changes, sometimes making it less competitive. Large national organisations like the NHS have tall hierarchies.

Wide and narrow structures

Organisations with many layers of management, supervisors and workers are referred to as tall organisations. As there are so many layers, the span of control of each manager is very **narrow**. There is a very long chain of command within tall and narrow organisations, which makes decision-making a very formal and long process. The benefits of a tall structure with a narrow span of control are that there will be clear lines of responsibility and lots of opportunity for promotion.

Flat organisations, like the one illustrated, have very few levels of management and are usually quite simple organisations. As such, the chain of command from the top to the bottom is short and the managers generally have a **wider** span of control. Wide structures are present in organisations where there are a range of values and ways of thinking that are taken for granted and influence decision-making and daily activities.

In the organisation illustrated, aspects of a wider structure may be reflected in the way all the therapists wear a similar uniform, or the routine with which they meet and greet their clients. They will do these things in the same way without really being aware of the routine that has been created and its value to their clients. In larger and taller organisations these routines may exist, but will have been planned and recorded as a set procedure. Over time these procedures become part of the organisation's deeper structure as they are carried out routinely and unconsciously by staff.

STRUCTURES, STRUCTURES EVERYWHERE!

What kinds of organisational structure can you recognise? Think about your school or college, societies and clubs and even the organisations you may work for part time.

TALL

FLAT

Hierarchical structures

Activity 2.4

Look at the example flat structure.

1 How many levels can you count?

2 Redraw the chart showing how it would look if the partners recruited two additional trainee therapists who are at a higher level than the receptionists.

3 Why do you think it is important that this business has a flat structure? List as many advantages as you can.

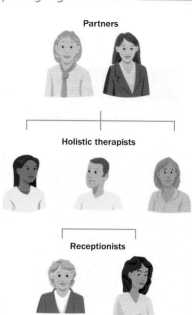

An example of a flat structure

Centralised and decentralised structures

In addition to the types of structure above, an organisation's structure can be further described as being centralised or decentralised. **Centralised** organisations are ones in which all the main support services are grouped together. For example, if you worked for your local council or in a large college of further education you might find that functions such as Reprographics, Administration, IT Support Services and Purchasing are centralised. This means, for example, that all the main photocopying and printing for the whole organisation is done centrally by one Reprographics function.

Decentralised organisations do not have any centralised functions. For example, each functional area will carry out their own photocopying, printing, filing and administration and IT support.

Activity 2.5

Consider the benefits and drawbacks for a large organisation considering changing from a decentralised structure to a centralised structure. Work in small groups and present your comments back to the class.

Centralisation of services

Summary

✳ Hierarchical structures are common in large and public sector organisations. They are characterised by many levels of authority.

✳ Hierarchical structures have many levels, so communication tends to be slower and quick change is difficult to achieve.

✳ Many organisations are moving towards flatter structures, taking whole levels of authority out of the organisation and passing on responsibility to lower levels of staff.

Types of organisational structure

So far we have considered hierarchical, narrow and wide, centralised and decentralised structures. There is one more widely known structure that is growing in popularity amongst certain types of businesses, which we will investigate here – matrix structures.

Matrix structures

Matrix structures are very different from other types of structure and are less common than hierarchical or flat structures. In matrix structures employees are grouped by their skills or function (department) rather than by their position of authority. The reason for this is that certain members of staff may have involvement with other functions. As an example, consider a large department store. It may be structured hierarchically (as in the diagram below), split into retail departments (such as Home and Electrical Goods and Men's Wear) and functional areas (such as Human Resources and Purchasing).

THE MATRIX STRUCTURE

Nothing ever stays the same in business. Some organisations have project teams consisting of specialists from all the functional areas (departments) within it. Can you suggest any possible disadvantages of using any of the previously discussed organisation structures in this situation?

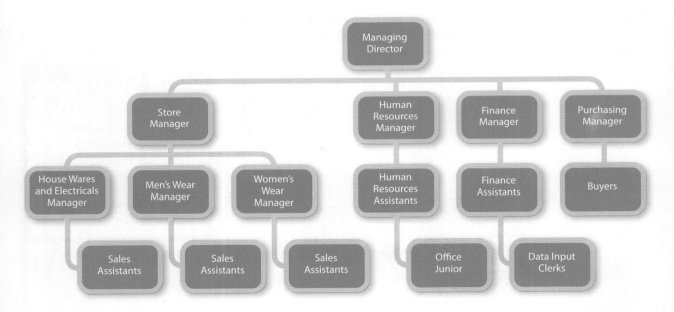

The hierarchical structure may work well but there may be conflict between departments. For example, what would happen if Men's Wear and Home and Electrical Goods both needed the buyers in the Purchasing function to research, source and purchase new ranges of products at the same time? The buyers may choose to prioritise Home and Electrical Goods and let Men's Wear wait. A matrix structure solves this problem by having key staff in each supporting department who work specifically with each retail department.

	Purchasing	Human Resources	Finance
Men's Wear	Staff looking after Men's Wear	Staff looking after Men's Wear	Staff looking after Men's Wear
House Wares	Staff looking after House Wares	Staff looking after House Wares	Staff looking after House Wares
Women's Wear	Staff looking after Women's Wear	Staff looking after Women's Wear	Staff looking after Women's Wear

Matrix structures are very common in organisations that specialise in one-off projects, such as construction and engineering companies that build bridges, commercial buildings and motorways. Teams of people formed from a range of specialists, functions and backgrounds will work together on one project easily within a matrix structure such as that shown below. The lines represent the relationships that occur in each project. One person in Finance, for example, could be accountable to several managers at once.

However, matrix structures do have limitations. Conflict between managers over key members of staff can occur. Also, members of staff who report to several managers can be overloaded with work because their managers are not aware of the workload placed on them by other managers.

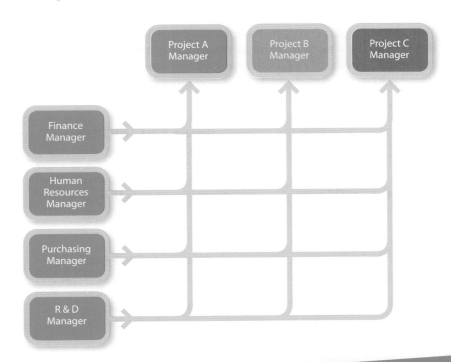

Activity 2.6

Consider your own school or college. Are there members of staff that operate in more than one teaching department or teach in more than one group? Are there any support staff that provide assistance to all teaching departments, for example a secretary? Draw a hierarchical and matrix structure for your school or college. For each, highlight one benefit and one limitation.

Summary

* Matrix structures are popular, particularly in organisations where activities or projects are carried out by teams of people with a variety of skills.

Organisational cultures

This section investigates organisational culture: the values and beliefs of organisations (their mission) as reflected in their brand identity, what their purposes are (their aims and objectives) and how they manage their employees (management style). These things combine to form the culture of an organisation.

Mission statements, beliefs and values, and brand identity

A *mission statement* is like a slogan. It concisely summarises an organisation's *beliefs and values*: what an organisation does and what it 'stands for'. The statement is very short, but embodies the promise that an organisation makes to its customers every day. You will see examples of mission statements in the box below.

The way an organisation develops and brands its products or services is also linked to its culture and the overall message it wishes to send to its customers. *Branding* is the process of creating a brand: the visual, emotional, and cultural image that a business wishes customers to associate with its services or products.

Take, for example, Weetabix. Weetabix is one of the strongest and most well known cereal brands in the UK and this is because of the Weetabix Food Company's successful marketing of it on a 'healthy platform'. The Weetabix Food Company have invested millions of pounds in developing the Weetabix brand identity, highlighting to customers the health benefits of its products so that any item with the Weetabix brand will be associated with healthy and nutritious imagery.

Mission statements

Government – NHS Direct
'To provide information and advice about health, illness and health services, to enable patients to make decisions about their healthcare and that of their families.'

Retail – ASDA
'To be the UK's best value retailer exceeding customer needs. Always.'

Manufacturing – Ford
'We are a global, diverse family with a proud heritage, passionately committed to providing outstanding products and services.'

Sport and Leisure – Total Fitness Health Clubs
'Your health and well being are our priority. It is our aim to offer you the best facilities and programmes with professional expertise in a friendly and caring atmosphere to help you achieve a unique health and fitness experience at an affordable price.'

Aims and objectives

Organisations operate simply to achieve the **aims** and **objectives** they have set. How successful an organisation is depends very much on how its aims and objectives have been achieved.

Organisations need aims and objectives for a number of reasons:

* so that all employees know what levels of performance they are all working towards

* so that decisions can be made with achievement of objectives in mind

* so that employee and organisational performance can be measured against them

Aims and objectives will vary depending on the type of organisation. Private-sector organisations such as ASDA (in food retail), Total Fitness Health Clubs (in sport and leisure) and Ford (in car manufacturing) are focused on earning maximum profits for their owners/shareholders. Public-sector organisations focus on maximising the levels of service offered to the public, such as when the NHS commits to reducing operation and treatment waiting times. Voluntary and charitable organisations, such as Oxfam, will also wish to maximise the money they make, but this isn't regarded as profit: it is surplus money used to carry out charitable work.

Aim

An aim is a general statement of what an organisation wishes to achieve. It is rarely specific or measurable, for example, 'We aim to provide outstanding customer service.'

Objective

Objectives are specific, measurable, achievable, realistic and time-constrained (SMART) statements of intended performance. For example, 'We will reduce customer complaints by 10 per cent by the end of 2008.'

Activity 2.8

Culture and Aims & Objectives

Working in pairs, consider the following statement and try to explain it using your knowledge of mission statements, values/beliefs and brand identity. You may wish to use the Weetabix illustration.

"The culture of an organisation contributes to the achievement of its aims and objectives."

Activity 2.9

A Business Investigation

Now is your chance to find out a little more about an organisation that interests you. On a large piece of paper, produce a poster detailing the following for your chosen organisation:

* the purpose of the organisation (what it does and for whom)

* its mission statement (and core values/beliefs, if you can find them)

* its brand identity (what it wants customers to believe about its products and services)

* its aims and its objectives (SMART)

Present your poster to the rest of your group. It might be worth checking if anyone else in your class is intending to investigate the same organisation.

Summary

* Every organisation has a mission. Some organisations record their missions in writing and communicate them to their staff and customers. They try to build the mission into every single activity carried out by the business.

* Every organisation has aims and objectives. Again, some have them written down so that an organisation's performance can be reviewed at some time in the future. Aims and objectives allow all the employees of an organisation to focus on achieving the same thing, for example improving customer service, reducing waste or increasing sales.

Management style

One way in which organisations can differ is in the management style adopted by their managers. The management style used is closely linked to the culture, values and beliefs of the organisation.

Managers are those people in an organisation tasked with the responsibility of overseeing workers and ensuring they carry out their duties. How effectively they do this will most certainly influence how successful the team, department and business is at achieving its aims and objectives (see pgs 46–47). The experience of managing will vary depending on the type of business a manager is operating within. For example, managers working in a retail outlet such as a clothes store or fast food restaurant will be concerned with the day to day smooth running of the store. This may involve receiving deliveries, planning staffing rotas and dealing with problems and staff-related issues as and when they occur. The table below describes some of the most widely recognised styles of management or leadership.

Autocratic	All decisions are taken by managers with little or no consultation with employees. They expect their orders to be carried out without question.
Democratic	Democratic managers involve employees in decision-making, considering everyone's viewpoint. This style is common in small and motivated teams but may not work where employees are used to having and like a lot of guidance from their managers.
Consultative	Consultative managers will listen to everyone's point of view but they make the decisions which they feel are best. Consultative managers increase the motivation of their staff and quality of teamwork by valuing what their team members have to say.
Paternalistic	Paternalistic managers are concerned with the feelings of their team members. In the same way as consultative managers, they make decisions taking workers' feelings into account.
Laissez-faire	This style of management is very different from the previous four in that there is very little direct management occurring. Laissez-faire managers let their employees self-manage. This style will only be effective where workers are motivated and can work independently with little or no guidance.

Managers have to perform a diverse range of duties. How they handle their staff will depend on their individual or personal style of management, the situations they are in and the kind of people they are managing.

They may believe that as a leader they are ultimately responsible for what happens and become autocratic in their management

TO MANAGE OR NOT TO MANAGE

Do you prefer to be told what to do? Or do you like to be asked for your opinions? What kind of manager would you be?

Management style
The term 'management style' refers to the approach adopted by managers in an organisation when exercising their authority, encouraging employees to contribute to decision-making and maintaining control so that performance targets can be achieved.

Organisational culture
Simply, the organisational culture is 'the way things are done' in the company. Culture is unique and will vary from one organisation to the next.

Activity 2.10

Consider the following situations and, for each, identify the style of management used, giving clear reasons for its appropriateness. The definitions in the table may be useful.
* school
* part-time employer
* organised group (for example Scouts, sports team etc.)
* home

style, making all the decisions and controlling the activities of every member in their team. Alternatively, they may believe in the increased motivation and performance of staff that comes from listening to and involving them in their decision making. This would make them democratic or consultative managers.

Remember that some styles may be inappropriate in certain situations. For example, a democratic style of management is less effective if your staff are accustomed to being told what to do and have no desire to contribute to decision making. Teams working in highly stressful emergency situations, such as a team of fire-fighters responding to a house fire, would be better handled by an autocratic style. Why do you think this would be the case? Effective managers take a flexible approach; they will select the style of management that best suits the situation and people they are managing.

Organisational culture

How an organisation is structured, its mission, aims and objectives, its brand identity and the style of management used within it all contribute to its overall **organisational culture**.

As an organisation develops and grows it develops expected patterns of behaviour which become part of its culture. The culture in a small organisation may be very different from the culture in a large organisation. It could extend from how telephone calls are answered to how staff are expected to dress. Everything that is done within the business reflects the values and mission of the organisation. Look at how Tesco describes its culture to perspective employees.

Personal Learning and Thinking Skills

By collaborating with others and working towards common goals you can develop your team working skills.

Case Study: Tesco's Culture

Three words sum up the culture at Tesco: 'Every Little Helps'.

* Working in small groups, consider the three words above. What do they mean to employees and customers and how do you think Tesco shows it?

* Think about any small local organisations or companies in your area. Are there any similarities in their culture to Tesco's? Are there any differences?

Summary

* Every organisation is different. Over time they develop their own style of managing people, often depending on the type of work carried out and the characteristics of their employees.

* The culture of an organisation is often linked to its values and mission. Therefore, if a company values its customers and wishes to provide the highest levels of service, it must first value its staff by training and developing them so that they possess the skills and the right attitudes to ensure customers are always satisfied.

2.2 Key business processes and 2.3 Technology used to support key business processes

This section introduces and discusses a range of key business processes that usually contribute to improved rates of customer satisfaction and so to the good image and overall success of organisations. It also explores and provides examples of the role and importance of information technology in carrying out and satisfying each key business process.

Key business processes and how they are linked

The diagram below details some, or all, of the key business processes you may have identified in your answer to Activity 2.11. These processes are the ones you need to be aware of for the purpose of this unit, but you may have identified many more. You will notice that the processes are linked by arrows. This highlights the fact that each process is dependent on others. For example, obtaining an in-depth understanding of customer needs, wants and behaviours through customer relationship management processes will support organisations in developing products, services and producing advertising and promotions that will attract customers, create interest in their goods or services, make customers desire them and actually act on these desires by purchasing them (marketing).

Customer Relationship Management (CRM) – Learning about the needs and behaviours of customers will allow organisations to identify ways to keep them as customers and attract new customers.

Marketing

Based on knowledge gained from CRM and market research, organisations are more able to develop products/services that customers desire at a price they are willing to pay, to make them available to customers in the right places and to attract customers using the right advertising and promotional techniques.

Service Delivery and Supply and Demand

How effectively an organisation satisfies its customers' needs depends on their ability to provide products and services when they are demanded and to deliver them to expected standards of service.

People management and performance management

How customers experience an organisation relies very much on the quality of service they receive from employees of the organisation and the quality of the products manufactured by employees of the organisation. By effectively managing the performance of employees and keeping them motivated the needs and expectations of customers will be achieved.

Key business processes

Importance of technology used to support key business processes

As organisations develop and grow they become increasingly reliant on information technology to support them in carrying out their daily activities and key processes. You will certainly be aware of some technological applications commonly used by businesses today such as the Internet and business websites. Established retail organisations such as Marks & Spencer have even accepted that if they are to compete they need to offer a variety of different ways to purchase goods including e-purchasing online. In addition, they use a variety of different technology to collect data on their customers' buying habits so that they can use it to develop and target products and services that will satisfy them in the future.

Case Study: The Technology of Loyalty

Loyalty cards have been around in one form or another for years. Your parents or carers may even carry one from Tesco on their keys in the form of a key fob! Essentially, these cards are used to reward customers for their loyalty, thus retaining them as customers and not losing them to the competition.

Supermarkets have probably been the most successful implementers of loyalty schemes, with Tesco offering 1 point for every £1 spent on shopping. Points are collected and exchanged for money-off vouchers that can be used to offset the cost of goods bought in the future. Other organisations, such as Caffe Nero, give their customers simple cards which are stamped every time they purchase a drink; when they collect nine stamps their tenth drink is free. GAME also have a reward card scheme offering customers 10 points for every £1 they spend – 1000 points can be exchanged for £2.50 off purchases.

The real benefit of loyalty cards, some feel, is the 'database potential' they offer. Customers provide organisations with lots of personal data, such as their age, profession and where they live. Every purchase made with a loyalty card will be stored on a database as data. The organisation can then use this data to understand the purchasing behaviour of customers, such as what beauty products or brands are commonly purchased by females aged 20–25. Most organisations will use this data to send vouchers and offers tailored to each individual customer.

However, there are some people who have serious concerns over the use and privacy of people's personal data collected by such organisations.

1. List the benefits of loyalty schemes to customers and organisations.
2. What do you think is meant by the phrase 'database potential' in the case study above?
3. What concerns should we have when providing organisations with our personal information?

Summary

* Successful organisations often have one thing in common: how much they value their customers.
* Establishing good relationships with existing customers and attracting new customers is dependent on a variety of different business processes including service delivery, people and performance management and, of course, marketing.
* As organisations grow they become increasingly reliant on information technology to help them carry out their key business processes.

Customer Relationship Management (CRM)

The term 'customer relationship management' refers to all the activities performed by an organisation to build and maintain long-term relationships with its customers. Customers of organisations that employ CRM have better experiences than those of organisations that do not; thereby, it is hoped, increasing sales and profits. Effective CRM is supported by complex IT systems that help an organisation to make the right marketing decisions (product/service design, price, promotion and distribution) to ensure customers' needs and expectations are being constantly met (and possibly surpassed!).

Market share

The percentage of total sales for a specific product or service achieved by an organisation is known as its market share. The higher the market share the greater the proportion of sales they have achieved.

Profitability

Profitability is a measure of financial success. Profit is the amount of money left after costs and expenses have been paid. The higher the profitability of an organisation the more profit it is making on every £1 of sales.

Customer Relationship Management

The better an organisation can manage the relationships it has with its customers the more successful it is likely to be. Successful organisations are ones that attempt to learn about their customers' needs and behaviours in order to develop an even stronger relationship with them and so be even more responsive to their needs.

Having effective **Customer Relationship Management (CRM)** means an organisation will be able to make changes that help it to keep its existing customers and attract new ones. Therefore, effective CRM can lead to an organisation increasing its **market share** and therefore its **profitability**, and can also contribute to increasing the efficiency of the organisation's business processes. In addition, it should lead to fewer customer complaints and an improved organisation image.

Stages of CRM

The next diagram shows the typical stages that an organisation may go through in managing its relationships with its customers.

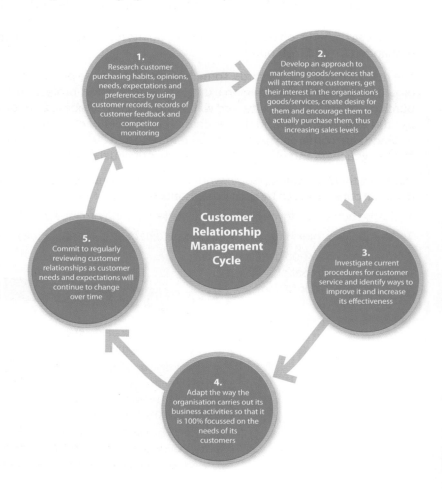

Customer Relationship Management Cycle

1. Research customer purchasing habits, opinions, needs, expectations and preferences by using customer records, records of customer feedback and competitor monitoring

2. Develop an approach to marketing goods/services that will attract more customers, get their interest in the organisation's goods/services, create desire for them and encourage them to actually purchase them, thus increasing sales levels

3. Investigate current procedures for customer service and identify ways to improve it and increase its effectiveness

4. Adapt the way the organisation carries out its business activities so that it is 100% focussed on the needs of its customers

5. Commit to regularly reviewing customer relationships as customer needs and expectations will continue to change over time

Commitment to customer service

Every time a customer is exposed to an organisation it should be seen as an opportunity to improve the image of the organisation and assure future sales. Organisations that listen to customer feedback and use schemes to increase customer loyalty will be more successful at retaining existing customers and increasing sales by attracting new customers. Organisations committed to customer service will:

* Invest money in conducting research to allow them to find out and understand exactly who their customers are and what their needs and expectations are.
* Develop products and services at a price and quality that satisfy customer needs and expectations.
* Develop a customer care policy. This is a statement of intentions towards customers. Customer care policies are regularly integrated with the overall mission of the organisation and staff are often trained in the meaning and delivery of the policy in their own area of responsibility. A commitment to customer care is a commitment to high quality and personalised service for every customer.
* Regularly measure customer satisfaction levels to monitor customer service effectiveness or efficiency. For example, organisations may monitor sales, complaints, returned and faulty goods, order fulfilment times, customer service feedback and surveys.
* Develop an established organisational procedure for promptly dealing with customer complaints so that the complaint will be avoided in the future.

Activity 2.12

Working in pairs or small groups, first list who the customers of your school/college are. For each customer, identify what the needs and expectations of the school/college are and then, using all the information you have, create a short customer care policy listing a range of promises your school/college will make to its customers. Present your policy back to the rest of the class and discuss it.

Summary

* There has never been a time when the importance of satisfying and keeping customers has been more important. After all, it actually costs a business more money to attract a new customer than it does to keep an existing one!

Customer Relationship Management Continued...

This section explores how organisations can use customer relationship management techniques to seek and secure customer loyalty.

HOW LOYAL ARE YOU?

Are you an independent consumer or are you influenced by the clever marketing tactics of some organisations?

There are many things an organisation can do to market itself and to enhance the image its existing and potential customers have of it. For example it can:

* choose a business name and company logo that reflect what the organisation does and convey its attitude to customer satisfaction
* develop products that customers value and desire and that meet their needs and expectations
* set prices at a reasonable level reflecting value for money and quality
* offer preferential discounts to existing and valued customers
* increase ways customers can access and purchase goods and services, for example by developing a presence on the Web (sometimes known as moving from 'brick to click')
* select advertising that communicates how much an organisation values its customers
* develop customer-friendly websites, on which all frequently asked questions could be answered and via which customers can easily make contact
* provide customers with free order and help lines
* provide free customer product samples
* notify customers of further purchasing possibilities such as the release of upgraded products
* introduce customer loyalty schemes rewarding existing customers for their continued purchases
* train all front-line (sales) staff so that they are knowledgeable and can aid customers in making the right decision for their needs

Personal Learning and Thinking Skills

If you are able to present a persuasive case for action to help an organisation improve its image, you will be able to apply your effective participation skills.

Activity 2.13

Working in pairs or small groups, identify two organisations that are known to you, one that you feel has a good organisational image and one that in your opinion does not. Explain for each what they do or do not do to enhance the customer service offered to existing and potential customers. Suggest possible actions that could be taken by the poor organisation to enhance its image. Feed your comments back to the rest of the class.

Use of technology in CRM and enhancing company image

Organisations are increasingly using technology to help them manage customer relationships. The most commonly used forms of technology in CRM are as follows.

- **Customer/marketing databases** – These are internal databases detailing customer sales histories and are used to identify the most profitable customers and product lines. This data helps organisations to identify who to focus their marketing efforts on. They also achieve a better understanding of the customers' needs and expectations and how to effectively communicate with them. Organisations wishing to set up their own CRM system may use affordable database packages such as Microsoft Access or more expensive specialised bespoke packages that are linked or integrated into an organisation's existing systems and that will automatically extract data and present it for managers to use and make decisions with. Retail organisations will use Electronic Point of Sale (EPOS) systems linked to loyalty card details in order to profile customers' purchasing patterns. This information can be used by retailers to offer special incentives to customers, such as money-off vouchers. **Benefits**: Improves efficiency, streamlines supply chains, cuts costs, enhances customer relationships and helps to identify improvements to products and services offered.

- **Websites** – Although these can be extremely expensive to set up and run, having a Web presence can be beneficial. Not only does a website give an organisation an additional outlet for distribution of goods and services, but it can also provide existing and potential customers with a wealth of product and service information and also provide good customer service. Good websites will have customer complaint or feedback/query forms to make customer contact with an organisation easier. In addition, websites can be provide data about the pages visited by customers and products considered but not actually purchased. This behaviour can be investigated and changes made to increase the chance of future purchases. Finally, websites can offer the user regular marketing material such as product or service update newsletters. This is called 'permission marketing'. In return for regular emails, customers provide personal information that organisations can use to fully understand who their customers really are and how best to communicate with them and satisfy their needs and expectations. **Benefits**: Enhances customer relationships and helps to identify improvements to the products and services offered.

Summary

* Retaining existing customers and attracting new ones is a difficult task particularly when there is a lot of competition for a limited number of customers.

* Larger organisations make great use of technology such as customer databases to help them identify who their customers are and what their purchasing history is like.

* This information is used to decide which marketing tactics should be used to encourage these customers to continue purchasing. For example, Tesco Loyalty Card holders will regularly receive vouchers to encourage them to go into their local store and make purchases.

People management

The people (employees) an organisation recruits, the training they receive and how valued they feel will all impact on the service provided by them to the organisation's customers.

Case Study: *The Sunday Times* 100 Best Companies to Work For

Every year *The Sunday Times* carries out a national survey to measure staff satisfaction levels. In 2006 and 2007, according to *The Sunday Times*, the best company with the best workplace standards was W.L. Gore & Associates. For two years running the survey revealed this company has offered its employees 'better personal growth, greater team spirit and a stronger sense of belonging'. W.L. Gore & Associates operates in the manufacturing sector, designing and producing high-technology fabrics and materials for a variety of applications. The company is best known for GORE-TEX® fabrics used in water-resistant hiking wear.

The survey looks at five aspects of organisational life:

* **leadership** – how employees feel about the head of their company and their senior management team
* **well-being** – how employees feel about stress, pressure and the balance between home and work
* **belonging** – how much employees feel they belong to and are welcomed by their company
* **giving back** – how much employees felt their companies put back into society and the local community
* **personal growth** – the extent to which employees felt challenged by their roles

Motivating Staff

How an organisation treats its staff says a lot about the company and its practices. It is fair to say that good employers will get a reputation for being fair employers that reward their staff and therefore will attract high-calibre candidates in future recruitment campaigns. This, in turn, will increase the quality of staff working for the organisation.

If you employ high-quality staff who feel challenged, valued and rewarded, they are likely to be highly motivated and thus the quality of their work will be high, ensuring customers are satisfied.

Organisations with effective people management will select a style of management and culture that will encourage staff to contribute to the operation and to help improve existing working practices. By consulting staff and listening to their views, managers ensure that their employees feel listened to, involved and valued. Different management styles are listed on page 44. The styles that would most likely lead to this are democratic, consultative and paternalistic. Remember though, not all members of staff wish to contribute to, or be involved in, decision-making and so an autocratic style might suit them.

Working for fair and effective leaders is far more rewarding than working for bad leaders. The qualities of a good leader include the following.

* acting as a role model and putting the organisation's mission statement, values and customer care policy into action at all times
* showing initiative and entrepreneurialism and identifying opportunities for continuous improvement
* the ability to encourage and inspire teams and individual staff members to grow and continuously improve
* the ability to listen to what others say and take their comments and ideas into consideration when making decisions

It is much easier to feel motivated in your job if you understand what your organisation requires from you. All jobs should have clear and concise job descriptions. A well-designed job will:

* have a clear list of duties to be performed by the job-holder
* offer opportunities to challenge and develop the job-holder
* use the qualities, skills and experience of the job-holder

Finally, it is in the interests of organisations to encourage employees to perform at their best and this is commonly achieved through **performance appraisals**.

Performance appraisals allow managers to recognise their team members' achievements and strengths. They are also an opportunity to discuss weaknesses and ways in which a team member could possibly improve their performance, such as by receiving training and development. Career aspirations are also often discussed and team members will understand what is required of them if they are to be considered for promotion in the future.

If carried out effectively, performance appraisals are an opportunity for managers to praise or reward a team member's performance and commitment. This will lead to better working relationships, which will mean that employees feel valued and therefore motivated to work harder and to perform better.

Performance appraisal

Organisations use regular (sometimes monthly or annual) meetings, known as performance appraisals, between an employee and line managers, to review the employee's work and achievements since the previous appraisal. The employee's performance is usually compared with targets or standards of performance expected and new targets are usually agreed to further improve the employee's performance. The appraisal system operates to improve the overall performance of the organisation.

Activity 2.15

Working in small groups, produce a list of benefits to employers and employees of performance appraisals. If you can, identify any possible drawbacks of performance appraisals faced by employers and employees. Present your list to the rest of the class.

Summary

* Some organisations say, 'people are our most valuable asset'. The reason for this is that without highly motivated and skilled staff it would be impossible to offer customers the goods and services they desire at the right quality and at the right price.
* The motivation of staff is linked to a variety of factors, one of which is the need for effective management with innovative and motivational leaders.
* Where the employees and their managers believe in the value of appraisals they can contribute to staff feeling more valued and recognised and therefore motivated in their work. When this is accomplished, staff performance increases and organisations can become more effective.

Recruiting and Retaining Suitable Staff

As well as motivational leadership, there are other factors that influence how effectively an organisation's employees perform.

Recruitment of the right staff

When an organisation has a position available they need to ensure they recruit the right person for the right post. Recruiting staff can be very expensive in terms of advertising, hiring specialist human resources agencies and even the time taken to sort through applications and to interview candidates. If the wrong person is chosen, the organisation may have to bear the cost of an ineffective person in the role for many years. Therefore, recruitment requires careful planning and consideration.

First, the post is thoroughly investigated and a **job description** is drawn up. Another important document, called a **person specification**, is produced at the same time. The job description and person specification will inform the content of a job advertisement so that only suitable people will apply. Those who most closely match the requirements will then be short-listed and invited to an **interview**. During the interview, interviewers decide which candidates will satisfy all the qualities desired in the post-holder and will fit into the existing culture and ethos of the organisation. This is a very complicated and time-consuming process and it needs to be done without any discrimination to applicants based on their ethnic background, gender, age, religion or other relevant factors.

Retention of staff

In businesses where it is difficult to find people with the right qualities, skills and experience, it is extremely important to retain staff within the organisation. This is even more important if the organisation is losing its highly trained and experienced staff to a competitor. Losing a member of staff is very costly: the organisation will have to recruit another person and provide cover for the position until it is filled. In addition, the new person will need to be trained and is unlikely to be as effective as the existing member of staff for months or even years. Therefore, if a business is losing its valuable staff they need to find out why and rectify it. Reasons could be as simple as a competitor offering a better package or better prospects for promotion. Organisations should then always try to maximise an employee's opportunities to develop and move up the hierarchy. Where this isn't possible the organisation should ensure the staff member has a varied job so that they do not become bored and unmotivated. They could also ensure they give their employees an opportunity to contribute to the running of the business by consulting everyone on where and how they feel the business should move and improve. Overall, employees need to feel valued by their organisation and this feeling can be created in many ways as discussed earlier in the section on motivation.

RECRUITING THE RIGHT PERSON FOR THE RIGHT JOB

'Quality people = Quality service'

Comment on this quote and explain what role effective recruitment and selection of employees has in organisations.

Job description

A document summarising the most important aspects of a job, and may include general duties performed, post holders' responsibilities, and level of skills required.

Person specification

A document summarising the specific skills, abilities and personal qualities desired by an ideal candidate.

Use of technology in people management

Even in terms of people management, technology can help organisations to keep records to help them manage staff performance. Human resource systems could include the following records for access and review at any time:

* personal details
* employment history
* records of absences, including lateness and sickness
* training attended
* appraisal documents with old and new performance targets
* details of disciplinary issues or actions taken

Small organisations might use a manual record system but as organisations grow they usually invest in a bespoke computerised record system, which is simply a database that is regularly updated by human resource administrators. For records to be accurate the human resources department will rely on managers notifying them of staff lateness, absences, disciplinary action, changes in job description and performance reviews.

Other people management technology includes:

* **360-degree Appraisals Systems** – These are computerised systems that are designed to compile all the data collected from a 360-degree appraisal on one member of staff. This kind of appraisal involves a member of staff's peers, subordinates, supervisors, managers and sometimes their internal and external customers rating their performance and their overall suitability for promotion or succession. **Benefits**: Improves efficiency, cuts costs, enhances customer relationships and helps to identify improvements to the services offered.

* **Payroll Systems –** These are computerised systems designed to speed up and increase the accuracy of wage and salary payments by an organisation to their employees. These systems will automatically calculate how many hours someone has worked, what they should be paid, how much tax, national insurance and other deductions should be deducted from an employee's pay before producing a wage slip with all the information on it and instructing the organisation's bank to make a payment into their employee's bank account. **Benefits**: Improves efficiency and accuracy, and cuts administration costs.

* **Intranets** – These are internal, secure, private networks shared by a group of users who work in the same organisation. In terms of people management they are a useful way of communicating in large organisations when a position has become available, just in case there is somebody with the desire and skills to do the job from within the business. This would save a lot of recruitment costs but the disadvantage is that the business would never experience the new ideas of someone from outside the business. **Benefits**: Improves efficiency and cuts potential recruitment costs.

* **e-training** – This is a very new and cheap training solution being used by organisations. By using on-line training courses, members of staff can update their skills and knowledge at their own pace without being away from work. **Benefits**: Improves efficiency, cuts training costs and enhances customer relationships as staff are still available.

* **Websites** – This technology can help reduce the high costs of recruitment and selection. Many organisations now advertise posts at little or no cost from their own well publicised websites. In fact, people searching for jobs in particular organisations will now automatically access organisations' websites to look for job opportunities. Quite often, interested applicants can fill out on-line application forms and send their curricula vitae electronically. This has sped up the whole process extensively. **Benefits**: Improves efficiency and cuts costs.

Summary

* Failing to recruit the right person for the right position can be extremely costly to an organisation.
* Retaining staff who have skills and qualities that are in short supply is essential. Businesses must do everything they can to ensure their staff are motivated and feel valued.

Supplier management

What is supplier management? It is the name given to all the activities of an organisation that ensure it has enough supplies and the resources it needs to meet its customers' demands constantly and consistently.

Meeting Customer Demands

Suppliers are organisations that provide products (raw materials and resources) or services to other organisations. An organisation's success is very much influenced by the availability of supplies, particularly in manufacturing where the running out of materials would halt the manufacturing process.

This would be extremely costly as the organisation is still paying its staff a wage and incurring the costs of heating and lighting its facilities but is unable to make products to sell to cover these costs.

Therefore, running out of stocks can be extremely costly to some organisations. In particular, if supplies were not received and production was halted, the manufacturer's own customers may then not receive their products on time, causing a knock-on effect.

A QUESTION OF 'SUPPLY AND DEMAND'

Consider your own school or college. Are there any departments or functions that rely heavily on suppliers supplying resources and materials so that it can go about its daily activities?

Activity 2.16

A taste of heaven or hell?

Working in small groups, read and discuss the situation faced by Taste of Heaven Cakes Ltd on page 57. They really do need to become more cost-effective and competitive.

Considering what you know about supplier management, list the potential benefits and drawbacks of each of the consultant's suggestions.

Consider the implications of each on the organisation's ability to satisfy the expectations and demands of its current customers. What would be the costs of not meeting these expectations? What would you recommend if you were the consultant?

Present your views and ideas back to the rest of the class.

Case Study: Taste of Heaven Cakes Ltd

Taste of Heaven Cakes Ltd was established in 1966 as a small bakery employing three people. It is now one of the Midlands' largest cake manufacturers, employing 96 people, of which 10 are dedicated to daily delivery and distribution of fresh cakes across the Midlands.

The cakes made only have a 24-hour shelf life. Over the years the owners of the business have taken advantage of the fact that supply has rarely ever met demand for high-quality fresh cream cakes and so business has been good. They have traded for years on their reputation for manufacturing and supplying the largest range of luxury cream cakes made from the highest-quality ingredients. They promise their customers that any order received will be delivered by 9am the next day.

Just recently, though, they have noticed a drop in sales. A number of smaller cake manufacturers have moved into the region and appear to be attracting some of Taste of Heaven Cakes' regular customers. The main reason for a swap in cake supplier has been price. Competitors are able to offer similar products at 20 per cent less than Taste of Heaven Cakes are charging, although the quality of the cakes is considerably lower. If Taste of Heaven were to drop its prices, it would struggle to continue to make a profit. They have hired a management consultant to investigate possible actions that could be taken to address this competitive pressure. Here are some of the consultant's ideas:

* reduce material costs by substituting some materials used for cheaper alternatives
* identify cheaper suppliers of raw materials (despite being with the current suppliers for decades!)
* close down the highly expensive distribution function and use a distributor instead
* decrease the average cost of cake manufacturing by automating the process and making fewer cakes by hand (this could provide the business with the opportunity to reduce its staffing overheads by 40 per cent)

Summary

* The supply and demand of goods, materials and components is central to all business operations.
* Organisations wish to purchase and manufacture their supplies at the lowest possible cost so that they potentially can make more profit on each item sold.

We know that supplier management ensures organisations have enough supplies and resources needed to meet its customers' demands but what exactly does it entail?

Controlling Quality

Supplier management, as we already know, is a very important aspect of business. In general it involves the following.

* building good relationships with suppliers based on commitment and trust
* agreeing and controlling the quality of service expected, such as delivery times
* agreeing and controlling the quality of materials, goods or components supplied
* ensuring that what has been agreed is adhered to, for example by having penalty clauses in the customer–supplier agreement

Larger organisations may find supplier management a little easier than smaller businesses as they have more power and influence over their suppliers. Suppliers are very motivated to keep large and valuable orders from large organisations or they risk going out of business. For example, Marks and Spencer are an example of a powerful customer. In March 2006 they sent a letter to all their suppliers asking for a 10 per cent discount in prices for goods. Suppliers responded by offering the discount but I wonder how much choice they had. Suppliers to Marks and Spencer have to comply with very high standards of quality and service if they are to be accredited as a Marks and Spencer supplier. However, if a supplier does not deliver what it promises the penalties can be high. Marks and Spencer have been known to reject whole batches of products if there is a slight imperfection or if delivery schedules have not been met.

Efficiency and Profitability

When an organisation has achieved effective supplier management and can rely on the quality and reliability of their suppliers the benefits are as follows.

* Organisations can reduce the amount of materials, components or goods they hold in stock just in case the supply chain fails. This means that less of the organisation's money is tied up in stock sitting on shelves. This money can be invested elsewhere within the organisation, such as in machinery which will have the impact of increasing production efficiency and therefore the profitability of the business.
* Organisations will need less storage space and warehousing, therefore they can save money by not renting warehouses or selling them if they own them. Alternatively, they could use the space to expand production operations. Overall, the cost of warehousing is reduced and money is either saved or invested in expanding production.

Use of technology in supplier management

In large organisations, supplier management relies heavily on technology. Some of the systems and software used to ensure customers' demands are satisfied include:

* **Stock control systems** – These are computerised systems for tracking and valuing stock levels of material, components and even finished goods which are ready to be sold. When manufacturing goods, the production department will request materials and components to be sent from the warehouse. This transfer will be recorded on the computerised stock control system and when levels of materials and components become low an automatic request to order some more will be made by the computer. Sophisticated stock control systems may do this automatically via **on-line ordering**. This is made possible by **electronic data interchange (EDI)**, which allows an organisation to partner with suppliers from all over the world via the Internet and make orders electronically and instantly. This speeds up the ordering process and dealing with partners in, for example, China, does not have to be marred by language or communication problems. As the process is done electronically, it is easy to track the progress of your order via **web-based order tracking**. For example, when you make an order with Amazon you can view the status of your order over the period of time it takes to get to you, which may include 'order being picked' and 'order sent'. Stock control systems are also usually linked to accounting and invoicing systems so that when a customer's order is entered on to the system, a document is raised to instruct someone in the warehouse to select a finished product and pack it so it is ready to be sent to a customer. When numbers of a particular finished product become low, the computerised stock control system will instruct the production department to make more! **Benefits**: Improves efficiency, streamlines supply chains, cuts costs and enhances customer relationships.

* **RFID** – Although Radio Frequency Identification (RFID) technology has been around for decades its use is only becoming common now. RFID involves tagging individual products or components with a microchip containing information so that they can be easily tracked. These microchips are most commonly used in retail to improve the accuracy of stock information held and to reduce theft. Radio signals can be transmitted to and from the tag so that whole pallets of items or racks of clothes can be entered accurately on to a stock system by waving an RFID reader near them. This technology is also used in manufacturing, with organisations such as Michelin putting the microchips inside tyres so that if they are stolen it is easy to track them back to the car they were stolen from. **Benefits**: Improves efficiency and security, streamlines supply chains and cuts costs.

Summary

* The key to effective supplier management is communication and negotiation. Businesses have certain expectations of their suppliers so that they can then meet the needs and expectations of their customers.

* Effective supplier relationships lead to businesses not needing to have so much stock. However, technology such as computerised stock control systems and on-line ordering are essential to speed up the process of ordering and delivery to ensure that organisations do not experience periods with no stock of an essential material or component.

Service delivery

Service delivery is important to the success and image of an organisation. As far as image and reputation is concerned, it is at the point of delivery of the goods or service that the customer is likely to experience satisfaction or dissatisfaction.

Organisations that are committed to high standards of service delivery will generate and agree a set of performance standards. These are communicated to their customers and form the basis of a customer service promise. Service standards will quite often have references to quality of service and targets of performance. Making sure they regularly meet their promised targets is important to an organisation so that they gain and retain a good reputation, leading to them gaining and retaining customers. Therefore, these standards are used to measure and improve the *operational efficiency* of the services offered by organisations to their customers. Organisations are likely to use a variety of different measures, sometimes referred to as *business intelligence*, to monitor service delivery performance, which may include customer surveys (phone calls and on-line surveys). They will also monitor aspects of customer experience, such as customer enquiries and complaints.

Case Study: Service Delivery Standards

The Three Rivers District Council Environmental Health Department

The following are our target response times to requests for service.

* Respond to telephone calls within 24 hours.
* Written responses to letter/fax/email within 5 working days.
* Out-of-hours service telephone response within 30 minutes or, if outside core hours, by 8 pm that day.
* Pest control treatment within 14 days.
* Collection of a found/stray dog, the same day if reported within office hours.
* Process licence applications within 2 days.

Source: Three Rivers District Council

The Co-Operative Bank

Our five promises to you.

* We promise to begin processing account applications within 48hrs and to open them without error.
* We promise to set up and pay your standing orders and direct debits as instructed without mistakes.
* We promise not to make any financial errors on your statements.
* We promise to automatically issue your cheque books and cards to make sure you never run out.
* We promise to calculate your charges and interest accurately and correct any errors without question.

This means you'll always know what you can expect when it comes to the level of service we provide. In the unlikely event that we break any of these promises, we'll apologise, correct our mistake and pay £25 into your account as compensation.

Source: The Co-operative Bank

Using web-based systems and computerised technology, they can measure how long it takes a customer's query or complaint to be addressed by a customer services representative. These measures are representative of the overall satisfaction of an organisation's customers. The information gathered may relate to all aspects of the organisation's activities, product design, delivery, sales administration and so on. Therefore, it is important that the *information collected is shared* with and accessed by all these relevant functions so that changes can be made to avoid customer dissatisfaction in the future.

It is common to see and read standards of service or service promises from government-run services such as the NHS or the police force. The standards of service delivery performance in the Rivers District Council example are typical of a government service and are very specific. It is easy for users of their service to see if promised standards are not being met so that they can complain. Although a different type of organisation, the Co-operative Bank also offer standards of performance that they call their 'Five Star Service Promise'. You will note that the promises are similar in each case but the Co-operative Bank are so committed that in the unlikely event they do not meet their promises they are willing to pay the customer a fine of £25.

Activity 2.18

1 In your own words, describe what you understand to be the meaning of the terms 'service delivery standards' and 'service promise'.

2 Service delivery standards are often referred to as 'targets to be achieved'. Explain what you understand by the term 'targets' in respect of service standards by referring to the examples opposite.

Use of technology in service delivery

Again, great emphasis is now placed upon the use of computerised technology to ensure the best service standards by organisations to their customers.

* Business Management Systems (BMS) – These are purpose-built computer systems that link (integrate) all the systems used in an organisation so that they communicate with each other. For example, if a car retailer sells a car, only one screen needs to be filled in and completed with the details; the appropriate entries in the accounting system and inventory system take place automatically. A BMS offers many benefits, including better monitoring and control of inventory so stock-outs are avoided. Mailing lists based upon customers' purchasing history could help a business target its advertising and promotions more accurately. In manufacturing organisations a BMS helps to plan production output and *work-flow* so that all orders are satisfied within required deadlines. The system will improve the customer experience by speeding up the overall response to customer orders, queries and complaints. The biggest value of an integrated BMS is the information and reports that can be compiled on all aspects of a business's performance so that managers within the business can make better and more informed decisions. For example, a product manager will monitor sales of each product line offered and when the number of requests to sell a particular item becomes too low they can decide whether to withdraw the product or to promote it to customers in the hope they will begin to sell more. **Benefits**: Improves efficiency, streamlines supply chains, cuts costs, enhances customer relationships and helps to identify improvements to products and services offered.

* Electronic document management and imaging systems – These are computer-based systems designed to store and track electronic and paper documents and media. Most organisations are still, even in this computer age, inundated with paper documents, which can be easily lost and take up a great deal of time, space and expense in storage. With electronic document management and imaging systems in place, paper documents can be scanned in the post room and sent quickly and efficiently electronically to the intended recipient. **Benefits**: Improves efficiency, cuts costs, reduces the organisation's carbon footprint and enhances customer relationships.

Summary

* Service delivery standards are a promise to the users of a service of the expected level of service they should experience and are expressed as targets that organisations aspire to satisfy.
* They are commonly found in public organisations, such as the NHS, who strive to offer the public value for money and the highest-quality service.

2.4 Understand that a number of factors contribute to the success of a business

The overall assessment for this unit comprises two activities. You will produce a report on an investigation into two different business organisations and how they use technology to support the key business activities and processes they carry out. You will also be asked to take part in a business simulation game and be assessed on your understanding, as a result of playing the business game, of key factors that distinguish a successful business from an unsuccessful one.

Business Simulations

Business simulations are a fun and interactive way to learn and understand how businesses are set up and managed. As you play you will learn the impact of common business decisions on the featured business, whether good or bad! By playing business games you will develop an understanding of a range of business strategies and tactics and their overall impact on business performance.

How is success measured? The objectives of the business simulation

In most business simulations success is measured in terms of the net profit (profit after all costs and expenses have been accounted for) generated by each team playing. Above all you must try NOT to go bust!

Decisions you will be encouraged to make

Most business simulation games will encourage you to make some or all of the following decisions. The idea is that you can observe the effect of your decisions on sales and the overall financial performance of the simulated business. This is not an exhaustive list but it will give you the idea before you get started:

* What are the business's objectives? Are they realistic and achievable? How do you plan to get there?
* How will you go about making decisions in your teams? This will highlight the importance of effective communication between team members to avoid conflict and ensure the best decisions are made.
* What products are you going to sell, when and how many? You will need to develop a good understanding of your market, identify who your customers are, what they buy and when they are likely to buy and, of course, who your competitors are and what they are doing to attract your customers away.

* What levels of stock of certain products, materials and ingredients will you require to satisfy demand? The worst thing you can do to dissatisfy customers is not have what they want in stock!

* How will you promote your business? Bearing in mind who your customers are and how much money you have to spend on advertising and promotion, how can you make your product stand out and appear unique against those of the competitors (differentiation)?

* What are the best ways you can improve sales? Examples include spending more on promotion, improving customer service, training staff or even reducing the price of your products.

* What are your staffing needs? How many people do you need, when and how much are you going to pay them?

* Do you need to take out loans to invest in new equipment, premises or web-based shops? Remember you will have to pay this money back with interest.

Team roles

Each simulation team formed in your class will consist of three or four team members. Your first task will be to decide which team members will carry out which roles. You will certainly need someone to monitor stock levels and someone to plan how the business will advertise and promote its products.

> ### Personal, Learning and Thinking Skills
>
> Taking part in a business simulation game will develop your ability to consider creative approaches and solutions to problems you will face.

Activity 2.19

Spend a little time considering your own personal strengths and weaknesses and make a list to be shared with the others in your group. Examples of strengths might include being good with numbers, creative and artistic, or having good attention to detail. Weaknesses might include a lack of personal organisational skills or not working well under pressure.

List the different roles required by the business simulation you have been provided with.

Consider each of your lists and agree which team member has the qualities to carry out the roles you have identified. Remember that this is a team activity but there still needs to be some structure to the time spent on the game. To avoid conflict, you must discuss and agree all decisions before going ahead.

> ### Personal, Learning and Thinking Skills
>
> Working as a team over a period of time requires organisation and time management if objectives are to be achieved.

Summary

* Successful simulation teams will be the ones which provide products or services that meet the needs and expectations of their customers. This should be equivalent to the team meeting its objectives.

Preparation for assessment

In this unit you will experience through the use of business simulation games what it is like to run a business. You will learn what key factors contribute to the success of a business and the impact of key decisions on its profitability and performance. In addition, you will carry out an investigation of two business organisations focusing on their key business processes.

How you will be assessed

This unit is assessed internally by your teacher. You will be expected to present evidence in the form of a portfolio, which for this unit will have two parts. Your portfolio for this unit will include the following:

Part 1 – An exploration of two different business organisations focusing on how they use technology to support key business processes, including customer relationship management, people management, supplier management and service delivery.

* You will produce profiles of two organisations clearly describing:
    * their organisational structure
    * their culture
    * the roles of key personnel
    * how the organisations' culture and the way in which they organise themselves helps them to achieve their objectives
* Using examples you will produce a report describing the purpose of key business processes in your chosen organisations, explaining how and why technology is used to support them.

Part 2 – Participation in a business simulation making observations on the key factors which distinguish a successful business from an unsuccessful one.

* You will take part in a business simulation game in order to find out what makes a business successful.
* Using your experience of playing the game, devise a set of recommendations for building a successful business.

Assessment tips

* **Report writing** is different from any other form of written communication in that it is very clearly structured, succinct and aims to deliver information in an efficient way.
* When writing your reports it is useful to consider the assessment criteria given in the following table. The criteria will clearly indicate what you need to put into your report in order to attract higher marks. Always bear in mind these criteria when planning an outline of what you want to include in your report and how you wish to structure it.
* Ensure your report has a clear introduction, a middle and a conclusion where you reflect or evaluate the points you have made and possibly make recommendations for improvement.

Unit-specific advice

* As you are contributing to and carrying out the business simulation, ensure you keep a note of any relationships between decision-making and successes experienced by the simulated business to draw upon later.

You must show that you:	Guidance	To gain higher marks you must:
2.1 Know that organisations have different structures, cultures and roles	* **Provide** some information about the structure, culture and roles of two organisations, including some **examples**	* **Provide** a full description of the structure, culture and roles of two organisations, using well-chosen **examples** * **Describe** how these help them achieve their objectives
2.2 Understand the purpose of key business processes and **2.3** Understand how and why technology is used to support business processes	* Show some **understanding** of key business processes and how technology is used to support these processes with some **examples**	* Give a **full explanation** of the purpose of key business processes and how technology is used to support these processes, illustrated with well-chosen **examples**
2.4 Understand that a number of factors contribute to the success of a business	* Make **several recommendations** for building a successful business, making some reference to the business simulation game	* Present a set of **well-reasoned recommendations** for building a successful business, drawing on your experiences of the business simulation game

3 Effective communication

Introduction

Businesses rely on **teams** of employees working together effectively and efficiently to meet objectives. The assessment for this unit will require you to work as part of a team on a task designed to communicate a message using IT. By doing this, you will learn how teams can be and are affected by the behaviour and actions of individuals within them. The foundation of good teamwork is **communication**, so in this unit you will be introduced to a range of methods that will help you to develop appropriate skills and to understand the importance of communication to the success of businesses.

THERE IS NO 'I' IN TEAM!

Do you belong to a team? How important is communication, cooperation and consideration of others to the success of your team?

Team
A team is a group of individuals that work together to achieve common objectives.

Communication
Communication is simply the exchange of information between two people or groups of people using a variety of different communication methods (written, verbal or electronic).

Learning outcomes

3.1 Understand why different types of communication media are used for different purposes

3.2 Be able to use confident, correct and contextually appropriate English in a range of business related communications

3.3 Understand how different behaviours, attitudes and actions impact on effective communication and performance between individuals and groups

3.4 Be able to work in a team to meet agreed objectives

3.5 Be able to evaluate their own performance as an individual and a member of a team

Case Study: The Snack Shack

As part of a mini-enterprise project some school friends decided to devise and develop a business idea that would address their break-time misery. Changes in school food standards had lead to the closure of their once loved 'tuck shop' with its array of sugary confectionery and salty snacks. The days of the traditional tuck

The Snack Shack

shop were well and truly over but coming up with a healthy, attractive and tasty alternative was all the challenge they needed. The results were amazing! Within months, their business, called 'The Snack Shack', had its own location and seating area, and the head teacher had even allowed them to play music at break times. On offer were fruit pouches, chew bars and smoothies to name but a few items. By working and communicating as a team they had performed market research, developed a product range that met customer needs and expectations and even devised an effective marketing and advertising campaign involving loyalty cards! Every team member contributed in a different way to the success of the project.

Activity 3.1

The Snack Shack

1 Consider the 'Snack Shack' case study. Discuss and explain how teamwork has contributed to the success of the project. List examples of possible teamwork that may have occurred at the idea stage, research stage, setting up stage and running stage.

2 The enterprise group held regular meetings where everyone was encouraged to share and express their views and opinions. How much do you think this contributed to the group's success?

3.1 Understand why different types of communication media are used for different purposes

Communication skills are essential to all aspects of our daily lives. We use them when speaking to friends, reading books like this one, writing assignments and contributing to the success of a team-based project like the one you will complete for this unit. In this section we will look at the purposes of communication and the communications media used to transmit and receive information.

Purpose of communication

In general and in business we communicate for a range of different purposes:

* **to inform** – e.g. an announcement to shareholders of what their dividend payments are going to be that year
* **to get a message across** – e.g. a poster on the staff notice board informing staff of a new menu in the canteen
* **to attract attention** – e.g. a neon sign advertising a restaurant
* **to entertain** – e.g. a humorous speech at a sales conference, which makes the speaker's message memorable
* **to educate** – e.g. an educational website aimed at primary school children learning about English history
* **to persuade** – e.g. a presentation recommending investment in local health services by a politician

Communications media & the communication process

The process of communication can be illustrated by the use of a simple model like the one shown. The medium selected is a means of transmitting and receiving information.

Appropriateness of communication and implications of poor communication

The diagram clearly shows that successful communication will occur when the sender selects the most appropriate communication method (medium) for the message that is being sent and for the person who is receiving it. For instance, if the message is short and to one person, a telephone call or email would be appropriate. If the message is detailed and technical and aimed at a group of people, a letter may be more effective because there will be a permanent record of what was communicated to refer to later. Whichever form of communication is chosen, the message needs to be clear for the desired audience and it must use the appropriate quality of language and presentation, as we will discuss later. Ask yourself the following questions when deciding how to communicate a message:

* What is the nature of my message? Is it an instruction, a request for product information or a confidential matter?

* How many people am I communicating with? Is it for one person, a group of people or a department?

* How quickly does the message need to be communicated? Does it need to be received immediately, today, tomorrow or by some other time?

* How long is the message and what level of detail does it contain?

* Is a permanent written record of the communication required?

Simple process of communication

1. SENDER
This is the person who wishes to send some form of message. They will decide on the content of the message and the method used to deliver it.

2. MESSAGE ENCODED
The sender's message is put into words that the person receiving it will understand.

3. MEDIUM SELECTED
The method of communicating the message is selected depending on the content of the message, amount of information, speed of communication etc.

4. MESSAGE RECEIVED AND DECODED BY RECEIVER
The message has been received and is interpreted and understood by the intended receiver(s).

5. FEEDBACK
This is simply the receiver's response confirming the message has been received and understood or not understood.

If communication is poor it is highly likely that the message will not be received or understood. The implications of this could be a misunderstanding between people which could ultimately lead to conflict. Communication can fail for a number of different reasons, called barriers to effective communication:

* **Poor relationships between two or more people.** This can lead to emotional conflict and people not listening to one another.

* **Communicators spread out geographically.** This means that people have little opportunity to meet and so communication can be difficult.

* **Language barriers and expertise differences.** People may speak different languages or have different levels of understanding of a technical issue.

* **Using the wrong communication medium for a purpose.** Examples of this include sending a letter when an immediate response was needed or giving lots of technical information during a phone conversation.

Summary

* Communication underpins effective teamwork in businesses and therefore can influence the overall performance of a business.
* We communicate for many reasons including to inform and to attract attention.
* Use a simple model of communication to analyse the process of communication and the effectiveness of the communications medium selected.
* Before we communicate we must consider a number of key factors to help us determine the best way to communicate our message.

Activity 3.2

Using the communications model

1 Consider the communication model and apply it to the lesson you are in now or to a typical lesson. Draw the circles on a plain piece of paper and insert who the sender and receivers are, what message is being communicated and in what ways (the communication method) and how receivers feed back to the sender that the message has been received and understood fully.

2 How suitable are the methods used to communicate the teaching message?

3 Are there any barriers to effective communication (that is, is there anything stopping you receiving and understanding the message being communicated)?

Types of communication media: Electronic media 1

A communication medium simply refers to the method in which a message is communicated. In this part of the unit we will investigate the main forms of communications media (electronic, print and voice media) and how they are used to communicate with groups of people such as customers. Media can be used to communicate news or information or to display advertising messages. Essentially, in this section we will look at the electronic media.

Electronic Media

What are electronic forms of media? If we were to define them we could say electronic media are all those types of communication where a message is being transmitted or broadcast electronically to its audience. They include websites, emails, text messaging and blogs. Essentially, electronic media are any electronic form of communication that is not paper-based or involves the recording and transmission of voices or films (moving images).

Websites

A website is a location owned or held by a private individual, charity, public organisation or business on the World Wide Web. Most websites contain a home page, which is usually the first page or document seen by a user who enters a site. More complicated websites may also contain or provide additional documents, information and files which can be downloaded, such as podcasts, brochures or reports which we will examine later.

The World Wide Web has given individuals, charities and public and private organisations the opportunity to connect to millions of people who are online. In March 2008, it was estimated that just over 20 per cent of the world's population (including developed and developing nations) had access to the Internet and this number is continuing to grow. This represents a massive audience to individuals and charities, or a potential market to online businesses. The Internet allows businesses to reach customers without the costs and overheads of running lots of expensive outlets. Also, outlets are physically restricted to a geographical location and therefore can only be accessed by customers in that area. In turn, the cost savings can be passed on to customers in the form of reduced prices. This is why you can quite often purchase products online more cheaply than in your local stores.

Case Study: teachICT.co.uk

Websites aren't just for businesses wishing to sell a product or service. Charities use websites to generate awareness of issues and to raise funds to help vulnerable people and animals. Governments use websites to communicate legislation and information to the public. Even teachers have websites to share their expertise and ideas about how to teach their subject. Go online and check out the exciting ICT education website called teachICT.co.uk, developed by ICT teachers. You will have probably been using such web-based resources in classes throughout your education. There are many interesting activities to have a go at including 'Project Earth' where you are asked to research the activities and purpose of a charity and then produce posters, letters, artwork, presentations, statistics in Excel and even your own web page concerning the charity's issues so that you can raise awareness of them in your own school, college, local community and who knows where else! Or you could participate in 'Star Struck' where you have to create your own band, decide on its members and image, make your own music tracks and produce letters to be sent to admiring fans to inform them of your first gig. Have a look at the website yourself. What do you think its main purposes are?

Activity 3.3

Assess the purpose of a variety of websites

For this activity you will need time to work in small teams and have access to the Internet to research a range of different websites. In your teams, identify five different websites you wish to investigate: one from a retailer, one from a manufacturer, one from a sport or leisure business, one from local government and one from a charity. Find examples of how they use the website to:

* inform
* communicate a specific message
* attract attention
* entertain
* educate
* persuade

Produce a handout, poster or PowerPoint presentation to communicate your findings back to your class. Comment on the overall importance of each communication purpose above to each type of organisation. For example, would 'entertainment' be an important part of the website design for your chosen charity? You might finish your investigation by commenting on how effective a website was for achieving all these purposes in each instance.

Functional Skills – English

You can practise your Functional English by presenting information concisely, logically and persuasively.

Summary

* Individuals, charities and businesses have a large range of communications media available to them.
* Websites as a means of communicating with customers and people in general have grown in importance. They can help individuals, charities and businesses inform, communicate important messages, attract attention, entertain, educate and persuade.

Types of communication media: Electronic media 2

In this section we will continue to investigate electronic forms of media used regularly by private individuals, charities, public organisations and private businesses to communicate with people.

Blogs

What are blogs? Well, blogs are a form of online journal created by 'bloggers' who are people with a special interest in one thing who want to share their thoughts, findings and views with other similar and like-minded people. Quite often blogs are set up as two-way communications where others can post responses to the originator of a blog message. Blogs have many uses.

Fan websites are common places to find blogs where stars of film, stage and sports keep their fans updated on what they are doing, where they are going and generally anything they are interested in at the time. Small charity groups may have their own blogs to keep people who are interested in their cause updated with progress and images related to their projects. There are even websites set up to help children who are bullied with a blog that details the latest information on projects to stop bullying.

It is only recently, however, that businesses have started to realise the potential of blogging. Businesses use blogs as a means of keeping customers updated on news or events to do with their business or their market in general. They may use blogs to notify customers of upcoming promotional activities. They may also use blogs to encourage customers to provide feedback on their products or services, which they can use to further improve what they offer their customers.

For example, why not visit South Penquite Farm's website at www.southpenquite.co.uk? This is a website all about the activities of the farm and a link to its blog where it announces and describes the success of their open days and general activities on the farm. Their blog is an interesting medium to generate interest in what they do and to encourage potential customers to visit in the future.

Emails

Every day, over 4 billion private and business email messages are sent. They are a fast, cheap and convenient means of communicating, particularly as almost everyone has their own email address.

Organisations have realised they can benefit greatly from this communication method as emails can be targeted specifically at potential or existing customers and, although emails can be deleted, they are not easily overlooked or ignored as the recipient will always see the message header. Companies such as Argos build up a database of customer details (usually via their website) and use this to send promotional 'blanket' emails. However, some Internet users do not like to receive unsolicited emails and can block them.

Text messaging

Text messaging has been around for years. Over 20 billion private and business texts are sent each year in the UK alone! Businesses are now realising the potential of SMS or mobile phone texts as a communications medium. Customers are encouraged to hand over their mobile numbers so that businesses can send texts notifying them of promotional offers and special events. One of the biggest companies to use text messaging as a communications medium is the mobile telecommunications giant Orange. They regularly send texts about new tariffs or services that they think their customers might be interested in, including mobile phone upgrades.

Using texts as a communications medium can offer private individuals, charities, public organisations and private businesses an opportunity to communicate instantly and cheaply with others, including customers. Text messaging can be used by businesses as a reminder tool for notifying customers of events or promotional offers made available for a limited time.

Activity 3.4

An electronic solution!

Consider the three examples of electronic communication covered here: South Penquite Farm's blog, Argos's marketing email and Orange's marketing text messages. In each case, assess the purpose of the communication giving clear reasons for your answer. Remember, the main purposes of communication media are to inform, to communicate a specific message, to attract attention, to entertain, to educate and to persuade. You may select more than one purpose in each case.

Summary

* Individuals, charities, public organisations and businesses have a large range of communications media available to them.
* Electronic communications media such as blogs, emails and text messaging that are used as a means of communicating with customers and people in general have grown in importance. They can help an individuals, charities, public organisations and businesses to inform, to communicate important messages, to attract attention, to entertain, to educate and to persuade.

ALL IN BLACK AND WHITE!

Many colleges are benefiting from extra funding to develop their services and in some cases totally rebuild their colleges. Why do you think they invite journalists and photographers from the local press to their opening events?

Types of communication media: Print media

Businesses, charities, private individuals and public organisations communicate messages continually. It is how they interact with customers and other groups of people. They will use a variety of different forms of printed media including newspapers, magazines, reports, brochures and posters, although the majority of these methods are mainly relevant to organisations (public, private and charitable). We will look briefly in this section at each of these.

Type of media	Advantages	Disadvantages
Regional newspapers **National newspapers**	* can reach a specific regional market place * costs are reasonable and cheaper than TV advertising * adverts can be seen again at a later time * can reach a very large audience * companies can benefit by building high-quality reputations and brands associated with good-quality newspapers * they have been proven to be a very successful medium * more product or service detail can be given	* it is difficult to find newspapers that appeal to a wide audience that includes, for example, young people * the quality of layout and printing may be poor * it is not very stimulating to read adverts in newspapers and they are usually limited to black and white printing
Magazines	* interesting colour adverts are possible * specialist magazines allow companies to target specific markets (customer groups) * one advert can cover international markets * adverts can be linked to informative features to be more persuasive * magazines can be referred to at a later date and passed on to others	* there is a long time between adverts being placed and magazines being printed and distributed * there is usually a large quantity of high-quality competitor adverts in the same publication * images have to be eye-catching to command the readers' attention
Posters (including billboards and transport vehicle livery)	* national and international advertisement campaigns are possible * most target markets (customer groups) can be reached * adverts are seen repeatedly to reinforce a message and make the reader remember it * excellent for short messages that remind customers of facts * scrolling digital billboards are particularly attention-grabbing and noticeable and are becoming a very popular medium	* it is difficult to measure how many customers see them and how effective they are for the company * they can be ruined by weather and vandalism * they need to be located where there is a lot of passing traffic
Leaflets, brochures and flyers	* good way to communicate vital information about the product, service or selling organisation that will help consumers make their purchasing decision * can easily be sent in the post in response to an enquiry * customers expect printed information and it adds to the credibility of the firm * can be very cheap to reproduce and to do leaflet drops through doors * cheap and easy to send via email as an attachment	* can be expensive to employ specialists to design professional standard materials * it is easy to include incorrect or outdated information * if dropping leaflets through doors, it may be difficult to ensure they are reaching the right people

Reports	* provide very detailed information so that potential customers can make informed decisions about whether to purchase a product or use a particular service * if the report shows excellence (in car safety or teaching for example) then this is a formal and genuine source that customers will believe entirely	* can be difficult to draw customers' attention to * could be very technical and difficult to read and understand by an average person * could highlight negative and damaging information that could ultimately affect the business and how successful it might be in the future

Printed media: an introduction

What are printed media? Printed media include newspapers, magazines, books, junk mail (direct mail), leaflets, brochures, reports, directories, school newspapers, programmes from sporting or theatre events and even comics, fanzines and e-zines (web-based magazines) to name but a few. Basically they are any form of communication that can be produced as a printed publication. Most of them (newspapers, magazines and comics) will provide a great deal of current affairs information and sell page space to businesses and organisations to advertise their products or services to the readers of that material.

Printed media: investigated

As we already know, individuals, charities and businesses will use a range of different printed media to achieve different purposes. Essentially, individuals use the media as a source of up-to-date information. Public and private businesses and charities may wish to inform the reader about their products or services (things that they offer that competitors do not), to communicate a message such as an upcoming special promotional offer or the launch of a new product or service, to attract attention (bringing awareness of their products and services where there previously wasn't any), to entertain (as the funniest adverts are the most memorable), to educate (such as providing instructions for the safe use of a product for example) and, above all, to persuade people to purchase, use or access their products or services. Here is a table investigating the advantages and disadvantages to businesses and charities of using various printed media to create awareness, to communicate a message, to attract attention, to entertain, to educate and to persuade.

Activity 3.5

Using what you have learnt so far in this unit, investigate the purpose of a range of printed media selected by you and your team. Working in small groups of about three or four, select at least one newspaper feature or advert related to a business's activities or products, one magazine advert, a report (such as your school's last OFSTED report), a brochure and a poster (you will have to take a digital picture of this to take into class).

Produce a presentation or brief report that addresses the following:

* A clear statement of why you chose each printed medium, including what attracted you to it in the first place.

* A summary of its purpose with a clear explanation and justification (to inform, to get a message across, to attract attention, to entertain, to educate or to persuade).

* Select one advert which you think is the most effective at achieving its purposes and explain your choice. You may want to comment on the use of colour, images and logos, the quality of the printed medium used, the chosen newspaper or magazine the advert was featured in, and how effectively it speaks to the business's customer groups.

Summary

* Organisations and individuals have a large range of printed communications media available such as newspapers, magazines, reports, brochures and posters. They can help an organisation to inform, to communicate important messages, to attract attention, to entertain, to educate and to persuade.

Types of communication media: Voice media 1

Individuals, charities and public and private organisations communicate messages continually. It is how they interact with customers and other groups of people. They will use a variety of different forms of voice media, including telephone, face-to-face communication, radio and podcasts. We will look briefly in this section at two of these media.

Voice media: an introduction

What are voice media? Voice media include all the verbal and audio (sound) means that individuals, charities and organisations use to communicate with groups of people and existing and potential customers. They include telephone conversations, face-to-face meetings, radio programmes and podcasts to name but a few.

Telephone

The telephone is probably the most commonly used communication medium. In the UK it has been estimated that over 25 million calls are made every working day. From a business perspective, because much telephone contact is with existing or potential customers, we realise that ensuring a business's employees have good phone skills is vital to the success and overall effectiveness of the business. It is also vital to the perception that customers have of the business they have communicated with. When a person starts a new job, it is highly likely that they will receive training on 'phone etiquette', that is to say, phone manners.

Many businesses use phones to conduct 'telesales' or 'telemarketing'. These terms simply describe the way a business contacts its existing and potential customers by telephone. Telemarketing can be a good method of communicating because the business is speaking directly with its customers and is therefore able to assess how interested customers are in their products or services. They can also use telemarketing to answer any complex questions customers or potential customers may have. Finally, the telephone call can help businesses learn a lot more about their customers' needs and expectations. However, telemarketing is a less commonly used communications technique than it used to be, with many customers finding the calls an intrusion. Telemarketing has obtained a very negative image with some telesales people bullying and cajoling people in their own homes. Businesses deciding whether to use telemarketing will have to determine whether the communication technique fits with their overall business image.

However, telemarketing is not entirely useless. Many businesses that sell specialised products, materials and services to other businesses still use it as a communication technique and it is an expected and common means of communicating with existing and potential new business customers.

Face-to-face communication

There are very few of us that can go through a day without having some face-to-face contact and communication with another person. This type of communication is essential to all businesses but even more so in retail businesses where customers have regular contact with the employees of the business. Customers expect staff to:

* be friendly, approachable and understanding
* treat them fairly and not discriminate (every customer is as important as the last)
* give them product and service information, options and alternatives that are relevant to the customers' needs

Therefore, staff who work face-to-face with customers and potential customers must try to:

* respond quickly to customers, serve them immediately, not rush them, and apologise if they have had to wait to be served
* smile at the customer and greet them respectfully on first meeting them (it is amazing how nice customers will become when treated in this way)
* where relevant, introduce themselves to offer a more personalised service
* be courteous and friendly regardless of how unfriendly and discourteous the customer is to them
* provide accurate and easy-to-understand information, but without being too pushy, so that customers can make purchase decisions
* develop knowledge about products and services they do not have so that they are better able to serve customers in future
* be aware of what their body language is communicating (if it is negative or aggressive, the customer might actually leave without making a purchase or getting the information they needed)
* end the service positively, saying goodbye to the customer (and not rushing on to the next!)
* treat customers as they would wish to be treated themselves

Activity 3.6

A little bit of research…

Just how good is the customer service in your local shop, supermarket or even in your school or college's canteen? Working in small teams, gather information on your experiences of being served as a customer in one chosen business or service provider. Using your knowledge of face-to-face communication, identify the strengths and weaknesses of your overall customer service experiences. Put your findings in a brief report and make suggestions as to how the service you received as a customer could be improved. Don't forget to explain the long-term consequences of poor customer service.

Personal, Learning and Thinking Skills

By presenting a persuasive case for action you can demonstrate your effective participation skills.

Summary

* Public and private organisations, charities and individuals have a large range of voice communications media available to them.
* Voice communications media such as telephone and face-to-face contact are used as a means of communicating with customers (new and old) and other groups of people. They can help organisations, charities and private individuals to inform, to communicate important messages, to attract attention, to entertain, to educate and to persuade.

Types of communication media: Voice media 2

Individuals, charities and organisations communicate messages continually. It is how they interact with customers and other groups of people. They will use a variety of different forms of voice media including telephone, face-to-face communication, radio and podcasts. We will look briefly in this section at two of these media.

Radio

Over the last 10 to 20 years there has been a massive growth in the number of commercial radio stations in the UK and internationally. Many have been developed to deliver types of music that appeal to particular groups of people such as classical music lovers and people into 'urban' sounds. This has provided businesses with a wide range of stations on which to advertise their products or services according to the type of person they understand will be listening to the show. For instance, if you had just set up an Internet business selling musical instruments you might want to advertise on a classical radio station and not on one that specialises in dance music. As many radio stations are regional (only covering a small area) it means smaller, more local businesses can use these radio stations to bring awareness of their products and services to the people in the area most likely to use them.

However, radio as a communications medium goes beyond traditional radio stations. Some large retailers such as Game, the games console and video gaming retailer, pipe their own radio station into their stores as a way of entertaining staff and customers but also as a means of informing customers of existing and future promotional offers, activities and gaming news. Game stores can receive over one million customers a week and their radio station offers an additional service in terms of providing up-to-date knowledge of gaming. Finally, online businesses are also offering radio entertainment while their customers browse their online stores. For example, www.urbanshop.co.uk, sellers of designer urban wear including skater clothes and organic clothing, have a link to their 'Urban Shop Radio' which allows customers to listen to urban music while making an order. The radio programme encourages browsers to look at particular items of clothing and brings their attention to promotional offers.

Podcasts

What are podcasts? They are digital audio files found on websites. People visiting the site can listen to the podcast and sometimes subscribe to it so that they receive new podcasts automatically via the Internet and email. Charities and people with their own websites produce podcasts as a means of communicating to anyone who is interested in what they have to say. However, businesses are starting to realise the powerful impact that podcasts can have on increasing an

OVER THE WAVES...

Do you have any experience with podcasts? Maybe you have produced one and posted it to your own website or, like most of us, at least watched a podcast on a website. What do podcasts do that printed information and pictures on a website don't?

awareness of their products and services. Also, as a communications method they are very cheap to produce and distribute. Let's look at the example below.

Case Study: Wiggly Wigglers

Wiggly Wigglers is a small online and mail-order garden company based in England. They sell rural goods such as seeds to grow your very own herb garden or a starter bee-keeping hive and kit. They operate with a green philosophy, encouraging their customers to be environmentally friendly. They struggled to generate awareness of their business and products through the traditional and somewhat expensive paper-based advertising communications media discussed earlier in this unit. They were then approached by a specialist company called sfpodcasting (http://podcastingpackage.com/default.aspx) who worked with Wigglers to save them £120,000 a year from their advertising expenses by moving from print-based media to a weekly podcast. The podcast is emailed and subscribed to by customers not only from the UK but from all around the world. If you have access to the Internet, go and listen to Wiggly Wigglers' recent podcast on www.wigglywigglers.co.uk. You can also listen to older podcasts in their archived section.

Activity 3.7

Podcasting: What's the purpose of that?

What would you say are the main purposes of Wiggly Wigglers' podcasts? How far in your opinion do the podcasts help Wiggly Wigglers to inform, to communicate important messages, to attract attention, to entertain, to educate and to persuade? Give examples and provide good explanations for the points you make.

Summary

* There is a large range of voice based communications media available.
* Voice communications media, such as telephone, face-to-face meetings, radio and podcasts are used as a means of communicating with customers and with people in general. They can help organisations, charities and private individuals to inform, to communicate important messages, to attract attention, to entertain, to educate and to persuade.

THE LANGUAGE OF BUSINESS

Is communicating in business, say with a customer, the same as communicating with a friend or relative? In what ways do they vary and why is it essential to use a different style of communication in business?

Functional Skills – English

For your assessed team activity you will be required to demonstrate you can communicate a message using a variety of different communication methods (using IT) with appropriate business English for each.

3.2 Be able to use confident and correct English in business

When working in business you will be expected to develop a confident and accurate use of business English in a range of different communications media. How well you communicate is a reflection of your professionalism.

Correct and confident business English

Writing business documents and contributing to team meetings requires a different use of language. This is to convey professionalism and because the communication of information is crucial to making business decisions and therefore to how well businesses perform. Therefore, you must ensure that you are:

* concise and clear about what is being communicated
* logical: communicating information in a logical order
* persuasive, as most business communication aims to influence decisions

The teacher who reads your documents will be looking for these three qualities, and at how well you are communicating using a variety of sentence structures, correct use of appropriate business terminology and, finally, the correct use of grammar and punctuation.

Sentence structures

There is a range of different ways to structure sentences. You will be required to demonstrate use of all of them.

* **Simple sentence structure** – This is the most common type of structure in the English language. It can be used effectively to grab someone's attention or to sum up an argument. In business communication it can be used at the end of a letter to make a firm statement, such as, 'With continued training we hope to improve standards of customer service.'

* **Compound sentence structure** – This is where two simple sentences are joined together with words known as conjunctions, such as 'and' and 'or'. It makes the communication sound a little more professional.

* **Complex sentence structure** – This structure is yet more advanced. In complex sentences the communicator gets to express things that are opposite. They are often used in business communications to make arguments or valid responses to suggestions.

Punctuation

You will be required to produce business documents that are correctly punctuated. Here are some tips:

* Use a full stop (.) at the end of a sentence. For example: Profits on sales of cars have doubled.

* Use a question mark (?) to show something is being asked. For example: How motivated are our employees?

* Use a comma (,) in lists or to separate two parts (clauses) of a sentence. For example: (1) We will stop selling the red, yellow and green trainers. (2) However, we have not considered the increased cost.

* Use an apostrophe (') to show possession or abbreviation. For example: (1) This is the sales director's responsibility. (2) The cleaners don't use this cupboard.

* Use speech marks (' ' or " ") when quoting spoken words. For example: In the last meeting the team leader stated, "There will only be two more meetings before Christmas."

* Use a colon (:) to expand on a sentence or to introduce a list. For example: (1) Shirley is a good typist: she makes few mistakes. (2) Following a recent meeting, staff have requested some extra equipment: two more computers, a colour printer and a new photocopier.

* Use a semicolon (;) to join or link two related sentences as a 'stronger' break in a sentence than a comma, but one that does not warrant a full stop. For example: Price is what we sell our goods for; cost is the burden on the customer.

Proofreading and checking for accuracy and meaning

In all written communication, it is important that you read your work thoroughly, checking for spelling, grammar and punctuation errors that may affect how the reader understands what is being communicated. This is called 'proofreading'. Not only does proofreading ensure that the communication is understood in the way it is intended (its meaning) and the information provided is accurate, it also reflects your professionalism.

Contextually appropriate communication

It is important that the correct communication method or media are used for the situation, the organisation for which it is created, the audience who is likely to receive it and, finally, the subject matter it deals with. You should also remember to use the correct level of English. For example, in a formal face-to-face meeting with senior colleagues you would express disagreement by saying, 'I am not sure that I agree totally with what is being said here' and not, 'I think this is all a load of rubbish', and when writing a reply to a letter of complaint from a customer you may say, 'On behalf of the company, I do apologise for the inconvenience you have suffered' and not, 'We are very sorry that you did not think our service was good.'

Activity 3.8

Using confident and business English

Working in pairs, provide examples of simple, compound and complex sentences using all the punctuation marks summarised above. The sentences must be based on a business or IT-related topic. Consider your last group activity or IT lesson for inspiration.

Functional Skills – English

An appreciation of appropriate business communication will enable you to develop an ability to write documents and materials that communicate information, ideas and opinions effectively and persuasively.

Summary

* To appear professional and to achieve the intended objectives of the communication (i.e. to persuade or inform), the message must be written or spoken using the correct business terminology, appropriate sentence structures and correct use of punctuation, so it is clear.

Business-related digital communications: Digital posters

Businesses communicate messages continually. It is how they interact with customers and other groups of people outside the business. We have already, in Section 3.1, investigated a wide range of communication media typically used by people in general, charities and business organisations. In this section we will begin to examine how we go about producing digital communication. Defined, digital communications refer to any communications media that make use of electronic digital signals (ones and zeros) to send information between electronic devices or computerised systems. Here we will look at digital posters as an example of digital communication.

Digital posters

Digital posters, otherwise known as digital signage, have been around for many years. They are LCD screens connected to a computer that pipes images to the screen in a set order. They can even be programmed to show certain images at certain times of the day. They satisfy many purposes but the predominant reason for their use is advertising. In retail outlets they can be set up and programmed to display adverts and promotional offers. If they have Hypertag technology, digital posters allow consumers to download things such as special store vouchers and offers to a PDA or mobile phone; these vouchers can be shown at checkout or printed and used later. If your mobile phone or PDA has Bluetooth technology enabled, the digital technology will automatically send the vouchers, information and offers to you.

Digital posters are not only used in retail. Remote Media, a business organisation that specialises in digital poster technology, has installed systems in hotels, pubs and even public buildings. Rugby Borough Council asked Remote Media to develop digital signage throughout their brand new visitor centre, which was home to a library, a museum and a tourist information centre. The digital signs were developed to provide visitors to the centre with information on events occurring on a particular day or in the future and to provide directions and signs to these events and activities. The digital posters were placed near windows so that even when the centre was closed they could still provide visitors with information.

The benefits of a digital poster or signage system are:

* they are flexible and can be used to display a wide variety of excellent-quality images and messages depending on what is going on in the business that day
* Hypertag technology offers even more opportunities to provide information by allowing visitors and customers to download vouchers and further information via wireless Bluetooth technology

The limitations are:

* they are very expensive to purchase and set up and usually require specialist software to run
* they will require some specialist maintenance and upkeep which can also be expensive

Produce your own digital posters using appropriate business English

Even if you do not have a large amount of money to spend on digital posters or signage you can still create the same effect using a monitor, a PC and some presentation software. Using software such as PowerPoint it is possible to put a series of slides together to create a moving slide show of information and directions for people to read in, for example, a reception area. You must ensure the material produced is suitable for the targeted audience and that correct business English is used. Poor English, punctuation and grammar will have a very negative impact on a business's image, which is the opposite of what is intended. As the digital poster is meant to be read quickly and to provide important information, the communication will:

* be succinct and to the point, using bullet points and short captions to communicate key information (the information is unlikely to be presented in the form of complex sentences)
* use language that all groups can understand (children and adults for example)
* use pictures and images (as a picture can say a thousand words!)
* be colourful, interesting and attractive so people are drawn to the communications medium and will use it appropriately

Activity 3.9

Your very own digital poster

Working in pairs or small groups, plan and produce a PowerPoint slide show containing lots of useful information and images about IT qualifications available in your school or college. Suppose it is to be displayed on a screen in the IT classroom during the next open evening at your school or college. List what information you think would be relevant to your audience (mostly existing and new parents) first before planning and producing the content of your slide show. When it is completed ask your teacher if it is possible to set it up in reception for the day as a 'digital poster'. Who knows? The School Head or College Principle may like your ideas.

Functional Skills – ICT

You can demonstrate your Functional ICT skills by using discrimination in selecting information that matches your requirements from a variety of sources and evaluating its fitness for purpose.

Summary

* Although they have existed for many years, digital posters are only just now becoming common in public places such as shopping centres and retail outlets. They are an excellent (but sometimes expensive) means of communication.

Business-related digital communications: Web pages and information points

In this section we will examine how businesses go about using the digital medium of web pages or websites and information points to communicate with customers and with people in general.

Web pages

As we are already aware, web pages offer businesses a mass form of communication. The benefits are:

* if the URL is well selected the website name can be easily remembered
* if well designed, websites can be easy to navigate
* they can have links to customer service email addresses so that customers can get in direct contact with the business
* they can communicate detailed information such as product specifications

The limitations of communicating via web pages are:

* not everybody uses the Internet, so an organisation cannot guarantee to reach all of its targeted customers via this method only
* they can be very expensive to design, set up, update and maintain

Setting up a simple web page using appropriate business English

Setting up your own web page or website couldn't be easier. Various easy-to-learn website authoring tools are available to individuals and small businesses, such as Microsoft Expression Web (the successor to FrontPage), Macromedia Dreamweaver and Macromedia Flash. You may have access to one or all of these in your school or college. To use them you do not need to be familiar with HTML (HyperText Markup Language, the programming code and language used to create web pages).

Some web-hosting services enable a small business or private individual to set up and host a professional-looking, effective and simple website in minutes; they may even provide instructions on how to build a web page or site, providing pre-prepared screen templates to be filled in, which are then hosted so that they can be viewed on the Internet.

As web pages provide people viewing them with a great deal of information, communicating via a website should be effective. Bear in mind the following tips:

* Make the web pages attractive and attention-grabbing by using appropriate colours and images.
* Use a font that is easy to read on the screen, such as Verdana.
* Don't insert too much text or the web pages will appear cluttered. Focus on communicating the main messages or information. You should bear your readers in mind when deciding on the content and how it will be expressed.

* Plan the structure of your website or pages so that they are easy to navigate. If people can't find the information they need quickly and easily they will get very impatient and switch to another site.

Information points

Information points, or digital kiosks, are electronic touch-screens that provide quick access to a range of information. Information points can be adapted for any type of service. Some cinemas have information points to provide film information and trailers and they also have the capability to accept payments and to print tickets.

Information points are also found in shopping malls, providing access to mall maps, retailer locations and other promotional material.

The benefits of information points are:

* they are flexible and can be used to display a wide variety of excellent-quality images and messages

* they are fairly simple to access and use

The limitations are:

* they are very expensive to purchase and set up and usually require specialist software to run

* information to be accessed through the portal has to be developed, kept secure and well managed

* they will require some specialist maintenance and upkeep

Setting up a simple information point using appropriate business English

Information points are very like websites. They consist of a large number of pages, containing lots of information, that are accessed via menu options. As information points provide people using them with a great deal of information, communicating via them should be effective. Bear in mind the following tips:

* Locate the information point where it is most likely to be needed, and can be easily identified.

* Design the information screens so that they are attractive and attention-grabbing by using appropriate colours and images.

* Use a font and font size that is easy to read, such as 14-point Verdana.

* Don't insert too much text or the information pages will appear cluttered. As information points will be accessed by a wide range of people (ages, technological capabilities, English not a first language etc.) you need to consider this when deciding on the content and how it will be expressed.

* Plan the structure of your information pages so that they are easy and logical to navigate. If people accessing the facility can't find the information they need quickly and easily they will get very impatient, opting to approach a member of staff instead.

Activity 3.10

Plan your very own web pages

Your teacher has asked you to plan the content and design of a web page specifically for IT diploma students like you to access as a source of support and information. It will provide examples of excellent resources created by teams who have recently completed the diploma. It will form part of your school's overall website and will be found in the IT Department's section. Consider the use of colour, layout, images and logos that would be expected so that the web pages fit into the overall site. Using paper and pens, work in small groups to draft out a front page and other pages clearly showing your menu options and clearly identifying exactly what information would be found where.

Functional Skills – ICT

You can practise your Functional ICT skills by using an appropriate page layout.

Summary

* Although they have existed for many years, digital posters and information points are only just now becoming common in public places such as shopping centres, retail outlets and local government buildings. They are an excellent (but sometimes expensive) means of communication.

Business-related spoken communications: Podcasts

Spoken methods of communication are most suitable where it is essential that information is communicated quickly and in person. They can be very cheap and encourage almost immediate feedback on issues and ideas, which in business may lead to faster and more effective decision-making. In this section we will examine how businesses are beginning to make use of the innovative 'podcast' medium.

Podcasts

Podcasts, as we learned earlier, are digital audio files found on websites. In certain cases, businesses will allow users to subscribe to receiving a regular podcast automatically via the Internet and email. Businesses are starting to realise the powerful impact that podcasts can have on their success.

Strengths of using podcasts as a communications tool are:

* they are a cheap and easy-to-distribute way of increasing awareness of a business's products and services
* they are still viewed as new and innovative so there is still a novelty factor attached to them
* most people will respond well to auditory (sound-based) communications as opposed to written or printed media

Limitations of using podcasts to communicate are:

* there is still a reliance on customers finding your website to access the podcast
* there is still a reliance on people signing up to a subscription to have the podcast sent via email on a regular basis
* to ensure the podcast doesn't sound amateurish, businesses will still need to employ the services of professional podcast specialists, which can be expensive (but is still cheap compared with running national newspaper adverts)
* the business needs to be committed to developing interesting and stimulating podcasts on a regular basis or customers will lose interest in the medium to long term

Creating a simple podcast using appropriate business English

Anyone can make a good podcast. All you need is the right equipment and interesting news to convey. The equipment you are likely to need includes a microphone and a digital recording device. You may have access to these at school or college. Some computers have a microphone point so that you can record your content straight on to your computer. Alternatively you can find MP3 players that will record voices and sounds. You will also need some editing software, such as Audacity which is free from http://audacity.sourceforge.net. Editing your recordings will enable you to create a podcast that flows just like a professional radio programme.

When planning your podcast, just like any other communications medium, you need to consider who your listeners are and what is the best way of communicating your message to them. You may use some humour or music but, essentially, how the person on the podcast expresses themselves will reflect on the business's image so using appropriate and correct business English is important. Here are some podcasting tips:

* Plan the structure and content of your podcast so that it has a clear introduction, middle and end and does not go on for too long (4 minutes is long enough). Otherwise, listeners may lose interest or even switch it off because they have too little time.

* Make your podcast interesting and engaging so that people will want to hear more. Use a variety of voices, but not too many.

* Talk to your listeners and find out what parts of your podcasts they enjoy so that you can do more of that material!

* If appropriate, try to make the podcast friendly as it is capturing an aspect of you or your business. The podcast can be an effective means of communicating your values and beliefs, which are not easy to communicate using other media.

Activity 3.11

Plan your very own podcast

Podcasts have many uses, even in your own school or college. They can be used to share news and information with learners and their families. The school or college's librarian could record their own podcast explaining how to use the library's referencing system for instance. Your Head Teacher or Principal could record a greeting at the start of a new academic year. Plan a four-minute podcast, which you will need to script, on any chosen subject to do with school life or your studies. It could be a podcast reviewing the success of a school open evening or disco. It must be interesting! If you have the facilities, record your podcast and share it with the rest of your class. Explain clearly why the podcast would be a more effective communications medium than, for example, a written piece of dialogue.

Functional Skills – English

Remember that functional English is not just about reading and writing – it includes speaking and listening too. When recording your podcast you should present your information and ideas clearly and persuasively.

Summary

* Podcasts are a new and innovative means of communicating. Only recently have businesses started to realise their effectiveness as a communications medium.

Business-related spoken communications: Telephone calls

Spoken methods of communication are most suitable where it is essential that information is communicated quickly and in person. In this section we will examine how businesses make use of the telephone as an effective communications medium.

Telephone calls

Telephone calls are mostly used to communicate quick and simple messages or requests when the people communicating are far away from each other. The benefits of using the telephone to communicate are:

* it's good where communication is between only two people
* it's a quick way of sharing ideas to develop solutions to problems
* immediate feedback is given
* there's an opportunity to ask questions and to check understanding
* it saves the time and cost of travelling to meetings

The limitations of using a telephone to communicate are:

* it can be difficult if more than two people need to be involved in the communication
* speakers are unable to see each other's body language
* it can be an impersonal way of communicating personal or sensitive messages
* there will be no written evidence of what was discussed to refer to later

Communicating on the telephone is one of the most widely used communication techniques in business. It is particularly suitable when a person needs a piece of information, such as the price of a particular product, before they can continue with their work. Calling someone directly will enable you to obtain the information needed in minutes. Telephone conversations are also used to discuss issues with people who are located far away or to arrange formal meetings. Telephone conversations can also be used to make requests or to give instructions. They are not appropriate if there is a lot of technical information to communicate. Learning how to communicate effectively on the telephone is one of the most important communication skills for business and IT students to develop. Learning the common phrases and structure of business calls, both as caller and as receiver, is a start, but telephone technique needs practice!

Making business telephone calls using appropriate business English

In business you may need to make phone calls to get information, for example for a project. Whether you are the caller or call-taker, your listening skills are as important as your speaking skills. Show that you are listening to the person speaking by occasionally confirming what is being said. If the phone call is more of a discussion then close the call by summarising the outcomes, for example, 'Just to check I've understood correctly, you need to order special high-quality paper for our advert, and that means you cannot deliver to us until Friday.'

When making professional business calls there are five things you need to consider:

* **Prepare** – Choose a quiet place with no distractions. Have all information you may need to hand. Know who you need to speak to and plan what you wish to say.

* **Hello** – First introduce who you are and who you work for and then ask to speak to somebody specific or someone from a particular department.

* **Obvious** – Speak clearly using appropriate business language. For example, 'I wonder if somebody could answer a query I have with my customer account?'

* **Notes** – Always have a pen and paper handy to make notes of names, numbers and other information you have received and may need later. You may check that your notes are correct at the end of the conversation.

* **Ending** – At the end of the conversation it is polite to thank the person for their time and assistance and to say goodbye.

Receiving business telephone calls using appropriate business English

How effectively telephone calls are received is critical for businesses. The callers are likely to be potential customers and how they are dealt with on the phone will be their first experience with the company. Therefore, when taking calls it is important to make a good first impression. Here are some tips on answering telephone enquiries:

1. Pick up the telephone before the third ring.

2. On answering the phone, show the caller you are enthusiastic and welcoming. Introduce yourself, for example by saying, 'Good morning, Snowcone Ltd., Sarah speaking. How may I help you?'

3. When speaking to the caller, use appropriate business language and not slang or jargon. For example, instead of saying, 'OK', use the word 'certainly'.

4. If you are unable to answer the caller's question, tell them that you need to consult someone else and would they mind waiting. You could also offer to call them back (but make sure you do, even if you don't have success finding an answer). If they are transferred from one person to another they are likely to get very upset.

5. When you have answered the caller's question it is polite to ask if there is anything else you can do for them. This is a polite way of bringing a call to an end.

6. Thank the caller for their enquiry and say goodbye.

Activity 3.12

A telephone role play

Get into groups of three. You will each have a turn at playing the caller, the call-taker and being an observer whose responsibility is to feed back on the performance of the other two.

Caller: You are planning to travel to New York this Thursday for a business meeting taking place on Friday. Call your travel agency to book a return flight from Heathrow to JFK airport and hotel accommodation for Thursday night only. You will need to know how much it is going to cost and what times you will depart from Heathrow on Thursday and JFK on Friday. Ask the travel agent to send an invoice to your company, SoulFeet Ltd.

Agent: You work in a travel agency and have access to a range of hotel and flight information. The cost of a return flight from Heathrow to JFK depends on the class of seat booked. Business Class costs £950 and Standard will be £525. There is a hotel close to the airport called The Reginald (4 star) that charges $200 a night. In pounds that is approximately £100 per night. Departures from Heathrow to JFK are at 10am, 1pm, 4pm and 8pm. Return flights from JFK to Heathrow depart at 2pm, 6pm, 8pm and 10pm. The next reservation number on your list is 25678345. This is the number that you will give to customers who make a booking with you.

Summary

* Using the telephone is a simple activity once you understand the typical structure of a call.

* Answering and making a business call requires a different approach and range of language compared with making a call to a friend, relative or carer.

* How well employees answer calls is linked closely to the impression customers and other callers will gain of the business.

WHAT MAKES A GOOD PRESENTATION?

Every day we are being presented to, in classrooms, on the television, in shops and by our friends. What makes one presentation better than another?

Business-related spoken communications: Presentations

A presentation, whether using a simple flip chart or software, is a frequently used means of communicating in business. If given professionally, presentations are an effective form of communication. The 'live' audience at a presentation provides an ideal opportunity to gain feedback.

Presentations

Presentations are a visual and highly effective way of communicating information. They are often used by people in business to persuade others to follow their plans or to make an argument. For instance, a sales person may give a presentation to the owners of a business to persuade them to buy their products rather than a competitor's. For your project you may be required to give presentations. You might fear doing them but being able to prepare and deliver effective presentations is an important and valuable skill. The key to getting a presentation right is your preparation. There is a very old saying that captures the importance of this, 'If you fail to prepare, prepare to fail!'

The strengths of presentations as a communication medium are:

* they can be visually stimulating and memorable
* the audience can ask questions and check understanding
* the presenter will receive feedback on their ideas and points, which will be invaluable in deciding whether to pursue certain ideas or not
* if certain people can not attend a presentation in person they can always view it by video or teleconferencing

The limitations of this approach are:

* the quality and effectiveness of the presentation depend on the presenting skills of the person making the presentation
* only a limited number of people can attend a presentation
* sometimes the equipment and environment are not conducive to effective presenting

Structuring and planning your presentation using appropriate business English

The success of a presentation relies on many things including how well the topic is researched and how well the presentation content is planned, structured and expressed.

* Understand the purpose of your presentation and research your topic thoroughly.
* Consider who your audience is going to be and how many people there will be. Develop presentation materials that will be appropriate to the level of understanding of the topic they are likely to have, using vocabulary, terminology and tone and expression which is appropriate.

* Plan an outline structure that has a clear introduction (statement of presentation objectives), middle (development of key presentation points) and conclusion (summary of the main presentation findings and any recommendations being made).

* Select images to make the presentation more interesting. You could also use models or have samples to pass around your audience.

* Select a presentation application, like Microsoft PowerPoint, to produce a professional slide presentation (but always have back-up OHP transparencies and handouts just in case the technology breaks or doesn't work on the day).

* And last but by no means least: practise, practise and practise some more!

Presenting tips

* Prepare a set of brief prompt cards or notes to help you remember what you want to say. These could be based on the structure you planned as you prepared. Beware: don't be tempted to read from them as this would make a very uninteresting presentation!

* Start your presentation with a 'bang'. An interesting fact or story will get your audience's attention.

* Keep good eye contact with your audience as their facial expressions will indicate whether they understand what you are saying. Also, this will stop you from reading directly from your notes or from a slide, which can become very boring for the audience.

* Speak clearly and ensure you project your voice so that everyone can hear you.

* Vary your presentation, making it interesting with pictures and diagrams, by telling stories or by demonstrating something.

* Allow time at the end of your presentation to answer any questions your audience may have.

INTRODUCTION

Slide 1 – Welcome and your name (and names of the team members if relevant) –
Hello and welcome to my presentation. My name is Lydia.

Slide 2 – State the purpose, aims or objectives of the presentation – The aim of this presentation is to ...

DEVELOPMENT

Slide 3 – State and make your first point clearly explaining its relevance to the overall aims of the presentation.

Slide 4 – State and make your second point clearly explaining its relevance to the overall aims of the presentation.

Slide 5 – State and make your third point clearly explaining its relevance to the overall aims of the presentation.

(You may use more slides here)

CONCLUSION & RECOMMENDATIONS

Slide 6 – Summarise the points you have made.
In conclusion, ...

Slide 7 – State and make your recommendations where necessary.
Overall, taking into account what I have said I would like to make the following recommendations ...

At the end of the presentation don't forget to thank your audience for listening to you and to ask if they have any questions.

Activity 3.13

A presentation structure

Using the example as a guide, spend 15 minutes planning the outline of a presentation. It could be a presentation on an area of your studies that you are particularly interested in or a hobby or sport you regularly take part in. Think about what you would like to put on each slide and any images, diagrams or other stimulating resources you would use to make your presentation interesting and engaging.

Functional Skills – ICT

When preparing presentations you will be developing a number of functional skills including the ability to select and use information, and to use IT to suitably present a message for a specific purpose and to an intended audience.

Summary

* Successful presentations require lots of research, lots of planning, lots of imagination and good presentation technique.
* Effective presentation technique involves projecting your voice, smiling (if you are not too afraid!), giving your audience eye-contact and knowing what you want to say (so you don't end up reading monotonously from a card, sheet of paper or slide).
* A good presentation style is a skill valued by many employers.

Business-related written communications: Business letters

Letters, reports and emails are the most frequently used forms of written communication in business. Learning to write them with the correct use of business English, tone and punctuation will reflect a lot about your professionalism. You will most certainly be required to produce one, if not all three, of them while completing your IT Diploma course.

Written business-related communications

A large amount of communication between and within businesses is written. Written methods of communication in business are suitable when it is essential to have a written record of what has been discussed or what is being communicated so it can be referred back to later.

Business letters

Letters in business are used to communicate detailed and usually formal messages. They are usually produced on headed paper with the company's business details and logo at the top. Letters generally provide important information or they are used to respond to customer enquiries or complaints. The benefits of using business letters as a form of business communication are:

* they provide a permanent written record that can be referred to later (for example, when there is a disagreement)
* they are also a confidential means of communicating with a customer, supplier or employee

Limitations of using business letters to communicate are:

* it can be expensive to produce and send business letters, particularly to a large number of customers
* in general, they may take a lot longer to produce because they are usually typed by administration staff

Writing business letters using appropriate business English

Letters are a method of communication with people outside a business, such as customers or suppliers. You wouldn't send a letter to someone working in the same department as you! Although, due to email, there is less emphasis on business letters these days, they are still an important form of communication and letter-writing skills are therefore important to develop.

Letters should have a clear structure with an introduction stating the reason for the letter, a main body of the letter providing the reader with information they need, and a conclusion (ending) which usually requests the reader to do something in response to the letter.

When writing letters it is always a good idea to draft them out first, checking for grammatical errors or confusion in meaning. Remember to use formal business language, as writing a letter to someone you do not know should be done with respect.

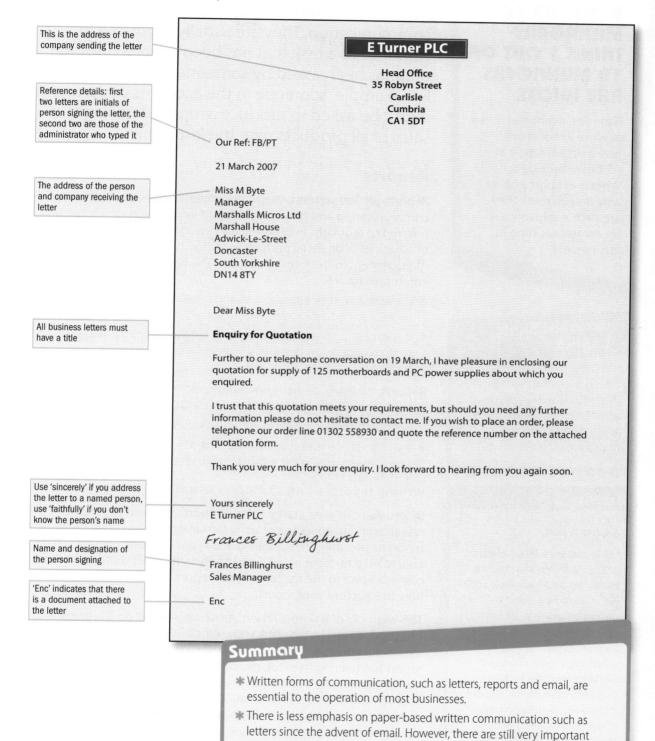

This is the address of the company sending the letter

Reference details: first two letters are initials of person signing the letter, the second two are those of the administrator who typed it

The address of the person and company receiving the letter

All business letters must have a title

Use 'sincerely' if you address the letter to a named person, use 'faithfully' if you don't know the person's name

Name and designation of the person signing

'Enc' indicates that there is a document attached to the letter

E Turner PLC

Head Office
35 Robyn Street
Carlisle
Cumbria
CA1 5DT

Our Ref: FB/PT

21 March 2007

Miss M Byte
Manager
Marshalls Micros Ltd
Marshall House
Adwick-Le-Street
Doncaster
South Yorkshire
DN14 8TY

Dear Miss Byte

Enquiry for Quotation

Further to our telephone conversation on 19 March, I have pleasure in enclosing our quotation for supply of 125 motherboards and PC power supplies about which you enquired.

I trust that this quotation meets your requirements, but should you need any further information please do not hesitate to contact me. If you wish to place an order, please telephone our order line 01302 558930 and quote the reference number on the attached quotation form.

Thank you very much for your enquiry. I look forward to hearing from you again soon.

Yours sincerely
E Turner PLC

Frances Billinghurst

Frances Billinghurst
Sales Manager

Enc

Summary

* Written forms of communication, such as letters, reports and email, are essential to the operation of most businesses.
* There is less emphasis on paper-based written communication such as letters since the advent of email. However, there are still very important circumstances when a paper document is essential, including when legal documents such as contracts are sent from one person or business to another to be signed and returned.

Business-related written communications: Reports

Reports are commonly used methods of business communication. They are usually produced in response to a task that has been set or a question that has been asked by someone in management. For example, someone in the accounts department might be asked to produce a report detailing the sales of all products over the last year.

Reports

Reports are formally structured documents. They are excellent for communicating and providing detailed information which can be referred to regularly. In business the results of some market research or a business's financial performance may be communicated to senior management in the form of a report. The benefits of using reports to communicate are:

* they provide structured, logical and detailed information presented in an easy-to-use and accessible format
* it is easy to turn to the section that contains the information you need to make a decision because the report will have a contents page at the beginning

Reports, however, do have limitations:

* they may be difficult for some people to read if there is a lot of specialist terminology and vocabulary used
* if a report is very long, it may never be read or referred to by busy employees, making the information and communication useless

Writing reports using appropriate business English

Before you can even start writing a report you need to conduct research and to collect as much information on the subject of your report as possible. Then, looking at all your information, you will be able to list a number of valid and important points that you wish to communicate to the readers of your report. You will then decide on how to structure your report.

This example of a simple report structure is based on the investigation of a production manager into how efficient production lines were in a particular business. You will note that it is clearly indicated who the report has been written for, the subject and purpose of the report, how the production manager researched the issue and what his findings and final recommendations were to his production director. The statements are short, easy to read and factual. You will also note a clear numbering system to make it easy to point out and refer to particular parts of the report. You may also be required to use a variety of punctuation marks, such as speech marks.

CONFIDENTIAL

For:	A Bailey, Production Director	Ref:PG
From:	P Guy, Production Manager	Date: 18 October 2008

The person who will receive the report

REPORT ON THE EFFICIENCY OF THE PRODUCTION LINE AT PHIL'S ELECTRICALS

The introduction. You should say what you are doing and why

1.0   TERMS OF REFERENCE

On 3 September you asked me to investigate production line efficiency on the shop floor. I was asked to comment on the current systems used, the mood amongst the production team and any recent developments that might help to improve performance.

The steps you took to gather the information

2.0   PROCEDURE

In order to obtain the relevant information and opinions, I followed the following procedures:

2.1   Observations were made on various occasions on the factory floor.
2.2   Interviews were conducted with staff members on the production line.
2.3   Extensive discussions were conducted with production line supervisors.
2.4   Those senior managers with experience of the production function were interviewed.
2.5   New technologies were evaluated off site.
2.6   Visits were conducted to RTK PLC and Middletons Ltd (Stockport).

This is the longest report section. It includes all of the information and opinions that you have gathered

3.0   FINDINGS

3.1   The mood of the staff of the production line is generally good, the managerial style used by the supervisors seems to suit the nature of the staff employed, however . . . .

3.2   Procedures implemented in the department work adequately well but many of them have not been reviewed for some considerable time . . . .

3.3   . . . .

3.4   . . . .

This should refer back to your Terms of Reference. What is the answer to the task that you have been set?

4.0   CONCLUSIONS

It is clear that the general management of the production function at the company is effective, however . . . .

What you think should happen as a result of your findings

5.0   RECOMMENDATIONS

As a result of my investigations, I recommend that the Board of Directors give active consideration to the following:

5.1   The introduction of JIT procedures would undoubtedly improve the efficiency of production . . . .

5.2   A variety of new technologies have become available in recent years, and the following seem to be the best of those available . . . .

Any attached documents referred to in the text should be included at the back of your report

APPENDICES

Summary

* Report writing is an essential business communication skill. You will be required to write a number of short reports on a variety of subjects concerning your mini-enterprise project.

* Understanding how they are structured and how sections are numbered is essential before starting to write any report.

* Report writing takes a great deal of research, organising and planning skills.

Business-related written communications: Emails

Billions of private and business email messages are sent every day. You sometimes can't purchase goods from websites if you do not have your own email address. Businesses have recognised its value as a medium to e-shot customers with their latest product and service offerings and promotional offers. The speed of emails has also contributed to employee's effectiveness and productivity in their work.

Emails

Emails are a very popular method of communication where messages can be sent between computers using a network. The benefits of using emails to communicate inside and outside a business are:

* messages are delivered almost instantaneously
* passwords make the communication more secure
* replies can be simple and speedy with just a click of the 'reply' button
* images, spreadsheets and documents can be sent as attachments
* messages can be one-to-one and one-to-many (sometimes using mailing lists)

However, there are disadvantages:

* you cannot guarantee that the email will be read
* important emails could be accidentally deleted
* an email could contain an attachment that harbours a virus

Writing emails using appropriate business English

There aren't many people who do not have their own email addresses these days. Emails are used as a less formal method of written communication and are usually short and concise messages, a little like memos but sent electronically. Emails are written as if you are directly speaking to the person and so the style is very like a business conversation. However, you must still use language appropriate to the recipient. For example, it might not be professional to use the text abbreviations you might use on your mobile phone or to use emoticons (smileys) when emailing a senior manager or important customer.

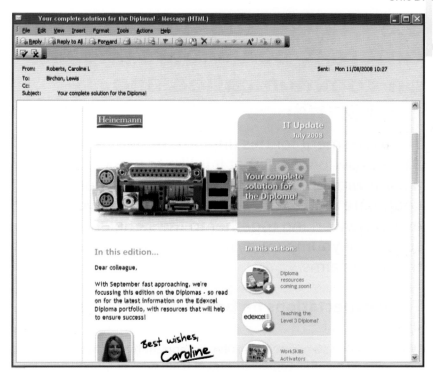

Many companies use emails for cost-effective marketing communications, but the language and presentation needs to be professional.

Functional Skills – English

You can demonstrate your Functional English skills by making sure your language, format and structure is suitable for your purpose and audience.

Activity 3.16

Send an email

For this activity you will be encouraged to work independently. You will need access to a networked computer and your own personal email address. You will also need your teacher's email address. Send your teacher an email with a document you have produced as part of your coursework for this unit attached. You will need to ask your teacher to look at your work and to provide you with some feedback and possible comments on how the document could be improved. Your tone and business English need to be appropriate for your teacher. He or she will send you an email commenting on your use of business English in your email communication and also in your chosen and sent document.

Summary

* Emails are a very quick, cheap and convenient means of communication.
* However, when sending an email we must be aware that the person receiving it will not necessarily know it is there for a long time and may not even read it at all!

3.3 Understand how different behaviours impact on communication and performance

The assessment for this unit is designed to provide a real experience of what it is like to work as part of a team with objectives to achieve. It is important to cooperate with each other. Cooperation involves everyone working together to the same end: the success of your team project and the achievement of the team's aims.

Team expectations on behaviour, attitudes and actions

When working as a new team it is very important that from the beginning all members agree on a set of team rules or ground rules for team behaviour. This is likely to be one of the first agenda items for your first meeting along with allocating roles and responsibilities. You could draw up and get everybody to sign a 'Team Expectations Agreement'.

Agreements on behaviour, attitudes and actions will improve the chances that a team will work well together. When drawing up your agreement you might want to consider the following.

Behaviour: what is expected from everyone in the team?

You could agree on:

* overall levels of professionalism expected from team members and what would constitute being unprofessional
* level of effort and helpfulness expected of team members and what would be construed as unhelpful
* quality of verbal and written communication expected within the team and with others outside and why it is important to the team's reputation
* expectations of team members' personal organisation skills and what would constitute being disorganised
* use of appropriate language and vocabulary in meetings (see below)

For example, it might be considered unacceptable for a team member to say things like, 'You are all talking rubbish!'

Action: what expectations do you have of fellow team members?

You could agree on:

* acceptable levels of attendance at meetings and the consequences of not attending them regularly
* deadlines for completion of tasks
* the consequences of work not being done or getting lost or not being completed to a satisfactory level of quality

* the consequences when a team member is not equally contributing to the goals and workload of the team

Lack of attendance or poor punctuality can stop the flow of a meeting while time is spent explaining to the late person what has been discussed, and the rest of the team get frustrated.

Attitude: what overall attitude to the project should be expected and how should this be communicated?

You could agree on:

* the general attitude of team members
* what constitutes a positive and negative approach to the team
* the expected use of verbal and body language in meetings to convey positive or negative feelings (see below)

For example, a team member may be reluctant to make contributions if someone else in the team yawns and speaks to the person next to them every time they speak. The attitude and body language of one team member can have a devastating effect on the motivation and attitudes of everyone else in the team.

Effective Communication & Performance: what are the expectations of communication and performance from each team member?

It is important that, as a team and before you start any work, you clearly agree on the aims and objectives of the task you have been set and how each person will contribute to their overall achievement. It is useful sometimes to set targets for each person so that at each meeting it can be checked whether targets set for individuals have been achieved and therefore deadlines met. You could agree on:

* what should be done by each team member and by when (objectives and targets to achieve by strict deadlines)
* when a team member finishes his or her work, what they should be expected to do
* what a team member should do if they do not possess certain skills, for example in an organisation this would mean training to ensure good company and product knowledge, understanding of procedures and the ability to treat colleagues and customers politely, helpfully and promptly

---

Personal, Learning and Thinking Skills

By studying this part of the unit you should be able to detail and demonstrate the skills and qualities of being a good team member.

Activity 3.17

Draw up your own 'Team Expectations Agreement'

Consider the content of this part of the unit. Working in your project teams, produce a thought shower identifying the desired expectations for behaviour, action, attitude and performance in your team. Present your agreement to the rest of the class, explaining the importance of each point.

Summary

* How team members behave, their actions and their attitudes can have a dramatic impact on the overall performance of the team.
* Agreeing what is acceptable and unacceptable behaviour is a positive starting point for any team. By drawing up a 'Team Expectations Agreement' all team members know what is expected of them in terms of their behaviour and the consequences of not fulfilling these agreements.

Personality types and how they influence teams

In most businesses people are expected to work within a team. A team can be described as a group working together to achieve shared objectives. Each team member is likely to bring certain skills and qualities essential for the overall team's success.

Characteristics of good teams

Good teams have many things in common. They:

* share commitment by working towards the same goal
* work collaboratively to share the load
* have the ability to compromise to reach a common agreement
* are fair and considerate to improve all member's experiences
* listen respectfully to ensure everyone has a voice
* take personal responsibility for the team's overall success.

Team members' personality types

The best teams have members with varied personalities, skills and qualities. This variety ensures good performance. Typical team roles are:

* **Leader/facilitator** – a person who has the natural ability, strength and confidence to coordinate the activities of the team and to monitor performance and team members' progress.
* **Recorder** – an organised and methodical person who records the results of all discussions, meetings, mind showers etc. They are usually also responsible for taking notes (minutes) of meetings, typing them up and distributing them to fellow team members. They may also assemble reports and other written documents.
* **Ideas person/innovator** – a person who has great vision and creativity, finding it easy to solve problems.
* **Team-workers/doers/producers** – these are the people who, once a plan is finalised, get on and do the work. They are happy to carry out the tasks and prefer not to put themselves forward as leaders. They implement the decisions that are made and ensure tasks are completed.
* **Compromiser/supporter/peace-maker** – this is a person who helps to develop team relationships so that members work harmoniously even at times of crisis. They will identify when members are conflicting and encourage them to see each other's perspective and to come to a compromise so that the team can move on.
* **Analyst** – this is a person with the ability to identify potential or existing problems or barriers to the success of the team. The problems are then usually solved by the innovators.

Some team members may carry out two or more of the team roles described. However, there are some roles such as the leader role that it is unwise to have two members conflicting for!

TOGETHER EVERYONE ACHIEVES MORE – TEAM!

What does the above acronym mean to you? Can you describe a personal example of a team's accomplishments because of the team members' ability to work together?

Collaborative working

Collaborative working is the process of working jointly with others so that everyone benefits.

Activity 3.18

What good team work means to you

Consider the characteristics of good teams. Working in small groups or your project teams discuss each characteristic and write in your own words what each means and how will they be achieved during your assessment project.

Belbin (1981), a famous British theorist, suggested that effective teams consist of members carrying out nine different but complementary roles as shown in the table below:

	Belbin roles	Description
Action oriented	Implementer	Well-organised and predictable. Takes basic ideas and makes them work in practice. Can be slow.
	Shaper	Lots of energy and action, challenging others to move forwards. Can be insensitive.
	Completer/Finisher	Reliably sees things through to the end, ironing out the wrinkles and ensuring everything works well. Can worry too much and not trust others.
Thought oriented	Plant	Solves problems with original and creative ideas. Can be poor communicator and may ignore the details.
	Monitor/Evaluator	Sees the big picture. Thinks carefully and accurately about things. May lack energy or ability to inspire others.
	Specialist	Has expert knowledge/skills in key areas and will solve problems here. Can be disinterested in all other areas.
People oriented	Coordinator	Respected leader who helps everyone focus on their task. Can be seen as excessively controlling.
	Team worker	Cares for individuals and the team. Good listener and works to resolve social problems. Can have problems making difficult decisions.
	Resource/investigator	Explores new ideas and possibilities with energy and with others. Good net-worker. Can be too optimistic and lose energy after the initial flush.

(Source: http://changingminds.org/explanations/preferences/belbin.htm)

Belbin developed a questionnaire called the Self Perception Inventory which can provide a detailed idea of a team member's typical behaviour and what they contribute to a team situation. Belbin suggests that people tend to adopt a particular team role depending on the situation, their own natural working style and their interrelationships with others and the work being done. You may behave and interact quite differently in different teams or when the members or work of the team changes.

Personal, Learning and Thinking Skills

Reflecting on the team role you are most comfortable with and those used most often by others in your team will help you to understand the value of team work and communication. When might it be appropriate to change your style in a team?

Activity 3.19

1 Read the team member descriptions in this section and decide which role you usually play and which roles you think your mini-enterprise team members usually play.

2 Compare and discuss your list with everyone else. For every person in your team agree a suitable role and list the responsibilities associated with each.

3 Good teams are ones in which there are a balance of roles. What would be the consequences for your group of not having a leader or innovator? What could your team do to overcome this?

Summary

✳ Good teams share common characteristics in that they work collaboratively to reach agreements in an atmosphere where everyone is treated fairly, considerately and feels listened to.

✳ Members of a team generally have different roles to fulfil and these roles are usually linked to their personalities. Successful teams are ones that possess members with a wide variety of skills and qualities.

The team leader or facilitator in your project team has an important role. Leadership and facilitating is about organising what needs to be done and motivating team members to carry out their duties so that the team is more likely to achieve its objectives.

Leadership

What is leadership?

Leadership is different from authority because authority is something that someone has because of their position or status, such as a manager of a department in a business. The leader in your mini-enterprise team is just one of the team and has no authority. However, the leader will need an ability to organise and motivate team members effectively without upsetting them or making them feel they are being bossed!

Skills and qualities of leadership

Many business theorists have asked what skills and qualities separate natural leaders from non-leaders. You may have already discussed some of these during the starter activity. Essentially, the skills of natural leaders are shown in the spider diagram.

> ## ARE YOU A BORN LEADER?
>
> Do you like to take responsibility for things? Do you naturally take charge and lead during school projects and activities? What qualities do natural leaders have and not have?

> **Leadership**
> Leadership is the process of influencing and directing the performance of team members towards the achievement of team goals and objectives.

> **Delegate**
> To allocate tasks or duties to team members who have the skills and qualities to carry them out.

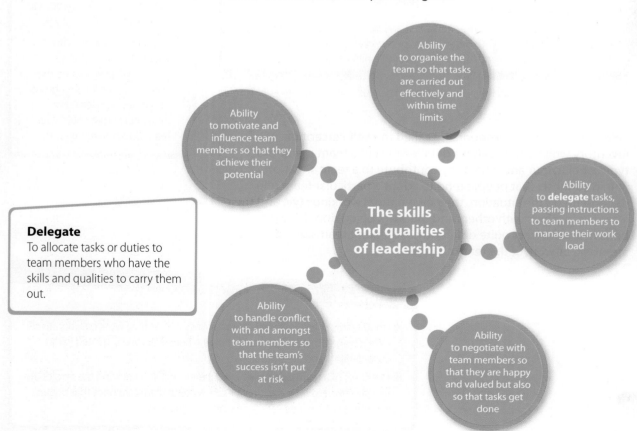

Ability to organise the team so that tasks are carried out effectively and within time limits

Ability to motivate and influence team members so that they achieve their potential

The skills and qualities of leadership

Ability to delegate tasks, passing instructions to team members to manage their work load

Ability to handle conflict with and amongst team members so that the team's success isn't put at risk

Ability to negotiate with team members so that they are happy and valued but also so that tasks get done

A natural leader is likely to possess some or all of the following qualities:

* trust of fellow team members and belief in the team
* approachability
* willingness to listen to others
* ability to deal with team members in a sensitive and tactful way
* ability to lead by example (carrying out duties as expected and on time)
* energy and enthusiasm even when things get difficult
* good communication skills

Activity 3.20

Qualities of a good leader

Consider one good and one bad leadership example known to you. Explain what the main differences between the good and bad leader were and how it contributed to your experience.

Summary

* Having the right leader or facilitator for your project team is important and it is not a task that should be taken lightly.
* Leaders/facilitators are usually elected. As a team you should decide on who you feel has the qualities and skills to carry out the role and ask them if they would be happy to perform the duty of leader.
* Leaders equally need to be supported by their team members by listening and respecting the decisions they make and trying as much as possible to do what the leader asks.

Objective

A specific, measurable, achievable, realistic and time-constrained (SMART) statement of intended performance. For example, 'We will reduce customer complaints by 10 per cent by the end of 2008'.

SMART

* **S**PECIFIC – be very clear about what is to be done and achieved, e.g. 'increase sales'

* **M**EASURABLE – have a quantitative element so achievements can be measured, e.g. 'by 10 per cent'

* **A**CHIEVABLE – reflecting on the task, the abilities of the team and the time provided, ensure each objective set is practically achievable

* **R**EALISTIC – be the most practical way of achieving the overall aims and goals of the team work

* **T**IME-CONSTRAINED – provide a clear indication of the time period over which the actions are to be accomplished (but remembering to be realistic!)

3.4 Be able to work in a team to meet agreed objectives

For this unit you will be asked to investigate how organisations use different media to get their messages across to others. You will research and explain the main types of communications media used by businesses, giving examples of their use. Using this knowledge you will then work as part of a team to produce a number of different communications for a given purpose. In this section we will explore the importance of agreeing objectives, planning and work execution to the overall success of a team-based project.

Agreeing objectives

Before we start let's ask ourselves a question. If a team does not know what it is trying to achieve (its **objectives**) then how can we expect it to achieve anything? It should be clear that one of the first and most important things that must be agreed once a team has been formed is the team's objectives.

Teams need objectives for a number of reasons:

* so that all team members know what levels of performance they are all working towards, for whom and by when

* so that decisions can be made with achievement of objectives in mind

* so that member and team performance can be measured and evaluated against them

In general, we say objectives are **SMART**. This is an acronym where each letter in the word SMART represents a quality that a good objective must possess.

Planning the team's work

Work planning is a very important part of managing a successful team. It involves working as a team to identify and agree what needs to be done, by when and by whom. We have already considered that team members bring different qualities and expertise. Roles, responsibilities and essentially each activity carried out, therefore, must be allocated appropriately to each team member depending on their specialist skills and qualities.

Effective teams are ones in which there is effective communication, negotiation and essentially fairness and equity. Therefore, the procedure for allocating work tasks needs to be formed and agreed by the team overall and not just by one person. Only when everyone is happy with the approach will everyone be committed to the process of work planning and scheduling.

Work schedules or plans are simple planning aids that help the leader of a team monitor team performance. Here is an example of a simple work plan. You can see that the overall team objectives are detailed at the top. We then list all the smaller tasks or targets that need to be achieved by individuals.

Team Work Plan

| Overall team objective(s) | Date set: _____ |
| | Team members: |

Work/Task Allocated	To Whom	By When	Achieved Y/N
1			
2			
3			
4			
5			
6			
7			
8			
etc.			

Executing the team's work

If team objectives are to be achieved then the work schedule or plan must be executed well. This involves:

* Working cooperatively and being willing to negotiate and to see things through other team members' eyes

* Communicating effectively and professionally so that team members understand what you are trying to say.

* Holding regular meetings. These are essential to agree roles, responsibilities, team objectives and individual tasks and later on to monitor progress.

* Showing consideration for others and the difficulties they may be having. This is linked to respecting your fellow team members.

* Providing feedback during meetings to team members on performance and the quality of their work and team members receiving and responding constructively to it.

Activity 3.21

Objective setting and work planning

Get into your teams and consider the task you have been set.

1. Using your understanding of SMART objectives, agree your team's overall objective(s).

2. Write each objective on a sheet of paper and, underneath it, start listing all the jobs or activities that need to be carried out in order to achieve it.

3. Next to each job or activity indicate a date by which it needs to be accomplished if the overall objective is to be achieved.

4. Next to each job start to agree and allocate the duties amongst the team members, remembering to share them fairly and according to the strengths of each team member. This process may take some time and agreement must be achieved. If an activity is allocated to someone who did not want to do it then there is a likelihood that it may never get done. Compromise and communication is the key here!

5. Using all this information, the team leader will be in a position to draw up the team's work plan or schedule. This document must be distributed to all team members and reviewed regularly at team meetings.

Summary

* Effective teams are ones that have a clear picture of what needs to be achieved (objectives) and how it is most likely to be achieved (work planning).

Team communication in meetings

We have already mentioned the importance of meetings to the success experienced by project teams. They are a useful form of communication providing a good venue for team members to agree what work needs to be done, to exchange views, to share ideas and to pass on information. They are particularly important to make sure that a project is progressing on the right track as part of the monitoring process. Discussions can occur that allow important decisions to be made and the responsibility for these decisions can be shared.

Preparing for a meeting

Once your team has decided that a meeting is required, the team leader or facilitator will need to decide on and communicate the topics or issues to be discussed, who needs to attend, where and when the meeting will be held, who will **chair** (lead) the meeting, who will be the timekeeper and who will be the recorder (note-taker).

The chair will then produce a key meeting document called the **agenda** and circulate it to all meeting participants by hand or email so that they can prepare for the meeting knowing what issues will be discussed. Here is an example of a typical agenda. Note the contents and structure of it when preparing your own agendas.

A MEETING OF MINDS

What have been your experiences of meetings? What distinguishes the good and effective meetings from the bad and ineffective ones?

Chair

The chair is the person nominated to run a meeting.

Agenda

An agenda is a list of items to be discussed at a meeting, sometimes with time limits placed to ensure the meeting runs to a schedule.

The next mini-enterprise meeting for the Snowcones group will be held in room 3B on Tuesday, 6 November from 12:30 till 1:10pm. All team members are asked to attend. Please send apologies to the chair if you are unable to attend.

AGENDA

1. Welcome and apologies for non-attendance.
2. Review and confirm accuracy of last meeting's minutes. (5 mins)
3. Review and allocation of team roles and responsibilities. (10 mins)
4. Sales forecasts for month 1 compared with actual performance. (5 mins)
5. Suggestions for improvements in sales. (10 mins)
6. Any other business. (10 mins)
7. Time, date and location of next meeting.

Chair: Sophie Blaser
Recorder: Lyndsey Looper
Time keeper: Tim Hollins

The meeting

Before a meeting, team members should ensure they have completed tasks they agreed to do at the last meeting. During the meeting they should be prepared to discuss the agenda items, and ensure they adhere to the 'Team Expectations Agreement' that they drew up on desired behaviour when the team was formed. They should aim to participate actively and listen to and consider the ideas and suggestions of other team members.

Recorders are often referred to as 'minute takers' or 'secretaries'. They take the minutes of the meeting, which are notes on what was discussed, stated or agreed and by whom. After the meeting the recorder writes or types up the minutes and distributes them to all team members, who should read them and correct any inaccuracies before the next team meeting. When minutes are reviewed at the start of each new meeting it is easy to spot those people who are dedicated and doing their duties and those who are not!

Often the outcome of discussion is that something needs to be done. For example, suppose it is decided that a poster needs to be placed on a school notice board, but nobody knows what permission they need to be allowed to do it. In this case, a team member will be tasked to find out the school procedure. The recorder shows this as an 'action' on the minutes, noting what needs to be done, by when and by whom. Actions serve as reminders to team members, and they can be reported on at subsequent meetings. These actions would most likely be added to the team work plan so that the activity is monitored carefully and ticked off once it has been completed.

Here is an example of meeting minutes to help you:

Minutes of meeting held on 6 November at 12:30 in room 3B
Snowcone Group

Present: Sophie, Lyndsey, Tim, Lydia and Charlotte
Apologies: John

Item 1 – Welcome and apologies
1. Apologies received from John who was unable to attend the meeting due to an inter-school rugby match.

Item 2 – Review of minutes from last meeting
2. Minutes have been approved by all team members present as accurate and consistent.
3. Tim expressed his apologies for not having the advertising posters to show at today's meeting. They have been completed but the printer in the computer suite is faulty. He will email the designs to everyone today.

Item 3 – Review of team roles and responsibilities
4. Etc.

Functional Skills – English

Attending meetings and contributing to them will develop your listening and speaking skills.

Activity 3.22

The first meeting

Working in your project teams, draft an agenda for your very first official meeting. Remember, this would normally be done by the chair or team leader but this person hasn't been chosen yet! What issues do you think would be important to discuss at the first meeting? Don't forget to use the suggested agenda structure to ensure the meeting is professionally structured. Consider everything we have discussed so far in this unit in helping you to decide on what to include or exclude from your first meeting. Structure is important or your meeting will become one long chat in which nothing will be achieved.

Summary

* Meetings are an important communication method for teams.
* It is important that they are conducted in an efficient and professional manner.

Personal, Learning and Thinking Skills

Personal evaluation encourages you to be reflective in assessing personal performance and identifying possible personal improvements.

Team evaluation encourages you to discuss concerns and issues and so learn how to resolve them.

Activity 3.23

SWOT

Draw lines to divide a piece of A4 paper into four and head each section with one of the following words: Strengths, Weaknesses, Opportunities, Threats. Write down as many of your positive (strengths) and negative (weaknesses) points as you can and then consider things you could do to improve (opportunities) and things that may be difficult to change about you that could stop you from achieving well in teams in the future (threats).

3.5 Be able to evaluate their own performance as an individual and as a member of a team

Part of becoming a better team member and improving performance is being able to evaluate what contribution you made to your team and to identify how you could possibly improve on it in the future.

Personal performance

Personal evaluation

For your Unit 3 assessment you are expected to evaluate how effectively you contributed to and performed in your team. This involves taking an honest look at your personal strengths and weaknesses (limitations). One way of approaching a self-evaluation is by constructing a 'Personal SWOT Analysis'. Ask yourself when conducting a personal analysis how well you contributed to the team.

Peer evaluation

A personal SWOT analysis contains only your own impressions. For a more effective evaluation it is important to also listen to the views of your team mates. You may like to carry out a 'Peer Assessment'. You can use a form similar to the one opposite.

Evaluating your performance by using feedback is similar to an organisation listening to its customers and acting on what they say about its products: it should be treated as an opportunity to improve your performance. For peer assessment to be of value you have to see the process as constructive and you need to respect the views of your peers. Your feedback to fellow team members needs to be honest but sensitive. The feedback would be of no use at all if you told the person they were fantastic when they were actually not.

If you were working in a business, the feedback on your performance in a team would be given to you by your team leader or manager via performance appraisals. These assessments will take place at regular intervals (for example monthly, six-monthly, or yearly). This means that the assessor and team member can easily see whether any criticisms have been addressed and, if performance is unchanged (or worsened), it provides an opportunity to find out why. You can provide evidence that you are responding constructively to feedback by asking your peers to assess you regularly during the team project. Hopefully, the assessments will show that you are constructively addressing your weaknesses; however, it is important that you also record why you might not have improved.

Peer Assessment Form for_____ by _____

Rate your team member according to the degree that he/she carried out their responsibilities during the mini-enterprise project.
Give a short reason for your choice.

Marks out of 5 = _____, where

5 is for **hard worker**, often doing more than their share and producing work of a high standard
4 is for **someone who did what was expected** and their work was of a good standard
3 is for **someone who sometimes failed to participate** in meetings and group activities and complete work by required deadlines
2 is for **someone who regularly failed to participate** in meetings and group activities and complete work by required deadlines
1 is for **someone whose contributions were minimal** or there was no participation at all

Reasons for mark awarded:

Team member's best qualities:

Opportunities for improvement:

Team performance

Once personal evaluations have been conducted, it is always good to consider how the team performed overall. This can also be done using the SWOT analysis tool. At the team's final meeting, it is worth reviewing the strengths (such as how well the team worked together and the performance levels achieved), weaknesses (such as conflict or poor leadership), opportunities (such as how communication could be improved) and threats to team performance (aspects of the team performance that would prevent them from being successful in the future). You may be in a position at the end of the meeting to highlight a list of key learning points about what it is like to work together as a team!

When reflecting on your team's overall performance it might be helpful to consider what went well, what went badly, how effective the team were overall, whether the mix of personalities contributed positively or negatively to the team's effectiveness, and whether all team members contributed equally. You might find your teacher's observations (as an independent reviewer) useful in helping you to assess the overall team performance.

Activity 3.24

Giving genuine feedback

When conducting peer assessments you must always think, 'How would I feel if someone said this about me?' One way to approach giving someone feedback is by considering everything they do well and key things that they could improve on. Give them a balanced feedback highlighting both their strengths and weaknesses. This is sometimes called 'sandwiching the negatives with the positives'. It involves saying something positive first, then highlighting something negative and then finishing with another positive. This doesn't leave the person receiving the feedback feeling demotivated and unhappy.

Working in pairs, give written and verbal feedback to a fictional fellow team member. She has sometimes failed to attend meetings and has been late producing work on several occasions. However, you are also aware she is always enthusiastic in team meetings and has contributed some great ideas in the past. Her written work is usually of a very good standard. You gave her 3 out of 5 marks on her peer assessment form.

Summary

* To do well in the business world we have to continuously improve and to improve we need to take an honest look at our personal strengths and weaknesses.

* Sometimes, we are not aware of the things we do that are negative, so peer assessments are an important part of that personal evaluation and continuous improvement process.

Preparation for assessment

In this unit you will experience what it is like to work as part of a team. You will be encouraged to investigate the use of different communications media for different business purposes and then to use the knowledge you have gained to work as part of a team, using IT to communicate a message for a purpose given to you by your teacher. The brief for this assessment will have a business-relevant context; it will specify the purpose of the communication, key requirements and the target audience.

How you will be assessed

This unit is assessed internally by your teacher. You will be expected to present assessment evidence in the form of a portfolio, which will for this unit have two parts:

Part 1 – An investigation into how organisations use different communication media to communicate messages.

* Research, describe and explain the main types of communication media used by organisations for different purposes and provide examples.
* Select with clear explanation which of the forms of business communication you will go on to produce as part of the work you will carry out with your challenge project team.

Part 2 – Working as part of an effective team (made up of three or four members), plan and execute a task that involves the team communicating a message in a business-related context by making use of appropriate communication media.

* Set up the team and keep accurate records of progress, such as minutes of meetings, how roles and responsibilities were allocated, to whom and why, a list of team objectives to be achieved, team work plans etc. It might be useful for one member of the team to keep a diary during the project to record discussions and decisions made.
* Work as a team using and utilising the team members' skills to achieve team objectives. Evidence of effective teams will be demonstrated by the success of team meetings where ideas are shared, progress is reviewed and decisions made on where the team will go next in developing and producing appropriate communications for the challenge. At least one form of communication must be as a result of a joint effort requiring contributions from all team members, such as a promotional website or podcast.
* Judge and evaluate the performance of your team and also how well you have contributed to the team's success.

Unit-specific advice

* As this unit is primarily concerned with communication and team work it is important that you clearly document and keep evidence of all communication within the team, in particular documentation relating to meetings such as agendas and minutes of meetings.
* It may be that these documents are created by one person in the team or, to be fair, the team may take it in turns to write up the minutes of the meetings, as this can be very time-consuming.

You must show that you:	Guidance	To gain higher marks you must:
3.1 Understand why different types of communication media are used for different purposes	* **Provide** some information about the three main types of communication media in business contexts and their use * **Comment** on the choice of business-related communications used for the team task	* **Explain** the three main types of communication media in business contexts, including examples of their use and some comments on benefits/ limitations * **Justify** the choice of business-related communications used for the team task
3.2 Are able to use confident, correct and contextually appropriate English in a range of business-related communications	* **Produce** some appropriate business-related communications and make a **useful contribution** to the team effort to communicate a message	* **Produce** several effective business-related communications and make a **strong contribution** to the team effort to communicate a message
3.3 Understand how different behaviours, attitudes and actions impact on effective communication and performance between individuals and groups and **3.4** Be able to work in a team to meet agreed objectives	* **Submit** a team plan * Keep a diary throughout the project with a **brief record** of team discussions (including initial meetings to agree objectives, allocate roles and plan a schedule), decisions made and your individual contribution to teamwork * **Communicate** reasonably effectively with other team members * **Provide** some support and constructive feedback to others * **Respond** sensibly to some feedback received from others * **Attempt** to adapt behaviour/ attitude to changing circumstances * Make a **reasonable contribution** to help the team meet its objectives	* **Submit** a team plan with detailed notes to track progress * Keep a diary throughout the project with a **detailed record** of team discussions (including initial meetings to agree objectives, allocate roles and plan a schedule), decisions made and your individual contribution to teamwork * **Communicate** very effectively with other team members * **Provide** good support and constructive feedback to others * **Respond** positively and constructively to all feedback received from others * **Adapt** behaviour/attitude effectively to changing circumstances * Make a **sound contribution** to help the team meet its objectives
3.5 Are able to evaluate your own performance as an individual and a member of a team	* **Comment** on your own performance and contribution to teamwork * **Comment** on the performance of the team, including the impact of behaviour, attitude and/or actions on communication	* **Evaluate** your own performance and contribution to teamwork, including the effectiveness of their communication with other team members and feedback given to and received from others * **Evaluate** the performance of the team, including the impact of behaviour, attitude and actions on teamwork and communication * **Suggest** opportunities for improvements

4 Skills for Innovation

Introduction

In business you will be faced with challenges and be presented with opportunities. To be successful, you will need to take advantage of both and turn them to your benefit.

LOOK AROUND YOU

Write down as many businesses as you can think of which have had an effect on the room you are in.

In this unit, you will use a lot of skills you already have, some of which you probably take for granted. Being able to manipulate numbers, especially currency, and the ability to communicate your ideas and persuade others of your way of thinking are important for any businessperson.

Creativity and innovation are skills that businesses regard highly and they are crucial to business success. Organisations frequently have to take risks in order to remain successful and grow, and often it is the creative solution that produces the highest profits.

However, the skills to be able to forecast and consider consequences of decisions are also important. A business that knows the probable outcomes of their choices is the one that can operate more confidently and with more foresight and understanding. Imagine getting on a bus: if you know where it is going you can be more confident about travelling on it.

Anyone can make a decision, but being able to make the *right* decision, and one that puts you ahead of the competition, is what makes you a successful businessperson.

Learning outcomes

4.1 Be able to use a wide range of numerical and graphical techniques to analyse and present business-relevant information, including the use of estimation and approximation to support ideas and proposals

4.2 Be able to use creative, investigative and numerical reasoning skills to present proposals to address business challenges and opportunities

4.3 Know about the key legal and ethical considerations in the IT environment, including data protection, health and safety, and copyright

Activity 4.1

1 List the skills you already have that might help you in this unit.

2 Why is it important to learn how to handle numbers?

3 How can innovation and creativity be used in business?

Hint: Keep your answers to these questions and look back on them at the end of the unit and see if you were right.

Case Study

When Walt Disney made his first full-length animation in the 1930s, *Snow White and The Seven Dwarfs*, the papers called it 'Disney's Folly', yet the film grossed $8 million (equivalent to $98 million today) and it is seen as a pivotal point in the history of animation and film-making. By taking a risk, by doing something no one else had done, Walt Disney shaped film history.

4.1 Numerical and graphical analysis techniques

Being able to understand and interpret numbers is a very important and highly valued skill in business.

NUMBERS, NUMBERS, EVERYWHERE

How many times do you work with numbers in a typical day? Consider reading the time, handling money and so on.

Imagine you've applied for a job that you really want and you're up against two other people. The first test in the job interview is an aptitude test in which your mental maths skills are assessed. You and one of the other applicants pass the test. The third person fails and is sent home. The test is followed by an interview with the Manager. He shows you sales figures for the last 12 months and asks you what they mean. You are able to explain that the business profit is steadily increasing and to identify which product is the best-seller. The other applicant couldn't, so you get the job. It's all down to being able to understand and interpret numbers.

At all levels of business you will be asked to use numbers:

* How many items have been manufactured today?
* Could you reduce these prices by 25 per cent?
* How much profit have we made this month?
* How much should we invest in this business?
* Every employee handles figures each time they are paid: salary, tax, pension etc. Will you know if you have been paid the correct amount?

So where does innovation come into it? By being able to understand numbers, you will begin to be able to predict the future. This isn't as mysterious and magical as it sounds. By seeing what has gone before, you will be able to estimate what may happen in the future.

Being able to come up with creative ideas, to present them clearly and to convince people to act on them are not things that everyone can do and therefore they are skills that are highly prized. An example could be seeing something others do not or cannot see, such as a gap in the market where there is potential profit.

In this section, you will be encouraged to create a spreadsheet – one of the most vital business tools for understanding numbers and figures. All the examples use Microsoft Excel, although other spreadsheet software can be used. You are advised to save your work frequently and make regular back-ups.

Activity 4.2

Sole is a shoe shop that specialises in designer and unusual footwear.

In pairs, do the following tasks.

1 List as many circumstances as you can think of where Sole might use numbers.

2 List what calculations Sole might perform with these numbers.

Summary

* Using mathematics is a skill that is important throughout business.
* By understanding figures, it may be possible to predict the future.
* Sometimes risks need to be taken in business: they can be profitable if they are successful.

Mathematical skills

All businesses, even non-profit organisations and charities, work with money and figures. For a multinational supermarket the figures would involve sales made, money taken, bills paid and so on. No matter how large or small the organisation, numbers are vital to understanding and improving it.

EVERYDAY MATHS

Think about a shop on your local high street. Write down all the calculations they might make in the course of their business.

Percentages

A **percentage** shows a figure in proportion to 100; for example 10 per cent (10%) is 10 in proportion to 100 ('per cent' meaning 'by the hundred').

Percentages are used in business to analyse figures and present them clearly. For example:

Percentage
A figure in proportion to 100, for example 10 per cent (10%).

Total sales of jumpers	Sales of red jumpers	Sales of yellow jumpers	Sales of other colour jumpers
719,260	539,445	107,889	71,926
100%	75%	15%	10%

It is much clearer to see that more red jumpers were sold and that they constituted three-quarters of the total sales when we use percentages.

To find a percentage, divide 100 by the total number to work out how much 1 per cent is worth, and then multiply it by the number of sales:

$$(100 \div 719,260) \times 539,445 = 75\%$$

Percentages are out of 100 and can be written like decimals (for example 75 per cent is 0.75). This can be used to work out a percentage of a number:

$$719,260 \times 0.75 = 539,445$$

Activity 4.3a

A charity has received £65,175 in donations of money. £12,490 has to be spent on utilities (such as electricity, gas etc.). 74% of the donations can be spent on aid.

1 What percentage of the donations is spent on utilities (to one decimal place)?

2 How much can be spent on aid (in pounds)?

Ratios

A **ratio** shows one number in relation to another, for example '1:4' means 'one to four'. If the ratio of customers who buy trousers to those who do not is 1:4, this means that in every five customers one would buy trousers.

Ratio
One number in relation to another, for example 1:4.

Total pairs of socks sold = 4,000
Total pairs of socks returned = 200
Ratio = 200:4,000 = 1:20

To calculate the final ratio, you divide both numbers by the highest common factor (the largest number that divides into both): in this case 200. It is clear to see that for every 20 pairs of socks sold, one pair was returned.

Statistics

Statistical analysis is a useful way of analysing the figures businesses have to deal with. If a business has sales of 500 items from 200 stores worldwide, there are many numbers to deal with. By calculating the statistics, these numbers become easier to handle.

Three methods of statistical analysis are 'mean', 'mode' and 'median'.

Example data set   2   49   12   2   100   56   7   1   24   9   2

Median: Line up the numbers in ascending order of magnitude. The centre one is the median. In the example the median is 9.

    1   2   2   2   7   9   12   24   49   56   100

Mode: Count how many there are of each number. The one that occurs most often is the mode. In this example the mode is 2.

    1, 7, 9, 12, 24, 49, 56, 100 all occur once.

    2 occurs three times.

Mean: Add up the total and divide by the number of figures. The mean is also called the 'average'. In this example, the mean is:

    $(2 + 49 + 12 + 2 + 100 + 56 + 7 + 1 + 24 + 9 + 2)/11 = 264/11 = 24$

Activity 4.3b

A local hospital is wondering whether it has enough beds to cope with the increase of patients during the winter.

1 In the last seven months, total number of patients per month has been 1,571, 1,443, 1,564, 1,521, 1,645, 1,498 and 1,396. Calculate how many patients in total are seen in an average month and what the mean number of patients per month is.

2 The hospital expects a 20 per cent increase in average patient numbers in December. How many patients are expected?

3 The hospital currently has 450 beds. What is the ratio of beds to patients in an average month? What is the ratio in December?

Functional Skills – Mathematics

You can practise your Functional Mathematics skills by carrying out calculations with numbers of any size in different practical contexts.

Summary

✱ Percentages show figures proportionally.

✱ Ratios compare two figures.

✱ Statistics allow large quantities of data to be analysed meaningfully.

✱ All three mathematical skills are frequently used in business.

Estimation and approximation

Computers are incredibly useful for performing mathematical tasks. However, you will not necessarily always have a computer, or even a calculator, with you when you need to perform calculations. By building your confidence with numbers you will be able to dazzle your colleagues with your mental maths skills.

Estimations

Estimation is performing a calculation as an approximation rather than being accurate either as a quick check or because accurate figures are not available.

Total sales of trainers = 548
Total sales of sandals = 423
Estimation of total sales of footwear = 550 + 420 = 970
Actual total sales of footwear = 548 + 423 = 971

Estimation allows a calculation to be done quickly to give an idea of the answer. In this case, the numbers were rounded to the nearest 10 – 548 rounding up to 550 and 423 rounding down to 420. A number ending in 5 usually rounds up.

Case Study: Accident and Emergency

The Accident and Emergency department of a local hospital must ensure it keeps track of all the items it has in stock. The department has a set budget each month to buy these items and must ensure it does not overspend.

Monthly budget: £1,000

Items needed	Price	Unit	Amount needed per month
Bandages	£10.15	per box	10
Slings	£6.98	per box	5
Cotton wool	£2.99	per roll	10
Syringes	£3.55	per box	20
Latex gloves	£10.97	per large box	50
Latex gloves	£6.56	per small box	50
Scissors	£1.21	each	10

Individually, answer the following questions without using a calculator or computer.

1   Using **rounding** to the nearest whole pound, estimate how much one month of supplies will cost.

2   Using rounding to the nearest ten pence, estimate how much one month of supplies will cost.

3   How much difference is there between the total for the monthly supplies and the monthly budget?

4   What does this mean yearly for the department?

5   If medical supplies were to go up by 10 per cent, what effect would there be on the department?

The Clinical Head of Emergency Medicine was interviewed:

'One of the biggest problems of running the A&E department, excluding patients and treatments, is managing the budget. A balance must be reached between ensuring we have enough stock and keeping spending within the budget. If we don't order enough stock, we risk running out when treating patients. If we spend too much, we are adding to the hospital's debt and possibly taking money from other departments. I have a meeting with the Trust board next week to discuss the situation and possible solutions.'

In a small team, investigate the situation further.

6   What business problem(s) exists in this situation?

7   Why is it important to investigate this problem? What are the potential consequences of not solving this problem?

An option with any business problem is to do nothing. This would mean continuing with the current situation.

8   Why would doing nothing not be a suitable solution in this situation?

With the Clinical Head meeting the Trust board soon, she will need to present solution(s) to solve the problem.

9   Suggest as many solutions as you can think of for the problem. Start logically and then think laterally and creatively.

10 For each solution, use figures to back it up. Use your previous estimations and approximate what may happen to the figures (for example if the budget is increased, if the stock costs change etc.).

Rounding

Approximating a number, for example 11 rounds down to 10, 15 rounds up to 20.

Functional Skills – English

Working in a team allows you to communicate by speaking, listening and exchanging information. By analysing a business situation together, you can produce solutions to practical problems.

Summary

* It is useful to be able to perform mental maths as well as using calculators and spreadsheets.
* Using techniques like rounding can make mental maths easier.

Spreadsheet skills

Most organisations now use spreadsheets to calculate their business figures, mostly financial. Without them larger businesses would not be able to cope with the vast amount of numbers that they have to deal with.

Data format

When inputting data it is important that it is in the correct **data format** so the software handles it correctly, for example a time format for hours, minutes and seconds, or a currency format for symbols such as pound (£).

The most common data formats include:

Format	Type	Features
Number	General number	✱ Can set number of decimal places
Currency	Financial figure	✱ Usually set to two decimal places ✱ Can choose symbol, for example £, €, $ etc.
Time / date	Time, day, month or year	✱ Can set format
Percentage	Percentage	✱ Adds a per cent sign (%) ✱ Can choose number of decimal places
Fractions	Fraction (for example ½)	✱ Can set format

A text type is also usually available for making titles, headings and other comments on the spreadsheet.

Operators

Mathematical operators are the symbols used in equations: plus, minus, multiply and divide. The addition (+) symbol is the same as in mathematics, but the subtraction, multiplication and division symbols change due to the limitations of the keyboard. The subtraction symbol which would normally be '−' becomes '-' (a hyphen), the multiplication symbol, normally '×', becomes '*' (an asterisk), and the division symbol, normally '÷', becomes '/' (a forward slash).

Relational operators are symbols used to compare two things, such as the equals sign. For example If T-shirt = dirty, don't wear it. The equals sign also shows where the answer is, in other words This calculation = this answer.

There are also logical operators, such as AND, NOT and OR, which can be used in equations to compare things. For example If left sock is green AND right sock is blue = not a pair.

Formulae

Formulae are equations which are used in spreadsheets. A formula is entered into a spreadsheet cell and the result is shown in that cell. Formulae always start with an equals sign.

Formulae can either use real figures: =10+20+30+40+50

Or they can reference figures in other cells: =A1+C2+M2

| **Formula** |
| An equation in a spreadsheet. |

Functions

Functions are formulae that use special words to perform complicated calculations without you having to enter whole formulae. For example =A1+A2+A3 could also be done with the function SUM().

So, =A1+A2+A3 now becomes =SUM(A1, A2, A3).

To make a formula even simpler, a range of cells could be used. If the cells are in a row or column, they can be referenced, for example, as A1:A3, which will include A1, A2 and A3.

So, =A1+A2+A3 now becomes =SUM(A1:A3).

Another function which is often used is AVERAGE(). This finds the average of a set of numbers.

So, =(A1+A2+A3)/3 becomes =AVERAGE(A1:A3).

| **Function** |
| A preset equation to make complex calculations easier to input into a cell. |

Activity 4.4

In pairs, create a spreadsheet for the local hospital using your figures from Activity 4.3b.

1 Create a worksheet with a title and the three categories and their patient numbers for an average month. Use the correct data format.

2 Use the function SUM() to calculate the total patient numbers for the average month.

3 Use a formula (without functions) to calculate a 20 per cent increase of patients for December.

Functional Skills – ICT

Spreadsheets can model a business, allowing you to enter, develop and format information, especially numbers. They allow you to bring together information from different places and combine it in an easily understood format.

Summary

* Spreadsheets are used in nearly all businesses.
* Figures are entered in cells and referenced in formulae.
* A formula always starts with an equals sign (=).
* Functions use special words to simplify complicated formulae.

Spreadsheet skills

Once you have mastered the basics of spreadsheets there are many more exciting things that can be done with them. They are very powerful applications and their uses are often underestimated.

Workbooks and worksheets

Each page of a spreadsheet is called a **worksheet** and a collection of worksheets is called a **workbook**. Worksheets can be linked to each other by connecting relevant cells. This is done by referencing to the worksheet name and cell, joined by an exclamation mark (!). For example Sheet1!A1 will reference to the top-left cell (cell A1) on Sheet1. To link between different workbooks: =[Book1]Sheet1!A1

Avoid using spaces in worksheet or workbook names: an underscore (_) can be used instead of a space.

IF() function

The IF() function will make different things happen depending on a situation (the **conditions**). For example IF the weather is sunny THEN wear sandals, ELSE take an umbrella.

The syntax of the IF() function is =IF(condition,true_action,false_action), for example:

> =IF(A1>20,"Over 20","Under 20")
> or   =IF(A1<=5000,"Under budget","Over budget")
> or   =IF(A1< A2,"less than A2","more than A2")

The true or false action is carried out in the cell in which the IF() function is placed.

It is possible to use IF() functions inside each other (to nest them), for example:

> =IF(A1>100,"Over 100",IF(A1>50,"Over 50",IF(A1>20,"Over 20","Under 20")))

LOOKUP() function

The LOOKUP() function will find one cell based on another. It is like looking something up in an index: first you look up the word you want, then you look across for the page number.

The syntax for LOOKUP() is =LOOKUP(value,where_the_value_is,where_the_result_is), for example:

> =LOOKUP(A5, A1:E1, A2:E2)
>
> where
>
> A5   is the value to be looked up
> A1:E1   is where the value is looked up
> A2:E2   is where the result is looked up

Worksheet
A single page in a spreadsheet.

Workbook
A collection of worksheets in a spreadsheet.

Condition
A certain situation, for example IF x > 10.

	A	B	C	D	E	F	G	H	I	J
1										
2										
3										
4										
5		1	hat	red		ID	Clothing	Colour		
6		2	jacket	blue		5	gloves	blue		
7		3	belt	red						
8		4	boots	black			= LOOKUP(F6,B5:B9,C5:C9)			
9		5	gloves	blue						
10							= LOOKUP(F6,B5:B9,D5:D9)			
11										
12			the data			the value				
13										
14										

The result is displayed in the cell in which the lookup is placed

Command buttons

Command buttons are interactive buttons which can give a user more control. They are often used to run macros, which are recorded actions, such as printing a worksheet.

In Microsoft Excel, use the Forms toolbar to add a command button and attach a macro to it.

Drop-down boxes

Drop-down boxes allow users to select an item from a list of entered data. Using drop-down menus makes data entry easier and also reduces the possibility of typing errors. Select **Data > Validation…** and allow the 'List' validation criterion.

Pivot tables

A **pivot table** is an interactive table which allows you to analyse large sets of data easily and clearly. Select **Data > PivotTable and PivotChart Report** and follow the wizard.

Security

When your spreadsheet is complete, you may want to lock certain cells or protect certain pages so users do not accidentally make changes and prevent it from operating correctly.

Select **Tools > Protection** and choose what type of protection you want. The protection will be applied next time you open the spreadsheet.

Functional Skills – ICT

Spreadsheets can effectively present complex information clearly. Make sure your spreadsheets are always suitable for their audience.

Pivot table
An interactive table which allows you to analyse large sets of data.

Activity 4.5

In pairs, add to your spreadsheet for the local hospital in Activity 4.4.

1 Use the IF() function to state whether the number of patients in an average month is "over 2,500" or "under 2,500". Repeat for December.

2 Add a column to your patient numbers table for ID numbers for each area (1, 2, 3). Create a drop-down list where these ID numbers can be selected.

3 Create two LOOKUPs beside the drop-down list to find the area and patient numbers based on the ID number selected.

Summary

* Spreadsheets are made up of worksheets and workbooks.
* Functions such as IF() and LOOKUP() can begin to automate data entry.
* Pivot tables allow data to be analysed in different ways interactively.
* Worksheets and workbooks can be locked to prevent users from making changes.

Graphical Techniques

By using graphs, it is easier to see patterns and trends in a set of numerical data. If there are hundreds or thousands of figures, it is difficult to get an overall picture. However, being able to look at a graphical representation of these numbers can help to give a clear picture of the situation.

Multi-series graphs and charts

Multi-series charts show more than one measurement at a time and can be useful for comparison of data sets.

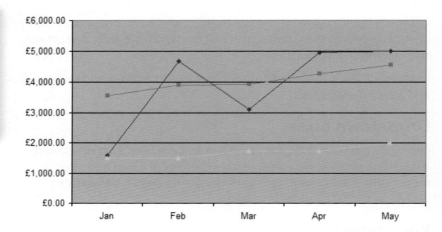

Trends

Trends create a **line of best fit** to existing numbers to show a general tendency. For example:

Sales	
January	£1,596
February	£4,659
March	£3,101
April	£4,955
May	£5,002

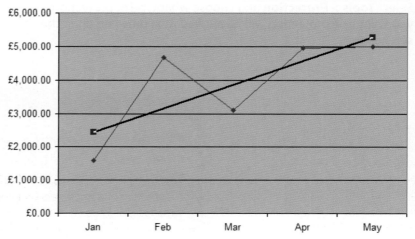

To create a line chart in Microsoft Excel, click in the data set and select **Insert > Chart…** . Follow the wizard, choosing a Line chart type.

To add a trend line in Microsoft Excel, make sure your chart is selected and click **Chart > Add Trendline…** .

By working out the trend of the figures, it becomes easier to predict the future.

Forecasts

Forecasting is using existing information to estimate what will happen in the future. By following a trend, a prediction of what will happen in the future can be made.

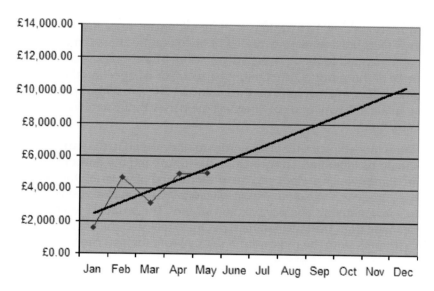

To forecast in Microsoft Excel, create a chart with a trend line. Double-click the trend line on the chart and select the Options tab.

The Forecast options (Forward or Backward) allow you to extend the trend line according to the pattern of the figures. As you can see in the figure, if sales continue in the same pattern, by December they will reach nearly £12,000.

Summary

* A graph can be used to represent large amounts of numbers visually.
* Once current data has been modelled, trends can be identified and future figures forecast.

Analysis using spreadsheet models

A model will allow a business to investigate a situation without exposing it to risk. Comprehensive analysis will provide the business with more information so that it can make well-informed decisions.

Models

Models are used to try things without taking any risks. Just as architects build miniature models of buildings, businesses model what could happen to them. These answer 'what if' questions, such as 'if I buy more of this product, what might happen?' or 'if I open another branch, what effect will that have on the business?' The aim of modelling is to simulate a situation to see what will happen without actually having to carry it out.

When modelling a situation in order to understand it, the variables should be identified. These include the inputs and the outputs. Inputs are things which are put into the business and outputs are the results they produce. For example money (capital) is put in to a business to buy raw materials and pay bills and salaries. The products will then be made from the raw materials, put into stock and then sold to the customers. With the money from sales a profit (or loss) can be made.

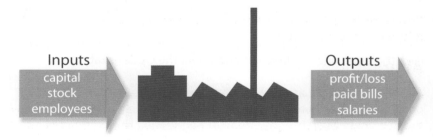

Inputs	Outputs
capital	profit/loss
stock	paid bills
employees	salaries

Sustainability

Sustainability is the consideration that any idea which is implemented should be for the long term. Everything should be future-proofed as there is no point spending time and money instigating a new solution if it will need to be changed in a few months' or even a few years' time.

Costs and returns

Cost-benefit analysis

A cost-benefit analysis identifies the advantages and disadvantages of a situation (usually from a financial perspective) and makes a recommendation as to whether a proposal should go ahead.

Costs and benefits can be tangible (physical) such as employing more shop assistants or intangible (not physical) such as improving customer service.

Cash flow forecast

One of the most important calculations in business is to work out profit:

PROFIT = REVENUE – COST

Revenue is the entire amount of money that has come in, before any deductions.

Cost is the total of outgoing money, including purchasing stock and utility bills, rent etc.

Profit is the money that remains from the income after costs have been deducted. This is the whole amount that can be pocketed or reinvested into the business.

Return on investment (ROI)

When starting a business, there is a certain amount of investment made; this is the money put into the business. This could be money from private savings, a bank loan or from another source, such as shareholders. This investment becomes the capital for the business and it can be used to buy premises and stock and to employ staff. More investment might be needed when changing a system or developing the business (such as breaking into a new market), but now the profit from previous trade can be used.

Investment is usually made with conditions in place, such as interest, a proportion of profits or equity in the business (owning a portion of the business).

Return on investment is the amount of money an investor gets in return for their investment.

Alternatives

Alternatives should also be considered and decided upon. They provide a fall-back position should the original idea not be accepted by the decision-makers, or give room for negotiation should that become necessary.

Business impact

The implementation of any solution will have an impact on the business. It is wise to try to reduce the amount of disruption caused so that normal trading can continue and the business can still gain customers and sell its products or services. Sometimes disruption cannot be avoided, such as when moving to new premises, but it can be minimised, and steps can be taken to reassure the current customer base that the disruption will only be temporary and that once the change is completed they will have an even better service.

Personal, Learning and Thinking Skills

By presenting a persuasive case for action you will demonstrate your effective participation skills.

Activity 4.7

The shoe shop Sole is doing well and wants to increase its business to make more profit.

In pairs, consider the following:

1 List, in a table, the inputs and outputs of Sole.

2 Describe three things Sole might do to increase its sales.

3 Choose which one it might take forward and explain why you have chosen that one.

4 Describe the impact this idea might have on the business.

Summary

* Models can demonstrate what will happen without taking any risks.
* It is important that propositions are backed up by numerical justification.
* The effect that implementing the idea will have on the business must be taken into consideration.

4.2 Legal and ethical considerations

You now have mathematical and spreadsheet skills and should be able to apply them to business situations. There are two further important things you must take account of in order to do this properly in the real world: the legal and ethical considerations.

A business must abide by legislation otherwise it could be fined or closed down or the owner could even be arrested and put in jail.

As computers were used more and more in business in the 1980s, it was realised that a great deal of personal data, such as customer details, was being stored on them. Therefore, in 1984, the Data Protection Act was passed and in 1998, with increased use of the Internet, it was updated, coming into force in 2000.

As the Data Protection Act only protects personal data, more legislation was needed to protect against the use of computers by people with malicious intent. The Computer Misuse Act was passed in 1990 to combat the spread of viruses and hacking.

A business should also be run ethically otherwise it may lose customers' trust and they may not purchase its products or services.

Ethical debates allow diverse views to be examined. Take different points of view and discuss the following topics. You can argue for either side, even if it's not what you actually believe.

* Should products be bought from developing countries? (Ideas: fair trade, air miles, cheap labour, … .)
* Should products be tested on animals? (Ideas: medicine, cosmetics, … .)
* Is it right for businesses to spy on their competitors? (Ideas: secret shoppers, reverse manufacturing, copyright, … .)

Activity 4.8

The shoe shop, Sole, in Activity 4.7, took on your recommendation and now has branches all over the UK and in Europe.

In pairs, consider the following questions:

1 What might happen to Sole if it does not abide by legislation?

2 What might happen to Sole if it does not act ethically?

Case study

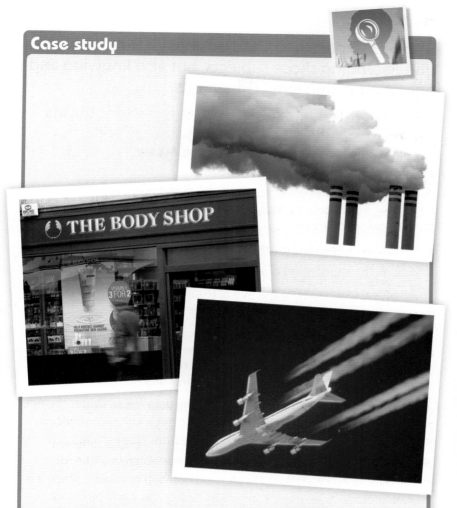

Ethics can be a difficult subject. In many cases there is no right answer and there will be several conflicting opinions. For instance, a business which manufactures a product can release a great deal of pollution into the air. The emissions may be under the legal limit, but environmentalists could still say the business should reduce them. The business is likely to incur a huge cost if it does so and this could mean it will have to put up prices. Will customers stay because the business is causing less harm to the environment or will they stop buying its products because the price is too high? This is an issue which has been faced in recent years by beauty product manufacturers. The Body Shop has a policy that none of its products have been tested on animals, but this makes its prices higher than equivalent high-street stores. However, Body Shop has successfully made a profit because customers support their ethical stance and are willing to pay more.

Summary

* Businesses must adhere to legislation and should act ethically.

Legislation

Being an expert in ICT and business not only involves understanding those subjects, but also knowing and operating within legal constraints.

Data Protection Act 1998

The eight principles of the **Data Protection Act** are:

* data must be stored fairly and legally
* data must be obtained for specified and lawful purposes
* data must be adequate, relevant and not excessive
* data must be accurate and up to date
* data must not be kept any longer than necessary
* data must be processed in accordance with the data subject's rights
* data must be reasonably securely kept
* data must not be transferred to any other country without adequate protection in place

Every business that plans to store sensitive data must register with the Information Commissioner, who is in charge of controlling data protection.

The 'data subject' is the person to whom the data refers. Under the Act, each person has several specific rights:

* the right to compensation for unauthorised disclosure of data
* the right to compensation for unauthorised inaccurate data
* the right to access data and apply for verification or erasure where it is inaccurate
* the right to compensation for unauthorised access, loss or destruction

Computer Misuse Act 1990

The **Computer Misuse Act** introduced three new offences:

* unauthorised access to computer programs or data
* unauthorised access with the intent to commit further offences
* unauthorised modification of computer material (for example programs or data)

A distinction is made between computer misuse and computer abuse:

* 'computer misuse' is an illegal act involving a computer
* 'computer abuse' is a legal but unethical act involving a computer

Freedom of Information Act 2000

The **Freedom of Information Act** was designed to give the public access to information held by public bodies, including the government, the police, schools and the NHS. Exceptions to this access include items which cannot be released in the interests of national security and items that it would exceed a certain cost to locate.

Data Protection Act 1998
Protects personal data held on computers.

For Your Project

All business is subject to legislation, especially when it involves computers. Make sure you understand these four Acts of Parliament.

Computer Misuse Act 1990
Protects computer systems against threats such as hackers and viruses.

Copyright, Designs and Patents Act 1988

Copyright protects all tangible works including business ideas, product designs, art, writing, music, creations made on computer etc. 'Tangible' means in a fixed form, such as printed, saved, written down or recorded on film.

Items do not have to be registered to be protected under copyright; the law comes into effect as soon as the work is tangible. The protection prevents actions such as reproducing, distributing or publicly displaying the work.

> **Copyright, Designs and Patents Act 1988**
> Protects all works which are tangible.
>
> **Freedom of Information Act 2000**
> Allows public access to data held by public bodies.

Case Study: 'Last Resort' Travel Agency

Last Resort is an independent travel agency that organises holidays and has branches all over the UK. When booking a holiday for a customer, an agent records the holiday and customer details on a computer and saves the data on a central server.

In pairs, analyse the situation.

1 Identify how the Data Protection Act 1998 could be applied to the travel agency's data.

2 Describe how the Computer Misuse Act 1990 could be applied to the travel agency's data.

3 The Last Resort logo is protected under copyright law. Discuss the value of it being protected by law and what might happen if another company used its logo.

Functional Skills – ICT

By recognising the importance and consequences of copyright and other constraints on the use of information you will be demonstrating your Functional ICT.

Summary

* The Data Protection Act 1998 protects sensitive and personal data.
* The Freedom of Information Act 2000 gives access to data.
* The Computer Misuse Act 1990 protects against viruses and hackers.
* The Copyright and Patents Act 1988 protects tangible works.

Health and safety

All employees have the right to work in a safe environment without threats to their health and risk of injury. Being a businessperson, it is important to understand health and safety legislation so you can keep yourself and your colleagues safe.

Health and safety legislation

The **Health And Safety At Work Act 1974** is legislation designed to protect the well-being of persons at work. It declares that it shall be the duty of every employer to ensure, so far as is reasonably practicable, the health, safety and welfare at work of all employees. Failure to uphold the Act could result in harm to an employee, who could potentially sue their employer and prosecute the business.

The employer's duties include:

* ensuring the workplace is safe
* ensuring machinery is safe and there are systems in place for its use
* ensuring substances are handled safely and procedures are in place for their safe use
* providing welfare facilities (such as toilets, wash basins, etc.)

Risk assessments should be carried out regularly, especially in work environments with more risks. For example in a school, all areas would need a risk assessment, but science laboratories, sports areas and IT rooms would need more detailed risk assessments.

There is other legislation that works in conjunction with the Health and Safety at Work Act, such as:

* the Workplace (Health Safety and Welfare) Regulations 1992
* the Display Screen Equipment Regulations 1992
* the Provision and Use of Work Equipment Regulations 1998
* the Manual Handling Regulations 1992
* the Personal Protective Equipment Regulations 1992

DANGER EVERYWHERE

Look around the room in which you are sitting. List all the possible ways you or the people around you could be hurt.

Health And Safety At Work Act 1974
Protects the well-being of people at work.

Ergonomics

Ergonomics means ensuring an environment is suitable for people to use and that an individual's capabilities and limitations are taken into account. The term is often associated with the design of cars or the use of machinery, but every workplace needs to consider ergonomics.

Ergonomics
Ensures a safe and comfortable environment.

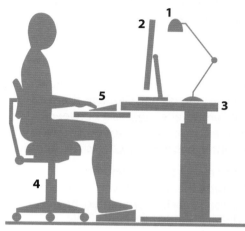

1. Correct lighting (usually filtered) so there is no glare on the screen.

2. Adjustable monitor so it can be changed to different user's eye level.

3. A desk at an appropriate working height.

4. An adjustable chair to move to the correct working position.

5. The ability to have wrists at a correct angle when typing on a keyboard, possibly with a wrist rest.

For Your Project

All businesses are subject to health and safety legislation. Make sure you understand it.

Activity 4.9

In pairs, create a reference leaflet for the Last Resort travel agency:

1a Identify how health and safety regulations affect an agent working at a computer in one of the branches.

1b Explain the effectiveness of the legislation and why it should be followed.

2 Are there any shortcomings to the health and safety regulations? Do you have any suggestions for changes?

Functional Skills – ICT

Remember to minimise physical stress when using computer equipment by using wrist rests and adjusting the arrangement of hardware.

Disability Discrimination Act 2005

The **Disability Discrimination Act** was implemented by the government in 2005 to prevent discrimination against anyone with disabilities. The act covers employment, education and transport. For example, a candidate for a position should not be discriminated against because of a disability, and an employer has a responsibility to adapt their work environment to meet the needs of the chosen candidate.

Disability Discrimination Act 2005
Prevents discrimination against those with disabilities.

Summary

* The Health And Safety at Work Act 1974 is designed to protect the well-being of persons at work.
* Ergonomics ensures the working environment is suitable and safe.
* The Disability Discrimination Act 2005 prevents discrimination against those with disabilities.

Ethical issues

In every area of business there are ethical decisions. It could be ensuring high-quality products for customers or reducing harmful emissions. To be truly successful in the real world you need to understand and follow an ethical moral code.

Digital divide

The **digital divide** refers to the gap between the people who have easy access to technology and those who do not. Globally, there is a difference in the distribution of computer equipment between developed and developing countries; for example, not every country, or even every person within a country, has equal access to the Internet.

In the UK there is a digital divide between socio-economic groups (rich versus poor) and geographically (broadband access versus no access). Many people in the UK take broadband access for granted, however there are still areas where only dial-up bandwidth is available.

Internet safety

Safe use of the Internet is crucial, especially for young people. Threats to Internet safety include cyberbullying and sexual predators (such as adults pretending to be children).

Ways to protect from these include:

* never giving out personal or contact details
* using blocking and parental-control software
* talking about your Internet use with your family or friends
* using your common sense and, if it seems wrong, not doing it

Businesses not only have a legal responsibility to protect customers' data, but also an ethical liability. For example, should a business sell its customers' contact details in order to raise revenue?

WHAT WOULD YOU DO?

A restaurant can offer only ten main meals on its menu. The range is determined by the money it has available for ingredients and the time it takes to cook them. How many should be vegetarian or vegan? How many should be suitable for allergy sufferers? Write a menu which you would consider ethical for the customers and explain why.

Digital divide
The gap between people who have easy access to technology and those who do not.

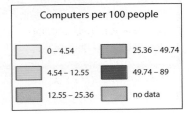

Computers per 100 people

0 – 4.54		25.36 – 49.74
4.54 – 12.55		49.74 – 89
12.55 – 25.36		no data

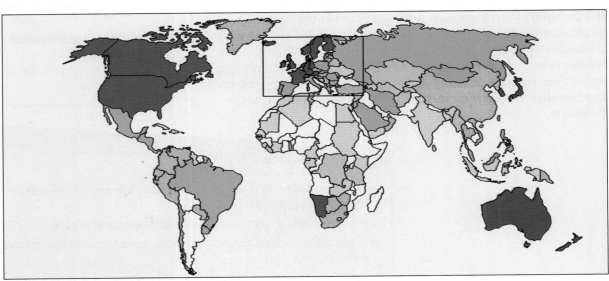

Environmental

Modern businesses must take environmental issues into consideration, as they concern a large proportion of the public. For example, a manufacturing business that has not taken steps to prevent air pollution may find its products boycotted and its factories the sites of protest.

Business culture and work–life balance

Employers have a duty to ensure their employees have a reasonable balance between their working lives and their personal time. If more commitment is required from employees than usual, businesses should consider other ways in which they could be repaid. For example, Google encourages a very high level of dedication from its employees, but in return offers flexible working hours and an enjoyable working environment. Business culture can have a huge effect on employees. It is often said that a happy employee is a productive employee. If a business invests in a culture which benefits its employees, those employees should, in turn, perform better.

Personal Learning and Thinking Skills

You can demonstrate your independent enquiry skills by trying to influence others and by negotiating and balancing diverse views to reach workable solutions.

Activity 4.10

When looking at ethical issues, there are usually many different opinions rather than one 'correct' answer. In pairs or small groups, debate the following issues. Take different points of view.

1 You have signed up to website, giving your name, address, date of birth and phone number. The website needs to raise profits and one way is to sell their customer list to a marketing organisation. Should they do it? What effect would it have on the business and on the customers?

2 Benetton often uses controversial advertising. What effects might this form of advertising have? Should it be used?

For more ethical problems, see Worksheet 4.14.

Functional Skills – English

By looking at situations from different points of view, you can gather information, form ideas and argue from several perspectives persuasively.

Summary

* The digital divide refers to the people who have access to technology and those who do not.
* Internet safety is paramount and users should never give out personal details.
* Businesses must also take into account their environmental impact and the work–life balance of their employees.

4.3 Be able to present successful business proposals and win support

Being able to analyse a situation and decide which way to act is not enough in business. In order for your ideas to be implemented you need to be able to put your case forward and persuade others that yours is the best solution.

The purpose of a proposal is to convince decision-makers not only that your idea is the best one available but also that you have considered all aspects of it. You should highlight the positives without omitting the negatives; instead you should aim to outline how the negatives can be overcome or converted into positives. For example, a large financial outlay could be presented as a one-off payment that will result in much higher profits, therefore recouping the capital spent.

Once the proposal has been presented, the people to whom you have demonstrated it may love the idea at once and wish to implement it in its entirety. However, they may not warm to the idea immediately, or they may like it but have concerns about certain aspects. In this situation you will need to use your persuasive skills to encourage them to change their minds. Alternatively you could reach a compromise whereby some parts of your idea remain the same whereas others are changed by negotiation.

Business proposals

A proposal is a document which outlines a new idea and is written persuasively with the aim of persuading the reader to invest in it.

Challenges and opportunities

When formulating the business **proposal**, all challenges and opportunities available to the business should be identified so they can be taken into account. These should include any major factors which could have a significant effect on the proposal. Also it is worth looking at factors which might be minor but should be considered in case they do become worse. It is best to identify in advance all elements which could affect the project, so that contingency plans can be drawn up, rather than being surprised partway through the project and having to adapt it during its execution.

Alternative costed solutions

As well as the main solution proposed, alternatives should be included. They should be costed and explained in detail. You could also provide other solutions should the primary one be rejected. If negotiations take place during the presentation, they can be brought forward as possible substitutes or merged with the main solution to produce a compromise.

Legal and other considerations

The proposal should contain all considerations which could affect the project. Laws which will have an effect on the project should be included, and also any other potential problems, whether ethical, environmental or cultural. Not only should the issues be identified but also the methods by which they are to be resolved. For example, if a new system is to hold customers' details, the proposal should detail how and when it will be registered with the Information Registrar and how to ensure it conforms with all eight principles of the Data Protection Act.

Recommended solution with justification

Along with the recommendation itself the proposal should offer rationalisation of why this solution would be the best for the business. Rationalisation could include forecasts of profits, a cost-benefit analysis or evidence of future benefit to the business. This section should be as persuasive as possible; this is when you 'sell' the idea.

SHORT AND SWEET

Come up with five new ideas which could be implemented in your school. Explain each idea fully but in only one sentence. Each sentence should be dynamic and inviting and able to enthuse those reading it, such as your teacher.

Proposal
A proposal document clearly outlines an idea and all related considerations.

Activity 4.11

In pairs, create a proposal for one of the ideas you came up with for your school.

1 Explain your idea in detail and justify it with persuasive reasoning.

2 Describe the challenges and opportunities related to this idea and how it would be implemented in the school.

3 Explain two alternatives which are similar to the primary idea.

4 State any legal or ethical barriers to the proposal and how they might be overcome.

Summary

* A business proposal is an important document which should outline the whole situation clearly and persuasively.

135

Business presentations

A business presentation may be to one person or a large group, but it must always be persuasive and professional.

Persuade

The whole presentation should be persuasive. The aim is to **persuade** the audience to believe in the solution and to want to implement it into the business.

In delivering a business presentation, the aim is to win the support of the decision-makers. This may be immediate, but, if not, it may be necessary to be more persuasive or come to a compromise. Sometimes these negotiations need to take place right at the end of a presentation, so the presenter must be confident about their idea and be able to think on their feet.

Presenting a business proposal involves several elements. One factor is the material which explains the idea. This needs to be well made, clear and appropriate for the audience; for example, technical jargon should be avoided if the audience won't understand it. Another element is your performance. Everything, from the way you dress to where you stand, your body language and the way you speak, can influence the reception of the presentation.

Negotiate and compromise to reach a workable solution

If the idea doesn't meet with support as a whole, it may be necessary to **negotiate**. Negotiation means coming to an agreement through discussion and reasoning. It may be that the decision-maker wants to impose certain restrictions on the idea or wants to make certain changes. Presentations customarily become open forums where ideas can be thrashed out and discussed. It may be necessary to reach a **compromise**, in which both parties meet each other half way. The desired result of this arbitration is to produce a workable solution with which all parties are happy.

Persuade
The idea should be compelling, able to be 'sold' to the audience to encourage them to commit to it.

Negotiate
Debate both sides of an idea with the aim of reaching an agreement.

Compromise
Change the proposed idea to one with which all parties can agree.

Activity 4.12

In pairs, present the proposal you created in activity 4.11. It should be persuasive and able to persuade your audience to adopt the idea. If they do not wish to accept the idea in its entirety you may need to negotiate or compromise.

Summary

* The presentation is the last part of this process and should include all the work which has gone before it.
* Although the presentation will bring this portion of the project to an end, it will be the beginning of the next phase, as once the proposal is agreed to, the business will need to start to implement it.

Preparation for assessment

In this unit you will learn skills to model business problems and develop realistic solutions. You should use creativity to come up with innovative solutions and justify which you select. You should also be able to draw on relevant legislation and ethical issues to further develop your business ideas.

How you will be assessed

This unit is assessed internally. You will be expected to present evidence in a portfolio, accessible by fifth-generation or equivalent web browsers.

Your work should be based on a case study of a business in one of the following fields: retail manufacturing, local government or sports and leisure.

Groupwork should be used to analyse the business to identify problems and generate a number of solutions. The results of this should consist of an e-portfolio which includes:

* analysis of a business using numerical and graphical modelling
* identification of a problem area or areas which would be suitable for improvement
* development of several solutions which are both realistic and innovative
* explanation of the solutions including details of the options available and their validity in the business environment

Individually, you will also be required to:

* model the situation of the business and the options available for improvement
* forecast to predict the future of a business, which should lead to supporting the selection of a solution
* explain in detail how the models and forecasts work
* present the information and justify a chosen method
* apply relevant legal and ethical considerations and produce a report for the company in the case study

Assessment tips

* Manage your time wisely throughout the project
* Keep your computer files in order, using sensible names. Keep all paperwork in an orderly fashion in a folder
* In your own time, practice with the software so that you are able to use the facilities efficiently in your project

Remember!

* Choose the business you analyse wisely
* Always remember the business's core aims
* Make all solutions realistic
* 'Doing nothing' is not a potential solution
* When presenting information, ensure it is suitable for the target audience
* Make sure legal and ethical issues are relevant to the business and the problem

You must show that you:	Guidance	To gain higher marks you must explain:
4.1 Are able to use a wide range of numerical and graphical techniques to analyse and present business relevant information, including the use of estimation and approximation to support ideas and proposals	* Analyse an existing business problem * Where are the areas for improvement? * Formulate a possible solution (other than 'doing nothing') * Why should they implement this solution?	* Which area or areas need improvement * Why you are investigating the area * Several options (at least three plus doing nothing) using estimation and approximation to support the options * The changes to be made for each option and the benefits to be gained
4.2 Are able to use creative, investigative and numerical reasoning skills to present proposals to address business challenges and opportunities	* Produce a model for the business problem * Explain how the model works * Outline the outcomes of the solution * Which solution do you recommend and why? * Seek agreement on the recommendation	* A well-designed model that is easy to use, contains relevant complex formulae or functions and is capable of producing relevant results * How the model works and how it will predict the outcomes of each option using examples to show what the formulae do * The outcomes of each option * Recommendations for future action showing an innovative approach * How to seek agreement on the recommendations demonstrating powers of persuasion and negotiation
Are able to explain key legal and ethical considerations in the IT environment, including data protection, health and safety and copyright **4.3** Are able to present successful business proposals and win support	* Produce a report describing some relevant legal and ethical issues * How will the legal and ethical issues specifically affect the business? * Formulate a proposal for a new idea * Present your proposal and persuade your audience	* In report form, the relevant legal and ethical considerations applying a balanced view * Why your proposal should be adopted, supporting your conclusions with reasoned arguments and evidence and proposing practical ways forward, breaking these down into manageable steps * How you might influence others, negotiating and balancing diverse views to reach workable solutions

5 Technology systems

Introduction

Technology systems are at the heart of many businesses and organisations, with a wide variety of approaches to how these systems are constructed and operated. This unit looks at a very common way of setting up and running one of these systems using a network, database and security.

NETWORKING

Think about where you study. Does it use a network? Consider what it is used for and how a network might be used in business. What threats are there to a system?

Firstly you will need to understand how components are used in a network and then assemble these components together to create a networked technology system. This system will need to have some software applications installed so the technology can actually be used.

Once this system is assembled, there will be a number of problems that you will need to overcome when it is set up and first run. You will then need to protect it from viruses as well as from users!

You will produce a database in this unit and configure it to produce forms and reports. User feedback can be used to help identify how the system might be improved.

You may find it useful to visit the learning resource centre and look for suitable books to help you carry out the network and database tasks needed for this unit.

Finally you will create a presentation explaining how to keep a business system secure.

Learning outcomes

5.1 Understand the role of key components of networked PC systems

5.2 Be able to assemble a business-relevant technology system including networked PCs and software applications

5.3 Be able to resolve problems within a small-scale technology environment, including viruses and simple user errors

5.4 Be able to design, develop and test simple systems (including programs) to meet identified business needs

5.5 Be able to create, search and sort single-table databases

5.6 Be able to write script programs and use macros

5.7 Know how to seek feedback, review the system and identify opportunities for improvement

5.8 Understand the principles of systems availability, including implementing appropriate file structures, security and back-up processes

5.1 Roles of key components

Networks give many benefits, especially helping people to work together and to share resources such as printers, the Internet and documents.

Modern computers are very often connected to other computers using a network. A network card converts data for transmission to a hub, switch or router using wireless or wired technology. This gives the network connection.

Routers are used to find the most effective path for data between systems. Many routers also include a DSL modem to give a computer a broadband connection as well as finding efficient routes for the data transmitted to another system.

Networked PC systems

A network is either peer-to-peer or client–server with PCs connected using cables, wireless or a combination of the two.

* Peer-to-peer systems do not have any servers to control the network. Each computer can be set to share resources such as a printer or folders.

* Client–server networks are most popular with organisations as they are far more secure and controllable, especially when there are a lot of computers attached.

Most networks use the **Ethernet** standards for addressing, protocols and cabling. The address ensures data arrives at the correct computer.

A protocol is used when computers communicate, making sure they have permission to connect, agreeing the speed data travels between them, requesting a re-transmission if the data gets corrupted etc. The Internet uses a protocol called TCP/IP (Transmission Control Protocol/Internet Protocol).

Every networked computer and device using the protocol has an IP address made from four numbers (each between 0 and 255) and separated by dots. Try entering 212.58.253.71 into the address bar of your web browser to reach a well-known website.

Most modern laptops have WiFi mobile technology built into them so they can connect to the Internet and other networks using wireless technology.

MAKE THE CONNECTION

As a group, discuss reasons why broadband is faster than dial-up.

Hubs and switches are used to connect computers and other devices in a network. Discuss any differences you know between hubs and switches.

Ethernet

A standard developed in the 1970s by Xerox to connect computers together. Ethernet uses frames to divide the data into small packets that can then be sent to another computer. The receiving computer can then assemble the packets back into the data.

Activity 5.1

1 Identify the components used in a network that you know of.

2 Describe the roles of the components you identified in Question 1.

3 Research and analyse reasons why switches are better than hubs.

Personal Learning and Thinking Skills

You can demonstrate self-manager skills by seeking advice and support when needed.

Summary

* The key components in a network are network cards, cabling and switches.
* The role of a network card is to connect the network cable to a PC.
* A network lets resources, such as printers and documents, be shared.

Key components

Networks are used at home, in small organisations and in large companies. Different network configurations have different benefits.

GETTING TOGETHER

Perhaps you have used a network at home. Suggest reasons why a home network might be unsuitable in a business environment.

Peer-to-peer
A simple network configuration that does not use a server. Each computer has equal status, sharing resources such as folders on their disks, printers or other devices.

The diagram shows a **peer-to-peer** network with three workstations.

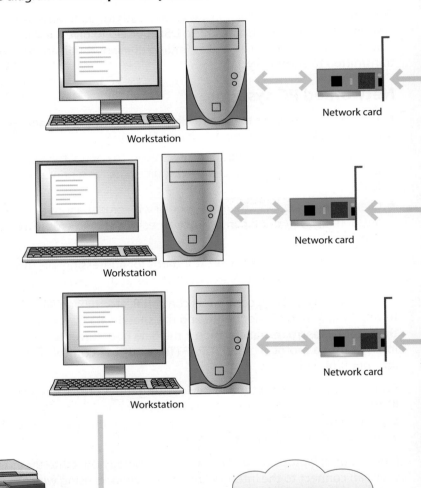

Workstation

Network card

Workstation

Network card

Workstation

Network card

Printer

Internet

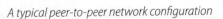

A typical peer-to-peer network configuration

Ethernet
Ethernet is the common standard used in networks to define the signals needed to let computers connect to each other and send data.

Broadband
Broadband is the name given to a modern, fast, always-on connection to the Internet.

Network card

A network card fits inside a computer and is used to connect the computer to a network. Network cards can be cable or wireless.

Switch

A switch is a box with RJ45 ports (sockets), so several network cables can plug into it to connect computers and other devices on a network.

Hub

A hub is a box with RJ45 ports (sockets), so several network cables can plug into it to connect computers and other devices on a network. A hub is not as good a switch because data arriving at a port is sent to all the other ports, thereby reducing how much data the system can carry.

Internet Service Provider (ISP)

A company that operates a technology system for connecting a computer to the Internet. Many ISPs also host websites, using software to store web pages and send them to anyone viewing the hosted website.

Switch or hub

DSL modem router

Modem

A modem is a device that converts computer data into a form that can be sent through a connection to another place. Two modems are required for this, one at each end of the connection.

ISP

The **Internet Service Provider** is an organisation that provides access to the Internet. Most people pay the ISP for this service, with their computers logging onto the ISP systems that connect to the Internet.

ISP

Functional Skills – ICT

You can practise your Functional ICT skills by accessing, navigating and searching the Internet purposefully and effectively.

Activity 5.2

1 The network diagram here shows a peer-to-peer network. Re-draw the diagram to show a client–server network.

2 Use the Web to find six ISP companies.

3 Describe the range of services offered by one of these ISPs.

4 Compare the services offered by three of these ISPs, then choose which you think offers the best package.

Router

A router finds out which routes are available between two computers then sends the data through the quickest. Many modern modems also have a router.

Summary

❋ Peer-to-peer networks do not have servers.

❋ Workstations are networked PCs.

❋ The addressing protocol allocates an IP address to each workstation.

5.2 Business-relevant technology systems

This learning outcome looks at some typical systems a home user or small business might network together. You need to recognise how hardware is connected, so you can assemble a business-relevant technology system and install software applications.

Technology systems

Networks

A typical technology system uses computers communicating inside a network and with the Internet. Networks are great at sharing resources such as printers, documents and the Internet.

Software

The network will use software, usually for word-processing and spreadsheets, and might include databases for storing an organisation's data. Databases are vital to many organisations as they not only store the data, but they can provide useful information when queried to display only data that is needed.

The user interface

A **user interface** can use forms to make the database much easier to control and operate, making data entry easy and accurate using validation techniques.

Programs

Programs are the software needed to control the system. Programming may be used in a database to help parts of a form work, such as making a combo box change the information shown on a form to match a selection from the combo box.

RELEVANT TO PURPOSE?

What is the main purpose of the technology system at your place of study? How does it deliver the main purpose? Can you think of any ways the system does not deliver?

User interface

Software which uses a mouse is said to have a Graphical User Interface (GUI), so most of the software in use today is of this type. Older software from the days before Windows became popular usually had a command-driven user interface, where the user typed instructions on a keyboard.

Business relevancy

A business-relevant technology system has a definite purpose, such as networking several computers together so folders on their hard drives can be shared allowing a team to work together.

A home user might set up a system so three networked computers can connect to the Internet via a broadband DSL modem, which might be a wireless DSL modem so there's no need to run cables. Each computer would need a (wireless) network card to connect to each other and the Internet.

A small business, such as a local estate agency, could network their computers into a business-relevant system. Such a system would allow staff to show customers up-to-date property details from any of the computers in the agency. A great strength of this system is that when a new property is added, every computer would be able to view the details almost immediately.

Functional Skills – ICT

The questions give you opportunity to present information in ways that are fit for purpose and audience.

Personal Learning and Thinking Skills

You can demonstrate self-manager skills by organising your time and prioritising tasks.

Activity 5.3

1 What is meant by business-relevant technology?

2 Identify advantages an estate agency might gain from using a network.

3 Find out why people say that ADSL is a type of DSL.

Summary

* Business-relevant technology includes home-user and small-business networks.
* A network is two or more machines connected together.
* Networks usually connect to the Internet using broadband connections.

Networked PCs

Networked PCs are becoming very wide spread, both in business and in the home. Many homes now benefit from network technology allowing shared Internet and printer access.

How to network

A network is when at least three PCs are connected using a cable or wireless connection. The network cable usually connects a network card to a switch. If you want to connect computers directly you will need a cross-over cable. In a Windows peer-to-peer network, each workstation should be in the same workgroup and have different computer names.

The main networking software is the operating system as this allows the computers to talk to each other. Modern operating systems, such as Windows, Linux and Mac OS, have networking capabilities built in. The operating system can be updated using a service pack from a manufacturer's website.

Networked applications

When you set up a network you must install certain software applications. The user will need applications such as Microsoft Office to do their work and the network will need software to protect it from online threats. This might include:

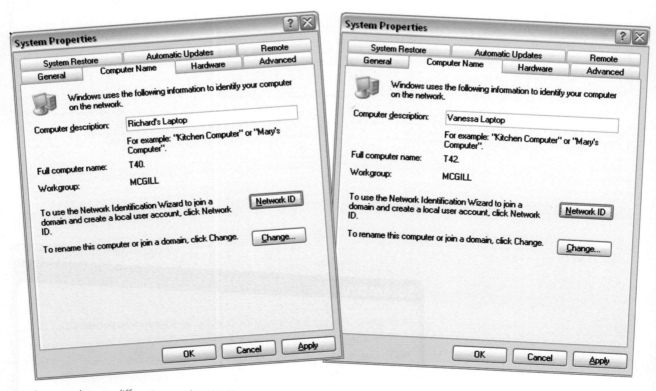

Same workgroup, different computer names

* anti-virus software to detect any viruses that enter the system
* anti-spyware software to prevent spyware programs from installing onto workstations and revealing anything on the workstation to hackers through the Internet
* pop-up blockers to stop annoying pop-up windows when using the Internet

Activity 5.4

* Create a small computer network using three PCs and two cross-over cables plugged into the network ports on each PC.
* Right click **My Computer** on each PC and click **Properties**. Use the **System Properties** > **Computer Name** dialogue box to set each PC to the same workgroup (for example, use your surname). Make sure each computer has a different **Full computer name**.
* Use **My Documents** to navigate to a folder that can be shared between the computers. Right-click this folder, choose **Sharing and security…**, then use the **Sharing** tab to share files.
* Use **My Computer** on the other PCs, then click the **Search** button to look for **Computers or people** > **A computer on the network**. Type in the name of the PC you're looking for. Click **Search** to find it and see if you can navigate to the shared folder.

Functional Skills – ICT

When assembling and testing a network system you can show you are able to follow and understand the need for safety and security practices.

Activity 5.5

1 Find the version of operating system your PC is running.

2 Describe any networking features your operating system offers.

3 Compare the networking features of another operating system with those you have identified in Question 2.

Personal Learning and Thinking Skills

You can demonstrate self-manager skills by dealing with competing pressures and responding positively to change.

Summary

* Networks need an appropriate operating system.
* Operating systems are upgraded with service packs from the manufacturer's website.
* Software can protect against viruses and spyware, and provide pop-up blocking.

Resolving problems

Making technology systems work correctly can sometimes be troublesome. This learning outcome identifies some of the many problems that can be caused by poor set-up, viruses and user errors. You are expected to be able to log problems, resolve them, make sure fixes actually work and document your solutions.

Problems

Problems often occur when creating a new system. You're expected to use structured techniques when resolving problems by logging errors, conducting proper tests and documenting your solutions. There are many different types of problem that prevent a technology system from running properly, and they might arise from many causes, including:

* poor configuration – when a system has been incorrectly set up
* hardware faults – when something breaks
* viruses and other external threats
* user errors – when the person using the system does something unexpected

Resolving problems

Sometimes a problem could have any one of several causes; for example, a non-functioning Internet connection may be caused by a hardware fault, or poor configuration, or the ISP may not be available, or some other reason. A skilled IT professional will carefully work through possible causes, documenting what is tried and the effects each action has.

Logging errors and resolutions is a very powerful problem-solving tool. The log can help solve problems the next time they crop up. It can also help identify recurring problems with software or hardware. Sometimes patterns emerge that are not obvious at the time, for example when a particular type of video card regularly gives problems to different computers.

Testing is important to ensure problems have been properly resolved. It is not enough to do something that will probably work and then leave! Each resolution should be properly tested to confirm all is fine.

Large organisations use help desk software to log requests from users for support. The person allocated the problem can search the software database for similar occurrences of a problem and look up how the problem was solved on the previous occasions. The software might also record the time taken to solve a problem as the support team are likely to be subject to service level agreements in the same way as in any business–customer relationship.

Name and Date	Problem and description	Time taken	Solution	Support name
Ian 7 July	Mouse stopped working. No error messages	30 mins	Checked mouse settings in control panel. No properties found. Turned off PC and swapped mouse. Now working.	Sue
Sally 12 August	Screen display looks different to normal	1 hour	Checked display properties in control panel. Graphics card only has 16 colour options available. Downloaded latest graphics driver from manufacturer and installed. Caused error message "Error in kernal 32". Ran MSConfig and removed driver from start-up. Problem solved.	Mike

A log of problems and the steps taken to resolve them

Smaller organisations that may not have a dedicated support team often insist that solutions to common problems are documented by the users. The documentation is posted on the company's intranet to be seen from any workstation so users can search for solutions.

Activity 5.6

1 Look for some examples of error logs then create your own design for an error log.

2 Find two examples of test logs. Which would you prefer to use? Why?

3 Identify three common user errors that would benefit from having their resolutions posted on an intranet.

Personal Learning and Thinking Skills

You can demonstrate self-manager skills by documenting the testing of a networked system.

Summary

* Logging errors can provide much useful information.
* Testing solutions is important to ensure they work properly.
* Documenting solutions to common problems helps both you and others.

Running a small-scale technology environment

Anybody running a small-scale technology environment needs to be able to cope with the many day-to-day problems that occur when resolving simple user errors and other issues.

SOLVING PROBLEMS

Think of 10 problems that might happen with a technology system. What do you think the solutions might be to these problems? Can you suggest any ways these problems could be avoided?

Viruses

Viruses are very common on the Internet. They try to enter any technology system with an Internet connection, so the technology system you assembled should be protected from viruses.

New viruses are being produced all the time, so any virus-checking software must be updated from the manufacturer's website to offer up-to-date protection which recognises and deals with current viruses. Virus-checking software should be configured to provide sensible protection for the way you use your computer. Many virus checkers are configured to:

* provide a resident shield, running in the background to detect any viruses as soon as they arrive
* automatically deal with detected viruses by deleting or moving them to a safe place such as a virus vault (quarantine)
* run a regular scan of the disk to check for viruses
* check emails for viruses

User errors

Users make mistakes! Sometimes a problem might have little or no consequence (for example, not noticing Caps Lock is on only means that part of a sentence needs retyping), but some user errors have big consequences (for example, saving a blank document over an important one could destroy weeks of work). You should be able to respond to common user errors including, for example, 'losing' a file or folder, forgetting a password and other possible errors. Your responses can be based on experience gained setting up the system, for example a forgotten password is easily reset so the user can log on again.

Many problems can be resolved if the system has a regular back-up routine, where copies of important documents are made to tape or optical disk. If a disaster strikes, documents can be restored from a recent back-up.

Dialog boxes help identify faults

Connection problems

A computer may lose connection to a network or the Internet. Often this is due to a dislodged cable or disrupted power. Rebooting the modem may restore a lost Internet connection.

Security violations

A security violation is when a computer system is accessed by something with no rights to it. The 'something' might be a virus entering the system from the Internet or somebody else logging on as if they were the real user.

Technology systems work best when protected from security violations.

Functional Skills – ICT

Designing, developing and testing the business system will give good opportunities to show troubleshooting skills.

Activity 5.7

1 Find out about the Klez virus. Produce a short report on how it causes damage to a computer system.

2 Compare the Klez virus with another virus of your choice.

3 Research virus-checking software. Analyse these products and report on which you find the most effective.

Personal Learning and Thinking Skills

You can demonstrate independent enquirer skills by investigating technical problems and finding solutions.

Summary

* Updating anti-virus software is essential as viruses change all the time.
* Expecting users to make errors is a good reason for taking regular back-ups.
* Systems should protect against security violations.

5.3 Principles of systems availability

Technology systems are an essential part of many organisations. If they stop working, the impact can quickly destroy the organisation. This learning outcome shows how security methods can help reduce such enormous risks.

Reliability of systems

Many technology systems need to be available **24/7** with uninterrupted service. This is known as 100 per cent up-time.

This level of reliability is achieved using many different methods depending on the type of system and its business requirement. For example, many important file servers have duplicated components, so if something fails inside the server, the duplicated component is instantly used instead, thereby keeping the system running.

Even with duplicate components in place, failures can still sometimes occur. Data might be lost through user error or data corruption. Data is core to many businesses and if records or systems are lost a company can potentially collapse. Data back-up is therefore essential, so if a disaster does happen, then valuable data can be restored and the system can function again. Some organisations define folder **tree structures** that users must use as this makes back-ups much easier to take and to retrieve if needed.

System security

Security is also key to achieving target reliability. Risks to security might be:

* unauthorised access to computers – passwords prevent people with no need to use a system from logging on. Users have different levels of access rights. A data-entry clerk would have a lot less access to the system than an IT professional. The log-on ID and password are used by the system to confirm who's logged on and what rights they have to the system

* viruses and hacking – anti-virus software and firewalls reduce risks from the Internet and from shared files

* **physical security** is used to allow only those people into a computer room who are entitled to be there. Different rooms have different levels of security, for example only IT professionals would have access to the server rooms

A folder tree structure can make back-up tasks easier

Activity 5.8

1 What are the advantages and disadvantages of a swipe card, access code or key to secure a room?

2 Compare door security systems. Which is the most secure?

3 What is needed to keep a system available 24/7?

Functional Skills – ICT

Producing a presentation on systems availability can show you can use ICT systems to meet a variety of needs.

Summary

* Many systems need to be available 24/7.
* Appropriately named folders are easy to back-up.
* Folders can be shared to give other users access to data files.

Security and back-up

Important data should be kept in folders that are backed-up regularly to another place such as disk or tape cartridges. Back-ups can be used to restore (bring back) data if a disaster strikes.

System availability

Technology systems are often so important that they need to be kept available or the organisation might cease trading. Imagine the impact of a business losing records of all money owed to it!

Organisations plan for the many types of disaster that could happen to a technology system including:

* hardware faults
* software crashes
* fire
* flood (often from overhead water pipes)
* theft (of hardware or data)
* building collapse (possible from earthquake, plane crashes, terrorism etc.)

Back-ups

The back-up process is when documents and other parts of a system are copied to tape or optical disk then kept in a safe place, so that if a disaster occurs, the system can be restored (brought back).

AVAILABILITY

Most people have a lot of personal information on their PCs including emails and bookmarked websites. How much information would you lose if your PC completely failed? What ways are used to make back-ups?

Case Study: Printing 4U

Printing 4U is a small printing business run by two partners with four staff. Everyone has a computer networked in a peer-to-peer system.

The owners use a software application for invoicing, accounts and payroll that other staff are not allowed to use.

One partner keeps clipart on their computer that's available to everyone. The other partner keeps a folder for each client on their computer where jobs are copied when completed. Jobs are allocated to staff, creating the work on their computers.

How would you structure the folders for Printing 4U?

It is important that restore procedures are checked periodically to make sure they actually work. Imagine needing a backed-up file after an emergency only to find that the back-up had failed or the restore procedure does not work!

Archiving is when old work is backed-up, but deleted from live systems, thereby freeing up space.

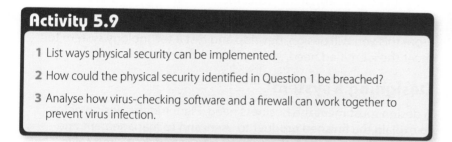

Functional Skills – ICT

You could show you are able to interact with and use ICT systems independently for a complex task to meet a variety of needs.

Activity 5.9

1 List ways physical security can be implemented.

2 How could the physical security identified in Question 1 be breached?

3 Analyse how virus-checking software and a firewall can work together to prevent virus infection.

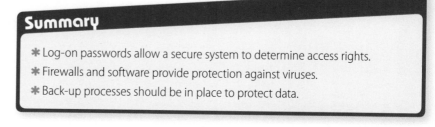

Summary

* Log-on passwords allow a secure system to determine access rights.
* Firewalls and software provide protection against viruses.
* Back-up processes should be in place to protect data.

5.4 Design, develop and test

This learning outcome shows how to design, develop and test a simple database system to meet identified business needs.

Introduction

For your assessment of this outcome you will be given a **business need**.

From this you will design, develop and test a technology system to meet the identified need.

Designing a system

A design must meet the business need. Planning the design helps to explain the finished product to users and to management and gives the IT professional the opportunity to anticipate and solve problems before spending time and money producing the end product. Planning is a lot quicker and cheaper than producing the full application and changing it after it is finished.

User interface

Data is entered into a database using forms. How a form looks and works needs to be planned. Designs can be produced using drawing software or pencil and paper (it is better not to use ink because pencil can be erased if changes are needed).

Database

The database table design will be a document naming the table and fields. The types of data for each field will be identified with any masks and validation rules needed to check entered data. Reports and queries must also be planned.

Programs

Any programs needed for the database will be planned. The starting event for each program will be identified, for example clicking on a combo box, with a description of what then happens.

Business need
The requirement an organisation needs a system to solve.

Developing a system

Development is when the table, queries, forms, reports, macros and programs are actually produced to meet the business needs. You will develop your system at the end of this learning outcome.

Testing a system

Every technology system should be thoroughly tested to ensure it works properly before handing it over to the users who will operate it. Unreliable, untested systems cost lots of money from wasted time, may lose or **corrupt** important data and even send out bad information to clients.

Testing should follow a test plan to make sure everything works properly. Quality is tested by the user to confirm the system looks good and is easy to operate. These tests should show the solution is correct, complete and secure.

> **Functional Skills – ICT**
>
> You could demonstrate that you're able to bring together information to suit content and purpose in your technology system.

> **Corrupt**
> When data is changed by a system without authorisation or it cannot be accessed because the way it is stored no longer makes sense to the accessing software.

Activity 5.10

1 What might be included in a database design?

2 What tests might be given to a form with validation on car number plates?

3 Analyse the benefits of designing a system before producing it.

> **Personal Learning and Thinking Skills**
>
> You can demonstrate skills as a creative thinker by generating ideas and exploring possibilities in their design and development of the system.

Summary

* A business need might be to keep membership fitness data for a gym.
* Designing a database can save time, then the end product is often right first time!
* The design is implemented as the database is developed.

Developing and testing a simple system

User requirements
Usually a document explaining what a user wants a system to do.

Designing a system means planning how objects (such as buttons) are used and identifying actions that trigger code with any wanted outcomes (such as showing a message box). New systems always need testing to check they work properly.

Requirements

Your cousin has been selling cars for some time and now wants a technology system for the business. The **user requirements** are that car details can be recorded and lists of stock can be printed to post to potential customers. There should be two types of stock list: by age of cars and by price. The system should be easy to use.

Design

User interface

There will be three forms: a main form to control the database, a form to search for cars and a data entry form. A macro named **autoexec** will show the main form when the database is opened.

Database

This table is named **Stock**. It shows the required fields and their format.

Reference (primary key)	AutoNumber
Make	Text
Model	Text
Year	Number
Price	Currency
Registration	Text
Photo	OLE Object

Mask and validation rules can be used with the Year and Registration fields.

Two reports are needed to show stock sorted by year and by price. A query will be needed for each report.

Programs

Program code will be written for the click event of a combo box on the search form to show cars younger than the selected date.

Developing

To implement the design the following will need to be produced:

1 The table with five or more records.
2 A query, **Year Sort**, sorting by year.
3 A report, **Sort Report**, using a wizard with **Year Sort** data.
4 A query, **Price Sort**, sorting by year.
5 A report, **Price Report**, using a wizard with **Price Sort** data.
6 A form, **Enter Stock**, using a wizard (columnar) with **Stock** table data.
7 A form, **Search Stock**, using a wizard (tabular) with **Stock** table data. A combo box named **cboYear** will have this code on a single line to show matching records using:

```
SQLtext = "select * from stock where year>= " &
cboYear.Text
```

8 A form, **Main Form**, with buttons using wizards to link to all the above objects.
9 A macro, **Autoexec**, to open **Main Form**.

The database can then be tested. Although individual components can be checked as they are built, the overall functionality (how the components work together) will also need to be checked.

Testing

Testing should use a plan to ensure:

* mask and validation rules allow good data and reject bad
* reports show the cars in correct orders
* the combo box shows selected records
* main form starts when the database is opened
* all buttons on the main form work
* all features work as expected

Functional Skills – English

You can show you can select and use a variety of sources of information independently for a complex task.

Personal Learning and Thinking Skills

You can demonstrate skills as a creative thinker by connecting your own and others' ideas and experiences in inventive ways to try out alternatives or new solutions and follow ideas through.

Summary

* Forms should be used in the user interface.
* The user interface should make the database easy to use.
* Solutions need to be fully tested for correctness.

Single-table databases

Databases are used by many businesses and organisations to hold data, to keep **records** and to provide information. This learning outcome requires you to create and construct a single-table database to meet a specific purpose.

Introduction

This learning outcome requires you to create, search and sort single-table databases. Your searches and sorts need to be shown both in datasheet view and as reports.

You may visit the learning resource centre and look for suitable books to help you carry out database tasks needed for this unit.

Creating a database

After planning the design, the first task in creating a database is a table to store the data. Professional database tables use techniques such as input masks and validation rules to reduce errors when entering data.

Table and field definitions

A table is part of a database used to store data – it looks like a spreadsheet. When a table is created you need to define suitable **fields** for storing data items, such as a music artist or the name of a CD. Each field needs a sensible field name, field length and data type, for example text, number, date or currency.

Tables normally have a field set as **primary key** to make sure there are no duplicate entries.

Input masks

Simple input masks can help keep bad data out of a database by preventing users from typing the wrong character. For example the Reference field mask L0000 will only accept data if it takes the form of a letter followed by four numbers.

Validation rules

Validation rules can work well with input masks to help the user enter good data.

REPORTING

Find out if there is anyone in your group who has used a database. What have they done with it?

How can a database reject bad data? What can a database report do that a spreadsheet cannot?

Field
The part of a table where an item of data is stored. A field could hold a date or almost any other type of data.

Primary key
Also known as the unique identifier. A field set to make it impossible to enter the same record twice and keep the table in correct order.

Record
A collection of fields for the same item, for example the name, artist and date of a single CD.

Validation rules
A check to make sure no invalid (obviously wrong) data is entered into a field.

Range checks

A range check is a validation rule to keep data within limits. A range check of **>0 AND <10** on a number field will only allow numbers larger than 0 and less than 10 to be entered.

Look ups

A look up can help the user enter data by offering a combo box with possible choices for the field.

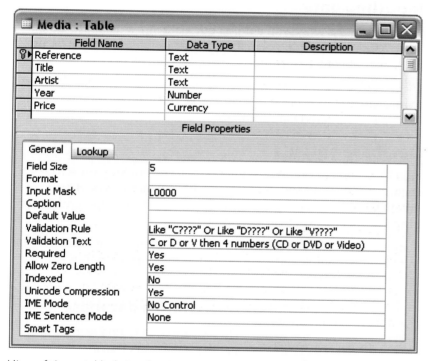

Microsoft Access table design showing an input mask and validation rule

Activity 5.11

1 Produce a short document listing the data types that can be used in a table with an example of the sort of data each could be used for.

2 Explain why data validation cannot be expected to ensure all data entries will be accurate.

3 Describe and justify a situation where a database has clear advantages over a paper-based system.

Summary

* Single-table database design includes fields for the table.
* Fields need to be suitable for the data that will be entered.
* Bad data can be screened out using input masks and validation.

Database skills

This learning outcome asks you to make your database user-friendly by using forms to control the system and to enter data. Your forms will offer searches for information and be able to show their results in reports.

NEEDLES AND HAYSTACKS

What do you think database forms are used for? How many examples of technology systems that search for information can you think of? Think of ways a database of student grades might be sorted into different orders.

Inputting data

Inputting data is when you enter or edit data into a database table using a form or by typing directly into the table. Many databases use forms for data entry and reports to display data brought out of the database so users can easily understand the information in them.

Forms automatically use any input masks and validation rules of tables to help keep entered data accurate.

Database outputs

Output is when information comes out of a technology system. Databases can produce a lot of information, which can be difficult to understand, especially if the information consists of pages and pages of spreadsheet-like data in a datasheet view.

Reports can make data much easier to understand by grouping similar information together with sub-headings. A report often uses a query to select the data it shows from the table.

Searching a database

Queries are used to find records in a database that match search criteria in the database. They can use multiple criteria for more complex searches, such as the query shown to the left, which finds media recorded after 1990 costing less than £6.

Sorting a database

Sorting is a very powerful feature of databases. It is used to sequence records in ascending (low to high) or descending (high to low) order. The example on the left shows a sort on price from low to high.

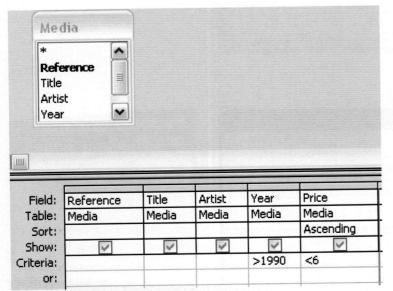

Microsoft Access query design showing multiple criteria finding media recorded after 1990 costing less than £6

Sorting can use multiple fields; for example, a database of students could be sorted by group then by surname.

This would keep all the students in the same group together with their names arranged in order for each group.

Activity 5.12

1 Create a new, blank database named **Entertainment**.

2 Create a new table in the database using design view, using the screenshot on page 161 as a guide.

3 Set the Reference field as the primary key.

4 Enter data validation for the Reference field as in the screenshot.

5 Close and save the table as **Media**.

6 Open the table then type some data into it.

7 See how the Reference field only accepts data that starts with C or D or V and then has four numbers.

8 Enter data including CDs, videos and DVDs. The screenshot below shows an example of this, but please do use your own choices.

9 Create a new query.

10 Use the datasheet view to confirm it works as expected. Try some other criteria, then change them back to those in the screenshot and save the query as **1990 query**.

Media : Table				
Reference	Title	Artist	Year	Price
C0001	Taste	Taste	1971	£6.99
C0002	Dark Side of the Moon	Pink Floyd	1973	£7.99
C0003	Achtung Baby	U2	1991	£7.99
D0001	Little Nicky	Adam Sandler	2000	£4.99
D0002	Momento	Guy Pearce, Carrie-Anne Moss	2001	£5.99
V0001	The Avengers (vol 5)	Dianna Rigg, Patrick MacNee	1993	£4.99
V0002	The Matrix	Keanu Reeves, Laurence Fishburne	1999	£8.99

Record: 1 of 7

Activity 5.13

1 How can sorting using multiple fields be used? Give examples from three different databases.

2 Explain some uses of a query.

3 Analyse differences between alphabetic and numeric sorts showing how they might produce unexpected results.

Functional Skills – ICT

You can evaluate the effectiveness of an ICT system you have used by testing and evaluating the business system you develop during assessment activities for this unit.

Personal Learning and Thinking Skills

You can demonstrate skills as a creative thinker by using your own and others' ideas and experiences in inventive ways to try out alternatives or new solutions and follow ideas through.

Summary

* Results of a search can be viewed as a datasheet or using reports.
* Searches can use multiple-criteria queries.
* Data can be sorted alphabetically or numerically.

Customising applications

Databases and other applications often use programming to produce the results needed by users. This learning outcome explores scripting and macros as programming approaches that could be implemented in your database application.

Introduction

This topic shows you how to write script programs and use macros. Macros are a lot easier to produce than script programs (**VBA**) which often need a skilled IT professional to write them. You may find it useful to visit the learning resource centre and look for suitable books to help you carry out the database customisation tasks needed for this unit.

Macros

A macro is a list of actions that the database is to do when the macro is called (started). The actions in a macro use Microsoft Access objects such as queries, forms and reports. A simple macro might carry out actions such as:

* run a query to create new records
* run a query to add the new records to a table
* run a report to show data from the table with the new records

A macro can be called from a VBA program; similarly a VBA program can be called from a macro.

Macros are more limited than a script as they need to use objects such as queries, whereas VBA can program a database to do almost anything!

Script programs

A script program uses code to create a **bespoke** business application.

Buttons

A simple script program could be behind a command button on a form using VBA to show only report pages relevant to a particular client for a database containing the data for all the company's clients.

Using SQL

Skilled IT professionals can add programming to a report or a form. A report could use VBA to place data across the report instead of down it. A form may have VBA code behind a combo box using the combo selection as part of a SQL query to change data shown by the form.

> **Bespoke**
> A bespoke application is a program that is written especially for an organisation. This takes a long time and is expensive compared with an 'off the shelf' application such as Microsoft Office.

> **Functional Skills – ICT**
> When you design, develop and test your business system you may show you can manage information storage to enable efficient retrieval.

Activity 5.14

1 Start a new macro in Microsoft Access to identify six types of objects that could be opened or run from a macro.

2 Identify a situation where using VBA would be more appropriate than a macro.

3 Using the event properties of a button on a form, explain how two different types of event might be used.

> **Personal Learning and Thinking Skills**
> You can demonstrate skills as a creative thinker by exploring possibilities in the design and development of your system.

Summary

* Script programs can be run from command buttons and other objects.
* VBA code can run SQL queries from a program.
* Reports and forms can run program code.

Script programs

Here are some techniques used to write script programs with SQL to search your table and to create macros.

A script program for a combo box

Code can be used with a combo box to change the data shown on a form.

1 Open the database you created on page 163.
2 Create a form using the wizard, based upon the **Media** table. The form will use all available fields in columnar layout. Name it **Media form**.
3 Enter the design view of this form.
4 Use the mouse to drag down between **Form Header** and **Detail** to open up some space in the **Form Header** band.
5 Place a combo box into the **Form Header** band. Select **I will type...** from the wizard. At the next screen, choose two columns then enter this:

Number of columns:	2

	Col1	Col2
	C	CDs
	D	DVDs
	V	Videos
▶		

6 Use mouse to reduce size of **Col1** until it cannot be seen, press **Next**.
7 Press **Next** on the next screen with **Col1** highlighted. Press **Finish** on the next screen to select **Remember...** and complete the wizard.
8 Show the combo box properties, name it **cboType,** select the **Event** tab, select **[Event Procedure] from Click,** then click the three dots to enter VBA editor where code can be typed. Edit this by typing the code in bold:

```
Private Sub cboType_Click()
  Dim SQLtext
  SQLtext = "SELECT Media.* FROM Media WHERE
  SQLtext = SQLtext + " Reference Like '"
  SQLtext = SQLtext + cboType.Value & "*';"
  Me.RecordSource = SQLtext
End Sub
```

9 Return to the form, use the view menu to bring up the form view then use the combo box. You'll see the data shown on the form change according to the combo box selection.

SCRIPT WRITING

VBA can be used to write script programs that help people use a database. What do you think the VBA statement *MsgBox "Update completed"* will do?

Discuss the contents of *Should I use a macro or Visual Basic?* from the Microsoft Access on-screen help pages.

A script program for a report

This code can be used to respond to the first letter of the reference to print whether an item is CD, DVD or video.

1 Create a report using the wizard, based on your query from page 163. The report will use all available fields in **Tabular** layout. Name it **1990 report**.

2 Enter the design view of this report. Show the detail band properties, select the **Event** tab, select **On Format**, then click the three dots to enter VBA editor where code can be typed. Edit this by typing the code in bold:

```
Private Sub Detail_Format(Cancel As Integer,
_FormatCount As Integer)
Dim MediaType
Me.ScaleMode = 7
Select Case Left(Reference, 1)
Case "C"
    MediaType = "CD"
Case "D"
    MediaType = "DVD"
Case "V"
    MediaType = "Video"
End Select
Me.CurrentX = 13
Me.Print MediaType
End Sub
```

3 Preview the report to see how the code has placed CD, DVD or Video into the report.

The autoexec macro

Some databases use a macro called **autoexec** to start a form automatically when the database is opened.

To do this:

1 Start a new macro.

2 Select an **OpenForm** action.

3 Select the name of the form to be opened from the **Form Name** box.

4 Select the **Maximize** action.

5 Close the macro, saving it as **autoexec**.

6 Close the database, then open it again. You'll see your form appear.

Personal Learning and Thinking Skills

You can demonstrate skills as a creative thinker by trying out alternative or new solutions and following ideas through when producing your application for assessment.

Activity 5.15

1 List some differences between design and form views of a form.

2 What does **ScaleMode = 7** do in VBA?

3 Compare the uses of forms and reports in a database.

Summary

* Macros can be called from VBA and vice versa.
* Macros are good at running a sequence of queries.
* Script needs skill and time to create and test.

5.5 Feedback and improvement

This learning outcome examines why the best designers of technology systems welcome feedback to confirm that user needs have been met and to identify anything that could be improved.

Introduction

Feedback about a technology system helps the producers review and improve the system. The feedback can be about the good or bad parts of a system. The views and opinions of people who use a system should be listened to as they can identify issues that have not been noticed or that have been considered unimportant.

A feedback cycle can be used to make a system much better and easier to use.

Seeking feedback

Feedback can be given using various methods including questionnaires, discussion and comment fields.

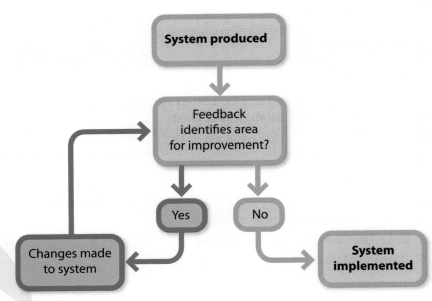

The feedback cycle

Questionnaires

Questionnaires can be paper-based or online. Paper-based questionnaires are very easy to use and don't need technology, which makes them available anywhere. Online questionnaires can be on a website, reaching out to anyone anywhere. They can quickly bring feedback to an organisation without any need for copying or retyping.

The design of a questionnaire is very important. The ways questions are asked have a big impact on the answers given. A questionnaire seeking feedback for a technology system should have some **open questions** to allow people to offer other comments.

Unfortunately, many people won't send back completed questionnaires, so this method can have a low return rate.

Comment fields

Comment fields can appear in many places, for example on guarantee cards, questionnaires etc. They can be a very effective method for getting genuine feedback, especially about anything that the producer has not already thought of.

Discussion

Discussion between the system designer and users can be very powerful as comments can then be explored so they're properly understood. It is likely to be an expensive method for gathering feedback as it involves a lot of employee time.

> **Open question**
> A question that does not prompt the answer. The question 'What can be improved?' is open because the reply could be anything. The question 'Could anything be improved?' is closed because the only answers are 'Yes', 'No' or 'Maybe'.

Activity 5.16

Produce a questionnaire seeking feedback from users of Windows on what they think of the operating system and identifying any parts they think could be improved.

Functional Skills – English

Carrying out a survey could show you can bring together information to suit content and purpose.

Activity 5.17

1 Produce three open and three closed questions.

2 Describe some situations where closed questions are the most appropriate.

3 Explain any disadvantages of comment fields.

Personal Learning and Thinking Skills

You can demonstrate skills as an effective participator by seeking feedback from users about the system in order to improve it.

Summary

* Feedback can be obtained through questionnaires.
* Questionnaires can include discussion and comment fields as open questions.
* Feedback helps when considering options and means of improvement.

Improving systems

Feedback can help you review the system you built and to identify where improvements can be made.

IMPROVING

Technology systems can always be improved. If you were asked to review the Microsoft Word application, what would you say? Are there any improvements you would like to see in this product?

Introduction

Reviewing systems should be an important part of the development cycle. This is because systems can usually be improved and fed-back comments can be considered for implementation.

Reviewing the feedback

As evidence for this outcome, you will have produced a technology system to meet an identified business need. You will need to obtain feedback on your system. From this feedback you will consider options to improve the system and identify where such improvements could be made. Remember, the feedback is on your system, not on you, so listen and consider how it can improve your system.

Many organisations analyse feedback to help understand it. Closed questions, such as 'Is the system easy to use?' can give useful statistics. For example if six out of 10 questionnaires gave the answer 'Yes', then the review could conclude that 60 per cent found it easy to use – for many organisations this would be a cause for concern!

Open questions can be very valuable for suggestions. Analysis of answers might show some that are similar and that can be grouped. For example a question such as 'How could the system be improved?' might be answered with 'by showing cheap cars' or 'by identifying cars under £500'.

Opportunities for improvement

There are likely to be many opportunities for improvement in your system. Remember, professional technology systems have a lot of skilled IT professionals working on them for many months or even years.

Improvements to the interface are often needed. Some examples might be:

* grouping related controls, for example putting forms buttons together and separate from reports buttons
* using matching fonts with bold or larger sizes used to identify more important words
* using the tab index properties of controls, so the tab key moves round the form in a sensible order

Your feedback may identify a need for more functionality such as:

* making one of the fields a primary key to avoid unwanted repeated records and to keep them in the correct order
* creating more queries to better meet user requirements, such as sorting data on a different field

Case Study: Improving John Lewis

John Lewis has an impressive online technology system offering a wide variety of quality products. Produce a brief review of their website with some suggestions on how you think it could be improved.

Personal Learning and Thinking Skills

You can demonstrate skills as a reflective learner by inviting feedback and acting on the outcomes.

Activity 5.18

1 Write three questions that could be used to get suggestions for improving a system.

2 Describe the advantages of using forms in a technology system.

3 Analyse the different ways people use forms in a technology system.

Summary

* Opportunities for improvement can result from feedback.
* A suggested improvement might be to improve the interface.
* Creating queries to meet user requirements can improve a database.

Preparation for assessment

In this unit you will need to understand how components are used in a network, assemble components together into a networked technology system, install software applications and protect the system from viruses, overcoming problems found when it is assembled and first run.

You will produce a database and use feedback to help you improve it.

You will also need to create a presentation on how to keep a business system secure.

How you will be assessed

For assessment in this unit you will produce the following documentation:

* the assembly and testing of a networked PC system
* the design, development, testing of a system to meet a defined need, including user interface, database and programmes
* feedback and review on how to improve your system

You may work as part of a team but evidence must be your own work and may be by witness statement, videos/photographs, screen prints and reports.

Your presentation on methods that can be implemented to protect data and systems from unauthorised access and corruption will be marked on content and delivery. This unit is assessed internally.

Assessment tips

You may work as part of a team for some of the assessment, but always make it clear in your documentation the parts you contributed to the technology system.

Practise your presentation beforehand, include audience participation if relevant to keep it engaging, and make sure it's succinct and to the point and fit for its intended audience.

Database development

You may find it useful to look in the library or a good bookshop for a book you find easy to understand for ideas and techniques that can be used to help you develop the database.

You must show that you **know:**	Guidance	To gain higher marks you must:
5.1 The key components of the networked PC system	* At least three of these key components will be described: modem, network card, switch, router, hub, broadband, ISP	* Explain the role of the key components of the networked PC system
5.2 How to assemble a business-relevant technology system including networked PCs by organising time and resources and prioritising actions, seeking advice and support when needed, showing initiative, commitment and perseverance and anticipating and managing risks and how to install a software application How to resolve virus infections and simple user errors	* You need clear evidence of the hardware assembly and testing the network connections, configuring at least one software application. * Organise your time and resources, prioritising tasks, anticipating and managing risks * Seek advice and support when needed * If no errors were encountered you could describe how such errors could be resolved	* Explain how you independently assembled a business-relevant technology system * Explain how you installed, tested and configured a software application * Explain how you resolved virus infections and simple user errors independently

You must show that you know:	Guidance	To gain higher marks you must:
5.3 The principles of systems availability Why suitable file/folder structures should be maintained Security processes How to backup and restore processes in the context of a business system	✳ How should file/folder structures be named? ✳ What are the benefits of file sharing? ✳ What are backup, restore and archiving procedures? ✳ Why are they used? ✳ Methods used to protect data and systems from unauthorised access and corruption include: password protection, user rights, virus protection and firewalls	✳ Produce a comprehensive presentation on systems availability ✳ Explain why suitable file/folder structures should be maintained ✳ Explain backup, restore and archiving processes ✳ Security processes ✳ For good marks present the information clearly with no errors
5.4 How to outline the user requirements for a simple system, to meet identified business needs by asking questions to extend their thinking How to design the simple system, including programs, by generating ideas and exploring possibilities and trying alternatives or new solutions to follow ideas through How to test the system How to carry out some validation checks on data entry How to create a single-table database for the system, and search and sort the data on at least one field How to include a script program and macro in the system	✳ Try to generate ideas and explore new possibilities in the design of your system ✳ Your description of the user requirements should reflect the expected outputs from the system's searches and sorts ✳ You will need evidence of fully testing the system against user requirements with any attempts made to optimise the performance ✳ Your printouts from the system will include evidence of data sorted on multiple fields and the results of at least one multiple-field search ✳ For high grades include input validation checks on two different types of data, along with at least one test for abnormal data ✳ The script program could be behind a form, changing the data displayed in response to a combo box being used ✳ The macro could automatically show a start form when the database loads	✳ Produce a detailed description of the user requirements for a business system, to meet identified business needs ✳ Design a simple system, including programs independently ✳ Create a single-table database for the system ✳ Sort and search the data on multiple fields using a multiple-field search and sort ✳ Include a script program essential to the running of the system, and a macro which enhances the system
5.5 How to implement some changes in response to feedback How to deal positively with praise, setbacks and criticism from user testing How to evaluate the system by evaluating experiences and learning to inform future progress	✳ You should invite feedback from the users ✳ You should produce a comprehensive evaluation of the system including strengths, limitations and suggestions for improvements	✳ Carry out comprehensive validation checks on data entry ✳ Fully test the system against the user requirements ✳ Explain how you implemented all changes in response to feedback from user testing, dealing positively with praise, setbacks and criticism ✳ Evaluate the system against user requirements and suggest an improvement ✳ How you worked independently

6 Multimedia

Introduction

Multimedia is an exciting field of ICT which is at the forefront of new technologies and progress. As it continues to be used more and more in business, the opportunities for careers in this field are multiplying.

YOUR THOUGHTS...

Write down as many types of multimedia you can think of. Keep this list and have a look at it when you have finished this unit. Assess how your knowledge has changed.

In this unit, you will first discover the many and wide-ranging uses for multimedia. Then you will investigate the technical considerations which must be taken into account when creating multimedia. Finally you will create a media product of your own and develop your skills in designing, implementing and testing.

Throughout this unit you are encouraged to be as creative as possible. In some activities there may be obvious relevancy to business problems, but try to be imaginative and come up with solutions which perhaps no one else has. In the design and media industry, it is those people who can be innovative that can really progress. Everyone can be creative, it may just be a matter of practising it and allowing yourself to develop those skills.

Thomas Edison (inventor of the lightbulb and forefather of cinema) once said, 'Genius is one per cent inspiration and 99 per cent perspiration.' Although the inspiration might be a small part of the process it is the most important and hopefully you will find that, although the work may be demanding, it is really fun as well.

A note on software

The instructions given in this unit are for using Adobe Dreamweaver for website design, Adobe Photoshop for image manipulation and Adobe Flash for animation.

Activity 6.1

1 List what skills you already have that might be helpful in this unit.

2 What do you think Edison meant when he said, 'Genius is one per cent inspiration and 99 per cent perspiration'?

3 Why do you think it is important to understand multimedia before beginning to create your own?

Learning outcomes

6.1 Understand the use of multimedia to meet different business-relevant objectives

6.2 Understand the technical knowledge and skills used to enhance multimedia products for a given purpose, through the use of multimedia content (such as images, graphics, timeline-based animation, video and sound)

6.3 Be able to design, develop and test a multimedia product which meets the needs of a specific audience and purpose

6.4 Know how to evaluate feedback from the target audience, identifying opportunities for improvement

6.1 Uses of multimedia in business

Multimedia is one of the newest and most exciting fields of ICT. A career in multimedia is one of the most exhilarating and creative professions, and one which also covers a huge range of skills.

Multimedia incorporates graphic design, animation, sound, video, digital photography, web design and several other areas. Each of these requires specialist skills, but all have a similar basis in techniques and creativity.

These areas could lead to a career in:

* film making (for example animated movies)
* television
* web design and development
* the computer games industry
* the music industry (for example music videos)
* photography and photo manipulation
* mobile technologies (for example content for mobile phones)
* advertising
* and many more

So what exactly is multimedia? The term derives from the words 'multiple' and 'media'. There are many types of media: they fall into the categories of print, audio/visual and digital.

* Print media includes printed static images such as books, posters, leaflets, brochures, magazines and newspapers.
* Audio/visual media are those which stimulate the senses of hearing and sight, and include film, television, music and computer games.
* Multimedia is relatively new, sometimes called 'new media', and includes websites, interactive TV and mobile phones.

Multimedia combines all these disciplines into one area and allows them to be mixed; for example, a website may use film and music and could be in a newspaper style.

WHAT IS MULTIMEDIA?

Think back over the last three days and write a list of all the multimedia with which you have come into contact. Consider what you have seen on the Internet, on television, even just walking down the street.

Activity 6.2

1 Name 10 specific print media products you have seen or read.

2 Describe the popularity of multimedia and how widespread it is.

3 Discuss the impact an audio/visual product may have on the audience.

Summary

* There are three categories of media products: print, audio/visual and digital.
* Multimedia is a combination of these three types.

Multimedia

The term 'multimedia' is used to refer to a variety of media products, but it also means the integration of these products. By combining two or more products, the message conveyed can be increasingly powerful.

Content

Some products naturally integrate media; for example, a website may involve text, graphics, photographs, sound, video and animation, all seamlessly working together to deliver a single message. A computer game that didn't combine animation and sound would seem strange.

The elements that make up a media product can come from a variety of places. Not all content is always generated by the developer. There are archives such as GettyImages and stock.xchng which provide stock photographs either gratis or for a fee. Clip art can be used as part of a media product as it is copyright-free, purposefully designed to be used by other people.

Understanding how multimedia products are made and used is only part of the journey. To attain a comprehensive understanding, you must also appreciate their technical aspect. Only then can you ensure that your products are fit for purpose and that their message is delivered efficiently and effectively.

If you wish to use other people's material, however, you must be careful not to infringe their **copyright**. The Copyright, Designs and Patents Act 1988 states that as soon as a piece of work is tangible (meaning 'in a fixed form') then copyright law applies to it and it cannot be used by other people without permission. The law can apply to a painting, a musical score, a novel, a website and any other piece of work, as long as it is in some physical form. Therefore, to use someone else's work you will need to obtain permission and possibly pay a fee. If you use a piece of work without permission, you could be prosecuted under the Act.

Interactivity

Often multimedia involves **interactivity**, whereby the user is involved in the product and can take some control over it. For example, a website may involve text hyperlinks, image hyperlinks, navigation buttons, rollovers, forms and other ways of allowing the user freedom in their experience of the site.

An interactive multimedia product must include some element of **navigation**, such as using hyperlinks in a website to move from page to page. Navigation should be instinctive and intuitive – so easy to use that the user has no need to refer to instructions.

WHAT YOU CAN USE

Make a list of ten ways you could use other people's work without breaking copyright law. Use the Internet to help you.

Copyright
Legal protection over tangible work so it cannot be copied.

Interactivity
Two-way communication between user and computer.

Navigation
Moving around the product such as using hyperlinks in a website.

Mix of digital components

Multimedia is often **integrated**, which means different types of media are combined in a single outcome. For example, a website might include video, animation, sound and images taken with a digital camera. Each element is integrated in a final product that should be more interesting and convey its message more clearly than a single type of media could.

> **Integrated multimedia**
> Different types of multimedia combined into one product.

Certain types of multimedia are integrated by their nature: for example, a digital photograph being edited in a digital graphics application, or sound being added to an animation. With increased developments in technology, integration has become more common. This has been especially noticeable in the case of mobile phone technologies: with every improvement more types of multimedia have been available, such as colour screens, better sound output, WAP or touch screens. With each development new possibilities have emerged.

The ultimate example of integrated multimedia is often considered to be the computer game, which draws on a wide range of methods to produce a complete sensory experience of sight, sound and touch.

Activity 6.3

Sampson's Automobiles are designing a website and wish to use a combination of some media which they have already. Do the following in pairs or small groups.

1 Sampson's have a short animation of a classic car and a CD called *Classic Driving Songs*. Describe how they could integrate these into a multimedia product.

2 They have several photographs of cars they have manufactured, a short text description of each one and another CD called *Classic Driving Songs 2*. Describe how they could integrate these into a multimedia product.

3 Design a three-page website for them including their two integrated multimedia products and others they may wish to create.

Summary

* Multimedia products can be more effective if they are integrated.
* Developers must be careful never to infringe copyright.
* Understanding how multimedia is made and used should be accompanied by an appreciation of the technical issues involved.

Uses of multimedia

Multimedia is all around us and impacts on our lives more and more. There are many uses of multimedia, but in business the two main ones are to promote and to entertain.

HERE, THERE AND EVERYWHERE

Multimedia is all around you. It's become so common you may not even notice it is there. Think back over the last hour and write down all the multimedia with which you have come into contact. Do the same for the last 24 hours.

Advertisement and promotion

Many businesses use multimedia when advertising their products or services, for example:

* a website, which could explain what they offer and why you should buy it
* an advert on television or before a movie in a cinema
* a billboard on a busy road or the side of a bus

These methods of promotion are now quite common, but there are more unusual ways of using multimedia to advertise, including:

* providing games on websites to encourage children to like the brand and persuade their parents to buy the product, such as on the McDonald's and the Haribo sites

* animated billboards such as those at Piccadilly Circus – they used to be made of neon and fluorescent lights, now they are made of digital screens which show animated adverts

Multimedia can be used to give a product the 'wow' factor. A recent series of Citroën adverts has featured a car that has morphed into a human shape and has danced, ice skated and done other activities. This makes the product look much more interesting than if they had just shown the car in its normal state and also reinforces their message that their car is 'Alive with technology'.

Training

Multimedia is useful in training. Situations can be simulated, meaning that activities can be demonstrated or even tried out without putting the trainee in harm's way; for example, when you learn to drive, you may use a simulator, perhaps for hazard perception. Similar systems are used to train pilots so they can learn the basic skills before taking to the air.

To promote and support a product, businesses can include advertising and training CDs or DVDs with their products. These might contain digital documents or even animations demonstrating how the product can be used. This is very common in software, where printed manuals, which are more costly to produce, are rare and have been replaced with interactive CDs.

Piccadilly Circus: then and now

In-store demonstrations

Presentations

A few years ago you may have seen people in stores demonstrating products, showing how effective they are and persuading people to buy. Now television screens can be used and presentations are shown above the product on sale. This is a much cheaper method than employing someone, and also more consistent as a digital advert will always be the same. However it does lose the selling techniques that the employee could have used and can be quite impersonal and more easily ignored by the customer.

Activity 6.4

1 CleanTeeth have asked you to create a new product for them. In pairs, create a design on paper for a new style of toothbrush. Be as imaginative as you can and give it a brand name. Briefly describe five ways in which multimedia could be used to promote your new toothbrush.

2 CleanTeeth can only afford to use two methods. Pick two from your five and state why you have chosen them.

3 State three advantages and three disadvantages of each of your two chosen methods.

Summary

* Businesses use multimedia to advertise their products and services.
* Some methods are becoming common but more unusual methods can give a business an edge over the competition.
* Multimedia can be used in training and as presentations to promote products and services.

Uses of multimedia in entertainment

From the beginnings of multimedia, entertainment has been high on the agenda and is often the reason that technology has been pushed further and further.

Games

In the last couple of decades, games have been one of the most important influences on the progression of multimedia technology. Due to the highly competitive market, the three main console makers (Microsoft, Sony and Nintendo) and producers of PC gaming machines are forever trying to outdo one another in terms of graphic and sound quality, memory, processing power and small case size.

Games studios are also constantly striving to produce the game that steals the largest market share. The UK video games industry is worth over £2.2 billion and there have been 25 million consoles sold in the UK in the last eight years, with worldwide sales of more than 350 million (not even including PCs used to play games).

Massively Multiplayer Online (MMO)
Computer games which involve thousands or millions of players globally, usually on PCs.

It is now easy to play games with people all around the world with **Massively Multiplayer Online (MMO)** games and other online PC systems, and also on consoles with Xbox Live, Playstation Home and Wii Online. Online gaming allows players from all over the world to compete, cooperate and communicate through in-game chat forums or through headsets with a microphone and headphones.

Television

The most popular form of multimedia on television is animation, shown in both advertisements and cartoons. As owning a television set became more commonplace, there was a remarkable rise of cartoon programmes in the TV schedule as schedulers realised there were prime times for children to watch, such as when they came home from school and on Saturday mornings.

Films

The film industry has always had the ability to introduce pioneering techniques. In the field of multimedia it is no different. The first animated film appeared in 1906 when a newspaper cartoonist translated his strip onto film. Since then, animation in film has taken off. In Japan, animation is widely popular for both children and adults.

Another use of multimedia has been the introduction and development of **CGI (computer-generated imagery)** to add special effects to films. CGI has improved dramatically in quality as computers have become more powerful. The animation process also advanced due to computers. Whereas previously each frame had to be drawn by hand, computer technology has made the process faster and made more effects available, such as 3D modelling. Today, the majority of cartoons and animated films use digital animation.

> **Computer-generated imagery (CGI)**
> Animated special effects often used in films.

Activity 6.5

CleanTeeth are thinking about producing some multimedia entertainment and have asked for your help. They hope to use them in order to attract new customers and to advertise their products and explain the importance of keeping your teeth healthy. Create the following designs in pairs on paper.

1 Design a home page for the CleanTeeth website. Annotate it to include the fonts used, colours, sizes, descriptions of images and all other components. Make it as interesting and attractive as possible.

2 Design a game to be included in the CleanTeeth website. It must promote their product and/or healthy teeth and include a character you have invented.

3 Design a storyboard for a short animated cartoon, which will be shown on Saturday morning television, starring the character from your game. The storyboard should be between 10 and 20 squares long and underneath each should be instructions of what is happening in that scene.

Personal Learning and Thinking Skills

You can develop your team working skills by collaborating with others to work towards common goals.

Summary

* Multimedia products can be used for entertainment and are incredibly popular.
* Media types such as games and film are pushing out the boundaries of what is possible at a tremendous rate.

Business relevant objectives

Multimedia has become integrated into business and is now an important part of beating competitors and making profit. This means that the opportunities to work in multimedia are increasing.

Multimedia in business

There are many uses of multimedia in businesses who are all trying to attract new customers, beat their competitors and ultimately make more profit. Some examples include:

* transactional websites – these allow a business to operate 24 hours a day, 7 days a week, and give access to a wider customer base. By using e-commerce, products and services can be sold over the Internet, which means customers can purchase from the comfort of their own homes

* training CDs/DVDs – for more complex products, a training CD or DVD could be produced. It is becoming more usual to provide software manuals on the disks with the program rather than as a book. If the product or instructions change, it is often cheaper to ask the user to download new documents than to reprint and distribute paper-based manuals. However, using this method means that the user must have a computer available for use and the CD/DVD must be playable on that computer

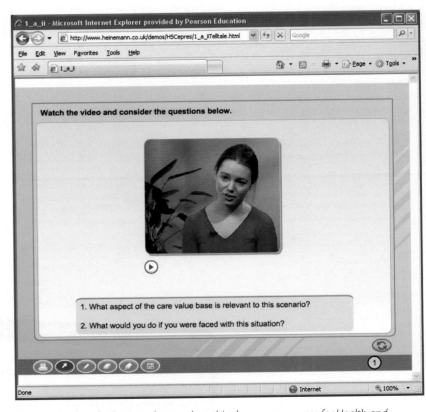

Multimedia can also be a product, such as this classroom resource for Health and Social Care

PURPOSES FOR MULTIMEDIA

Think about the decision process businesses must go through to choose the best type of multimedia for the job they want to do. Consider three multimedia products you have seen recently. What other types of product might they have used instead? Would these have delivered the message more or less effectively?

* video on websites – an alternative to a training CD or DVD might be to put a video on a website. This way the files can be updated whenever necessary and it is much easier as all users are accessing one copy, so only one copy needs to be updated. It also means that the user is responsible for ensuring they can access it, removing potential problems caused by incorrect formats. However, it does assume that the user has Internet access

* promotional CDs/DVDs – businesses sometimes use these as a promotional tool, similar to the way they use training media. Although using a CD/DVD has certain issues attached, this method can encourage users to look at the product where they may not have considered it before. Using CDs/DVDs can be expensive as each one has the cost of being burnt, packaged and posted

* virtual tours – these are becoming a popular way of giving users an experience of something without actually being there. It is popularly used in the fields of housing and holidays, although colleges and universities are also beginning to take advantage of the technology

* television or cinema adverts – multimedia is being used more in order to promote products and services. This is often done with animation or CGI. The audience likely to be watching a TV programme or film needs to be taken into account when choosing the advert to show. Advertising space, generally sold in units of time, is subject to various factors; for example, it will be expensive to advertise on television during a prime-time Saturday family show or in the cinema before a Hollywood blockbuster. However, it would be cheaper to advertise on television during the day or late at night, or perhaps just to one region. Cinema advertising is cheaper for more specialist films

For Your Project

When you create your project, remember it is important to choose the right tool for the job. Always bear in mind the core purpose and your target audience.

Activity 6.6

For each business described below, in pairs or small groups, choose a suitable multimedia product and produce a design for the product. Describe why you have chosen it and how it would be used.

1 Sampson's Automobiles manufacture quality traditional cars based on designs from the 1920s. Their target market is older drivers who want to invest in a classic car. They wish to promote their products, aiming specifically for the target market.

2 Blitz is a nightclub for over-21s which aims to attract sophisticated customers. They have a famous DJ playing next month and want to promote this to a wide target audience.

3 Belle Hotels are opening a new complex in Monte Carlo. They wish to advertise this new hotel on their website to attract holiday-makers.

Summary

* Multimedia can be used in a variety of ways by business, to advertise, sell and inform.
* Each method has both pros and cons and must be chosen wisely to be effective and cost-efficient.

6.2 Design and develop a multimedia product

Now you have a detailed understanding of the use of multimedia and the technical considerations, it is time to start applying that knowledge to the practical creation and development of an actual product.

Pre-production

Pre-production is essentially the design stage of the process. It can include everything from the conception of the initial idea to the creation of detailed plans.

Generally in multimedia, a product will start with an idea. This could be spotting a gap in the market, for example a new e-commerce website, or creative inspiration, for example a storyline for an animation. This idea will be sketched out and developed further.

The pre-production can sometimes take a disproportionate amount of time compared with the development time, like in advertising where people creating a three-minute TV advert can take six months to come up with ideas, choose the best and plan it fully. However, if the resulting product is successful, it is most often worth the time it took to develop.

Designs at the end of pre-production should be detailed enough to be implemented immediately and a designer should always work on the premise that they might not be the person creating the product, therefore the designs should be as detailed and clear as possible.

Production

Production is the creation of the product itself. This could be the making of the website, the shooting of the film or the generating of the animation.

Developers should not make the mistake of thinking that production is one big phase. It should always be broken down into separate tasks. For example, when creating a computer game, the stages might include drawing the characters, animating the characters, modelling the environment, putting the characters into the environment, building in the interactivity and so on.

The construction of a multimedia product should be divided into as many parts as possible. After each part has been completed, a developer can assess whether they are still on target in terms of the product requirement and the time frame. This is the stage where time can become problematic as components of the project can take longer to develop than anticipated or problems can occur, such as computer failure.

THE PROCESS

Think about a multimedia product you have seen recently (a website, computer game, animation etc.) and write down all the things the developer had to do to create that product.

Pre-production
The planning stage of a media product.

Production
The implementation stage of a media product.

Post-production

Post-production is the final stage of the creative process and consists of making the product suitable for the audience. This can include editing, testing and delivery.

If the multimedia product is a film with CGI, the film will have been shot and the bulk of the animation created during production. In the post-production stage the CGI is added to the film and made into one complete product ready for viewing.

For a product like a website, post-production will involve testing and **uploading**. Testing is vitally important because delivering a 'buggy' product is very unprofessional, reflects badly on you as a developer and could make the client's product look bad and prevent it from selling. Uploading the website means it is placed on servers so the general public can access it (also known as '**going live**').

Post-production
The finalising and testing stage of a media product.

Uploading/Going live
Putting a website onto a web server and allowing the public to view it.

Activity 6.10

What similarities and differences can you see between developing multimedia products and developing computer systems?

Summary

* Creating multimedia products involves three stages: pre-production, production and post-production.
* These three stages are essentially design, build and test/deliver.

Pre-production: Audience and purpose

The most important people to consider when creating a multimedia product are the audience. What do they want from it? How will you attract and hold their interest? What is the reason for the product?

Audience

The **target audience** generally comprises the people who will make the product successful or not, such as the buyers on an e-commerce website, cinema-goers watching a movie or gamers purchasing a computer game. Therefore, when designing a product, it is important to understand who the audience is and what it wants.

Consumers can be segmented into **demographics** which place them in bands in terms of employment, disposable income and other factors. These are categorised as letters, so demographic group A are high earners such as lawyers and bankers, whereas group E include students, pensioners and the unemployed. Each group can be further broken down into particular sections, so a product could be targeted just at students, then even further to just female students between the ages of 19 and 22. The more specific your target audience, the fewer potential consumers will be available.

No matter how you have defined your target audience, during the whole development process you should have a clear idea for whom you are creating it. A popular technique in business is to invent your typical customer and give them a name and a detailed description.

Your decisions are affected by your target audience (for example whether it comprises business or leisure users, whether it is young or old, male or female, etc.) and take account of its level of experience (such as for a 'silver surfer' who has minimal experience of websites but wants to learn more).

REASONS AND REQUIREMENTS

Write down three websites you visited recently. Why did you go there? What did you hope to find? Did they deliver?

Target audience
The potential users of a product.

Demographics
Putting the population into groups in order to understand it and so target specific sections.

When discussing audience needs it is often the users or viewers of a product that become the priority, but it is important to take into account the needs of the client as well. Both will have certain requirements for the product, some the same, some different. Some requirements will perhaps conflict and you may need to negotiate a solution with your client.

Purpose

In addition to understanding your target audience, throughout development it is important always to stay true to the purpose of your product: the reason you are creating it. For example, if you are building an e-commerce site, the purpose is to promote the product and establish sales. The final product may be the best-looking website ever, but if it does not sell the product then it has not been very successful.

By the end of the design, you should have a clearly defined purpose for your product. Will it be informative, functional or purely entertaining? Is it a product in its own right or is it promoting something? What is the reason for its creation?

For Your Project

When creating your project, always keep the purpose at the forefront of your mind so that the final product fulfils the original brief. Also remember that the most important people are your target audience.

Activity 6.11

Prepare4College is a new service which will advise students who plan to continue their education beyond Year 11. It will provide helpful tips on how to choose the right courses, where to find support, what to expect, reasons to continue with education and alternative routes other than sixth form college. They have asked you individually to design, build and test a website for them that is to contain a home page and five other pages.

1 Describe the purpose of the site.

2 Describe the target audience of the site

3 Write five requirements the target audience will have.

4 Write five requirements the client will have.

Summary

* At the start of a multimedia project, the target audience should be defined and their requirements identified.

* A multimedia product should always fulfil the desired purpose to make it effective and useful.

Pre-production: Design documents

By creating clear and accurate designs, a developer is less likely to make mistakes during production and therefore the product will be made better and without wasting time. Your designs are the ideas from your head put down on paper and turned into reality.

FROM HEAD TO HARDCOPY

Practise drawing the pictures you imagine. Try thinking up a new breed of animal, an alien and a new plant and sketch them on paper.

Visuals
Translating an idea to something physical, for example creating concept art or a mood board.

Concept art and mood boards

These tools are often referred to as **visuals** because they help the developers and client visualise the product.

Concept art is used to show the core idea of a product. What it entails will vary depending on the type of product and its central concept. For example a website with a distinctive layout might have rough outlines of that design, whereas a computer game character is usually sketched in pencil before drawing it in 2D on a computer, then modelling it in 3D.

A mood board is used to demonstrate how a multimedia product should 'feel', that is the effect it should have on the audience. Usually they are A3 and a collage of existing images such as from magazines. The choice of images should be based on the core idea of the product.

Storyboard
A series of panels showing what will happen in each scene or page.

Storyboard

A **storyboard** illustrates a multimedia product's actions. This is most important for dynamic and interactive multimedia such as animations and websites. It can show the different stages through which an animation may move, scene by scene, or it could show the effect of a user on a site, such as where they will go if they click a certain button.

Site map

A **site map** is used in website design to explain all the pages and their interaction in one easy-to-read, visual diagram. It should start with the homepage and follow through all the buttons until all pages are included. It could be shown as a hierarchical diagram or similarly to a mind map.

Site map
The design of pages of a website and how they will interact.

Interaction

Even at this early stage you should consider the interaction in the multimedia as it will need to be built in as part of it, rather than added on as an afterthought, so that it is seamlessly used within the product.

This might involve using **pseudocode**, especially for products such as websites (using languages such as JavaScript), animation (using facilities such as ActionScript in Adobe Flash) and computer games. Pseudocode can be used to plan what the code will do without having to worry about using the correct words or syntax.

Designing the interaction could also include the control mechanism for the product. This would be especially important in computer games where interaction plays a critical role.

Screen designs

To demonstrate precisely what the product will look like once it is made, a screen design shows where the elements will be placed. For example, the screen designs for a website would show the layout of the text, images, buttons and all the other components, and there would be one screen design for each web page.

Pseudocode
A form of language which is between proper English and a programming language. Pseudocode gives the functionality required by the full and final code in an easy-to-read form but it cannot be executed (run).

Activity 6.12

Individually, design the website for Prepare4College.

1 Create a mood board to show the concept of the website.

2 Draw a storyboard or site map to show how the pages will interrelate.

3 Create screen designs for the homepage and one other page. Annotate them to show colours, fonts and other formatting.

Summary

* All parts of the product must be designed before beginning to build it.
* Using images and diagrams can help the developer and client understand what the final product will look like.

Production: Static multimedia

Not all multimedia is about interactivity and movement. Static images, photographs and presentations are used every day in the business world and are a powerful tool to sell products or to get across a message.

Graphics

Graphics are digital images which are either created or edited on a computer. They could begin as hand-drawn pieces of art which are scanned into a computer, or they could be drawn straight into a graphics package such as Adobe Illustrator or CorelDRAW. Images can be manipulated in packages such as Adobe Photoshop or Corel Paint Shop Pro. They can range from simple line drawings to full-colour detailed images.

When working with graphics, understanding the difference between bitmaps and vectors is important (see Worksheet 6.1(3)).

Key skills when working with digital graphics include:

* **cropping**
* altering size and shape
* changing colours
* adding **layer styles**
* applying **filters**

For instructions on working with digital graphics, see Worksheets 6.1(4).

Digital photographs

Digital cameras are used throughout industry due to their ability to store numerous photographs which can be transferred easily to a computer for editing. You will need a cable (often a USB cable) to connect the camera to a computer.

The quality of a digital photograph is a function of the resolution of the digital camera used. This is measured in **megapixels** (one million pixels). For high-quality photographs it is advisable to use a camera with no fewer than five megapixels.

A digital camera case houses the control buttons, a lens, a flash and an LCD screen (which will show what the lens is 'seeing' so you know what picture you will take when you press the 'shutter' button). Modern digital cameras often do not have a viewfinder and the photographer relies totally on the LCD screen.

Presentations

Presentations are generally used to inform or persuade. They can be delivered by a person or can be automated to run by themselves. Microsoft PowerPoint is the most popular presentation software and it uses a similar environment to the other applications in the Office suite.

PICTURES, PHOTOS, PRESENTATIONS

Think back over the last couple of days, at school, at home, out and about. List all the times you came into contact with a digital picture, a photograph or a presentation.

Cropping
Cutting an image down to a selected area.

Layer styles
Pre-made styles, such as shadows, glows and bevels, which can be added to layers.

Filters
Pre-made styles which can be simply applied to an image to allow complex effects.

Megapixel
One million pixels, used to measure quality of digital camera photographs.

However, presentations made in Adobe Flash are becoming more popular, especially in the design industry. To access the presentation templates in Flash, select **File > New** and click the **Template** tab.

Activity 6.13

Individually, create a presentation about yourself to give to Prepare4College as a digital CV.

1 On paper, write your name clearly. Scan it and then use a graphics package to edit it.

2 Take a digital photograph of yourself. Transfer the photograph to a computer and edit it.

3 Create a presentation about yourself. Use your name graphic on the first slide and your photograph and details on the second slide. Create three more slides which describe your skills, your hobbies/interests and your favourite multimedia product (website, game, animation etc).

Summary

* Not all multimedia is about movement. Static multimedia includes graphics, digital photographs and presentations.

Production: Dynamic multimedia

As technology continues to develop at a tremendous rate, methods of dynamic multimedia become more accessible. The Internet has been a huge inspiration in this development, and going from text-based to graphical browsers was a huge leap. This is an exciting time for dynamic multimedia as it becomes easier to use and more widespread.

Websites

The Internet contains millions of websites, all of which are battling for the attention of users. Some are selling products or services, some are to inform and some are to entertain.

To create a website you could **hard code** it in a text editor like Microsoft Notepad, but nowadays it is more common to use a web-development application such as Microsoft FrontPage or, the industry standard, Adobe Dreamweaver.

To upload a website to be viewed by the public you need a domain name, like www.google.com, and a web server on which to host the site.

Animation

In the early days of animation, hand-drawing frame by frame was time-consuming and also a very specialist task. Although some movies and television shows are still created this way, digital animation is becoming the standard. Animated movies are becoming available on the Internet, often freely available to watch.

Animation is also a crucial part of computer games and this is an area which is pushing the field further and further in terms of design, technique and technology.

As animation packages become easier to use and more widely available, it is possible for the amateur to create animations as the field becomes less specialised. Applications like Adobe Flash are bringing the public the possibility of creating their own animations.

A core concept of digital animation is **tweening**. In traditional animation each frame is drawn by hand, which is very difficult and time-consuming. Tweening allows the animator to put in a start point and end point and the program will work out the frames in between.

Video

Video, like animation, was once exclusively the area of specialists, with equipment being expensive and difficult to use. However, with the advent of the camcorder, hand-held cameras with recorders built-in, and with their prices becoming lower, it is now possible to purchase a video camera for personal use.

ACROSS SPACE AND TIME

It might sound like science fiction, but dynamic multimedia usually operates across more dimensions than static. Use the Internet to research 2D, 3D and 4D. What is the fourth dimension?

Hard code
Code written directly and in full, without using an editing environment.

Tweening
When a computer works out the frames needed between two user-defined points.

Digital video became popular in the 1990s and is becoming the standard format to use. Like digital cameras, digital video cameras provide an easier method to transfer film to a computer for editing. Packages such as Adobe Premiere and Sony Vegas have allowed high-end video editing to be more accessible. The Windows operating systems come with Windows Movie Maker and all Macintosh machines include the iLife suite which includes iMovie.

Websites like YouTube and Google Video are cultural phenomena and have provided a forum for amateur film makers.

To create a video, you will need a camera and its required storage media, such as a **DV tape**. You will also need a cable to connect it to a computer.

DV tape
Digital video tape used to record film in some camcorders.

Sound

Sound exists in analogue sound waves but these can be recorded and converted into digital waves on computer. Sound can be captured in several ways, most commonly by using a microphone. Audio recording and editing packages can be used to alter the sounds, even down to the tiniest part of the sound wave, using applications such as Sony Sound Forge or Audacity (which is available for free).

Activity 6.14

Individually, build the website you have designed for Prepare4College.

1 Create the layouts and hyperlinks of the web pages.

2 Add static multimedia such as graphics and photographs.

3 Add the text, formatting it appropriately.

4 Create an animated logo and add that to the home page.

5 Add any other elements to your website so it looks professional and complete.

Summary

* As technology and software become more available, more people can get involved in dynamic multimedia.

Production: Multimedia elements

Each multimedia element in itself is interesting, but by combining them a product can be made which is more effective at delivering its message and which will have a more powerful impact on the audience.

INTEGRATION

Multimedia is essentially the mixing of different media in one product. Find five websites which use at least two types of multimedia within them.

Activity 6.15

Prepare4College have asked you to create an advertisement which will promote the website you are building. This will use integrated multimedia and must deliver their message effectively. It will take the form of a single web page to be displayed at Prepare4College.com until the launch of the full website.

1 Create a screen design for the webpage. It must include:
   * the name Prepare4College
   * an animated tag line
   * the animated logo
   * a photograph of happy students
   * a short video
   * background music

2 Create the layout of the web page.

3 Draw the name Prepare4College on paper and scan it into a computer. Edit it and add it to the web page (hint: **Insert > Image**).

4 Add the animated logo you have created (hint: **Insert > Media > Flash**).

5 The tag line of the advert is 'Be ready for your future!'. Create an animation of this and add it to the website.

6 Take a photograph of some students looking happy, edit it if necessary and add it to the webpage (hint: **Insert > Image**).

7 Take a short video, or use one that has already been made, of a suitable topic and add it to the web page.

Adding a video to a web page

If the video is from a website, use the HTML code provided and insert it into the code at the point you want it to appear on the page. If it is not from a website, you can use **Insert > Media > Plugin**. The following HTML code can also be used:

```
<embed src="filename"></embed>
```

8 Add the background music to the web page.

Adding music to a web page

Music can be added to a website to play all the time while on a specific page or to play when a link is clicked.

* To add background music, use **Insert > Media > Plugin**. The HTML that can also be used is

```
<embed src="musicfile.mp3"></embed>
```

between the `<head>` and `</head>` tags of the page.

* To add to link, highlight the text or image to be used as the link. In the **Behaviors** panel, click the **+** symbol. Select **Play Sound**, browse to the sound file and select it. Set the sound to **onClick**, so it will be played when the link is clicked. The HTML code that can also be used is

```
<a href="musicfile.mp3">Text of link</a>
```

at the point where the link should be displayed.

Activity 6.15a

Creating videos can be a real challenge for your team skills. You may have a crew of director, camera operator and lighting operator behind the camera, then you may need to work with actors who are in front of the camera. It can be challenging to ensure that everyone gets what they want from the project and are able to have an input into the production. As practice, make a mini film of a classic fairy tale, such as *Cinderella* or *Hansel and Gretel*. Have three people in your crew and two or three actors. You might also want to take turns at different roles – this can also make it look like you have a bigger cast.

Summary

* By integrating multimedia elements, a product can become more effective.

6.3 Post-production: Testing

If a product is released to the public and it contains 'bugs' or incorrect content, the result could be very serious. If an interactive animation doesn't work, the audience will not want to use it and it will become unpopular. If content on an e-commerce site is incorrect, the company could be penalised under the Trade Descriptions Act (1968). Testing could be the difference between damage to your reputation and a successful project leading to more opportunities.

Original requirements

At the beginning of the project, if you designed it thoroughly, you will have declared the core purpose of the product and the needs of the audience and the client. Once it has been created, you can go back and compare the finished product with those fundamental requirements.

Does the product fulfil its purpose? If a website was designed to sell a product, does it demonstrate the benefits of it, do photographs of it look good, is there a facility to purchase the product? If an interactive animation is to educate Year 7 pupils about Science, is it appropriate for that age range, is it factually correct, will they learn from using it?

To test whether the purpose requirements have been met, analyse each one individually against the final product. For example, if you have stated a website must have a functioning feedback form which emails the results, you can test this by filling in the form and clicking submit. Requirements which are more intangible, such as the need for it to be user-friendly, might require a focus group to decide if it is suitable.

In analysing the finished product against the audience and client requirements, you may find that some have not been fulfilled, but you should always be able to justify why that is. Perhaps the client asked for a certain colour scheme which turned out to be inappropriate during production and was renegotiated with the client. Maybe the language was changed to make it easier for younger people to understand.

Prototyping

It is common in the multimedia industry, as in others such as the IT industry, to build a prototype of a product before commencing on the production in its entirety. A **prototype** is a miniature version of a product, similar to how an architect would make a small model before constructing a full-scale building. Its purpose is to test whether a design will work in practice. It is possible to conceive anything because the imagination is limitless; however, in reality there are things which are impossible. Prototyping is especially important for more daring or innovative projects.

Prototype
A small version of a product used to test whether a product will work when developed in full.

A prototype of a multimedia product

A prototype of a website with complex hyperlinks might be built to test whether it is user-friendly. The structure of the site could be made but with blank web pages, having only the buttons on white backgrounds. This means that if it does need to be redesigned, time has not been wasted on the formatting of all the images and text only to have to reconstruct the site again.

Activity 6.16

1 Compare your website with the original purpose. Does it fulfil its objectives?

2 Compare your website with the audience and client requirements. State whether they have or have not been met.

3 For those requirements which have not been met, explain why this has happened.

For Your Project

At the end of implementation you should be able to prove that your product meets its original requirements.

Summary

* When a multimedia product has been completed, it should be checked to make sure it fulfils its purpose and meets audience and client requirements.

* Prototyping can be used to save time and effort, especially for innovative projects.

Post-production: Opportunities for improvement

TEST, TEST AND TEST AGAIN

Find a piece of text you have written, either by hand or on a computer. Proofread it and mark the spelling, grammar and formatting mistakes in red. Then ask someone else to check it and mark any mistakes you missed in green. Nearly every time testing is done, it won't pick up every single mistake, which is why you should always test more than once.

As you know, testing is important, but remember to take every opportunity to improve the product to make sure it is the best it can possibly be.

Test plan

When testing, it is useful to use a plan so that the tests are organised, you do not repeat any and nothing is omitted.

A test plan such as this could be used to test a website:

Test Number	Test Element	On Page	Test Data	Expected Result	Actual Result	Success or Failure	Screenshot Reference
1	Home button	About.html	Left click	Load index.html	Load index.html	Success	S1
2	Logo.gif	Index.html	Load page	Appear in top left corner	Appear in centre of page	Failure	S2

On a website, the tests could include checking that:

* buttons are hyperlinked to the correct places
* images are correct and are in the right places
* colours are displayed as expected
* text is error-free and readable

Platforms

A multimedia product may be expected to be used on many different **platforms** although you created it on only one. It is therefore important to check that it works on as many different platforms as possible. A product, such as an interactive CD, might be widely distributed, therefore testing should be done to ensure it will work on different hardware and operating systems. If it does not, changes might need to be made or instructions or system requirements added.

A website will be expected to perform on different software platforms, such as Microsoft Internet Explorer, Mozilla Firefox and Opera, therefore it is important to test it on different browsers to ensure it works correctly on each.

Platform
A system. Different computer hardware with different operating systems.

Improve and retest

Once testing has been done, analyse the results and see where failures have occurred. This is an opportunity to improve the product. Then retest the whole thing, focusing in detail on the new parts. This should be done as many times as possible until all the errors you can find are eliminated.

It is common in testing to try to break the product by a variety of methods. Testing will start by using the product the way it is supposed to work; for example, on a website the buttons will be clicked once to make sure they go to the correct pages. To thoroughly test it, the buttons should also be doubled-clicked, continuously clicked, clicked around the button area and so on. Trying every possible action, both normal and abnormal, will examine whether the product is completely **robust**.

Functional Skills – ICT

Being able to test logically and thoroughly is a skill that can be used in every product you make.

Robust
Thoroughly tested and able to withstand any method of use.

Activity 6.17

1 Create a test plan with which to test the site.

2 Carry out the testing and complete the test plan.

3 For the tests which failed, make improvements.

For Your Project

Testing is very important as it removes errors and faults from your product. If a product contains errors when it is published/released, it could mean the purpose is not fulfilled and users will not like it.

Summary

✳ When testing, always use a plan.

✳ Test, improve and retest as many times as possible.

Post-production: Feedback

Even if you think your media product is the best ever, it is important to get feedback to find out if other people agree. It could highlight areas for improvement, or build your confidence if they think it is as good as you think it is.

Audience testing

A good way to test your product further is to gain the opinions of a small proportion of your target audience before releasing it to everyone. This can test intangible elements such as user-friendliness and appropriateness, which cannot be measured scientifically.

There are two main ways to gain audience feedback: individually or in focus groups. In the individual method, people would be invited by themselves to try the product. It may be that they are asked to go to a location to test it or they could do it from home. A focus group brings people to one place to test a product and discuss it. For example, The Walt Disney Studios invite groups of children and their parents to watch newly completed animated movies and then discuss their opinions of them, maybe even making changes from the feedback. In both cases, individually and in focus groups, the testers are selected from the target audience.

When using a target audience to test a product, its purpose should be considered. If a product is meant to be informative, not only will its usability need to be tested, but also whether the testers have learnt from its content. If a product is interactive, this needs to be added into the feedback from the testers and they should be instructed as to how they should test it (for example, to use it correctly or to test its robustness by trying to break the product).

Having collected all this feedback, it is vital that improvements are made. There is no point going to all this trouble unless you use this new knowledge to make your product better.

Gathering methods

You can use several methods to get feedback, each with their own advantages and disadvantages (see table on next page).

The questionnaire method could be on paper or online.

Evaluation

At the end of every project it is important to evaluate it, to say what parts were successful and what parts were not. By carrying out this process, you can learn from your mistakes and improve your own skills.

An evaluation identifies good points, bad points and areas for improvement. You should look at both the finished product and the process you took to produce it, evaluating each separately.

	Advantages	Disadvantages
Interview	* can build a rapport between interviewer and interviewee * can adjust the questions as interview progresses * the information gathered is usually quite in-depth	* are time-consuming, therefore costly * poor interview skills can mean poor information * because it takes time, you can only see a limited number of people, therefore there are fewer opinions
Group meeting	* can get information from several people at once * can adjust questions as meeting progresses * the information gathered is usually quite in-depth	* are time-consuming, therefore costly * poor meeting skills can mean poor information * meeting members may not want to criticise the product in front of developers
Questionnaire	* many people are asked same questions, so comparisons are easy * cheaper and quicker than interviewing large numbers of people * anonymity may encourage honest answers	* questions need careful design (for example open/closed) * ambiguous questions can lead to incorrect information * cannot guarantee 100% return rate

The improvements should be based on the bad points you have identified, but also give a reason as to how they will make a difference. It is insufficient just to say you will change the background from bright blue to pastel blue; you should also add that this is because it will make the text clearer to read. Reasons for improving should include making the content clearer, the navigation more intuitive, the site easier to use etc. Consider all types of users: some may be experienced users of websites, some may be virtually computer-illiterate. Never disregard any as they are all important – perhaps the person who cannot use websites very well will spend hundreds of pounds on the product you are selling!

Activity 6.18

1 Choose an information gathering method and carry it out: either interview two people, carry out a focus group discussion with four people or distribute 20 questionnaires.

2 Analyse your feedback. What have you learned from this process? What changes would you make to the website having carried out this audience testing?

3 Evaluate your project using the following structure:

Process

* good points
* bad points
* improvements

Product

* good points
* bad points
* improvements

For Your Project

As well as removing errors and testing it yourself, it is useful to gain the opinions of others, especially those of your target audience. This provides more proof that your product is successful, or can identify areas for improvement.

Summary

* Audience testing is a great way to find out the opinions of your target audience before releasing your product.
* Choose your method of information gathering wisely.

Preparation for assessment

In this unit you will learn how to create a variety of multimedia products. You should analyse existing products to further understand how they are created. Using this information, you should create your own multimedia product following a creation cycle including designing, implementation, testing and evaluation.

How you will be assessed

This unit is assessed externally. You will be expected to present evidence in an e-portfolio, accessible by fifth-generation or equivalent web browsers. You will be assessed through:

* a report and presentation analysis of the uses of existing multimedia products to meet different objectives based on thorough research. You should compare areas such as multimedia in advertising, film and gaming. Your audience for both pieces is a group of businesses you are trying to persuade to use your company to create their multimedia products. The report should be used as a handout to delegates during the presentation and therefore needs to be suitable for this purpose with appropriate use of English. The presentation should be approximately six or seven slides in length and be based on the report.

* your production of a working multimedia product. This must include the design, development and testing to create a complete and functioning product.

* evaluation of your product based on feedback from the target audience

Assessment tips

* Manage your time wisely throughout the project
* Keep your computer files in order, using sensible names. Keep all paperwork in an orderly fashion in a folder.
* In your own time, practise with the software so that you are able to use the facilities e ciently in your project

Remember!

* Analyse as many multimedia products as possible and gain experience in a broad variety of styles and approaches
* Ensure your documentation is thorough. It should be possible for another multimedia developer to build your product from your design documentation alone
* When creating your own product, remember the target audience at all times and make sure it is appropriate to them
* Learn how to incorporate different multimedia elements into one product
* Allow yourself to be creative in order to produce a more innovative product

You must show that you:	Guidance	To gain higher marks you must explain:
6.1 Understand the use of multimedia to meet different business-relevant objectives	* Produce a report and give a presentation explaining uses of multimedia * How and why are different types of multimedia used for different purposes?	* Comprehensively and using analysis, the different uses of multimedia considering different uses for different objectives
6.2 Understand the technical knowledge and skills used to enhance multimedia products for a given purpose, through the use of multimedia content (such as images, graphics, timeline-based animation, video and sound) **6.3** Are able to design, develop and test a multimedia product which meets the needs of a specific audience and purpose	* Produce design documents for a multimedia product * What technical aspects must be taken into consideration in this product? * Create the product which incorporates at least three multimedia types * Create a test plan and carry it out	* Using **comprehensive** storyboard designs, how the product meets specific business objectives and audience needs * Using a **clear** sitemap/structure chart where the interaction occurs between the different pages * The creation of a **fully working** multimedia product, integrating at least three different types of multimedia components and including user interaction in some form * The **comprehensive** testing documentation and evidence of several prototypes
6.4 Are able to evaluate feedback from the target audience, identifying opportunities for improvement	* Gain feedback from at least one member of the target audience * How will that feedback be obtained? How will it be analysed? What have you learned from your feedback? * Evaluate the product including strengths and weaknesses * Where could the product be improved?	* The feedback from several members of the target audience * The comprehensive evaluation of the feedback * **Comprehensively**, how the multimedia product created can be improved, with consideration of HCI issues

7 Managing Projects

IT has had a major effect on business over the last few years. With the help of IT, many organisations now do things very differently from how they used to. However, none of the changes have happened without planning a project's designs, time schedules and finances. This unit, together with your project, gives you ideas on how you can best tackle IT work. This ranges from small pieces of work, just for your own benefit, up to working as part of a team on a major IT project.

PROJECT MANAGEMENT

Many of the units you have done so far can be seen themselves as projects. Look again at the units and your project and compare them with a major IT project, for example an online banking service, and list anything similar that might be needed to manage each.

Your local fast food restaurant is likely to have electronic tills linked to an IT system to analyse sales. Access to many local government services is often through IT systems. To make these and other IT systems happen, many IT projects have been run. In this unit you will learn the best way to run these projects to make them, and your part in them, a success. However, not all IT projects are successful. We have all heard of projects that have never worked, have been abandoned part way through or have been very late or over-budget. This unit will tell you how your project can avoid many of these failures.

Make sure you use what you learn here in your project.

Learning outcomes

7.1 Understand the key factors that determine the success of IT projects and reasons why some projects fail

7.2 Be able to produce a project proposal and develop a project plan for a small-scale IT project

7.3 Be able to manage a successful project

7.4 Be able to carry out an end-of-project review

Defining success

A successful project is commonly defined as one where all objectives have been achieved, all deliverables delivered within budget and on time and where the customer is satisfied with the outcome. It all sounds very simple, but there is a wide range of factors that affect the success or failure of a project, and it is possible for a project to be a success in some regards and a failure in others.

However, even if a project goes wrong, the lessons learnt from the experience can help avoid repeating the same mistakes and help you make a success next time round.

Cost
What needs to be spent as money, manpower or other resources.

Budget
How much money and other resources a project needs for success.

Variable factors
Financial items such as inflation and the cost of raw materials, over which the project manager has little control, but which may impact the project.

7.1 Determining factors for success

In this section you will learn about the key factors that lead to the success or failure of a business project.

Budget

In a business project, all the resources have a **cost**. The project manager is expected to keep the total cost within the overall **budget**.

A budget might be divided into costs, **variable factors** and revenue.

Costs

* Materials and equipment – many projects take existing software and put these in place in a business. Projects often need new desktop computers, servers and cabling.
* Labour – this is often the largest part of an IT project. There is the cost of the IT professionals who analyse, specify, design, build, test and put in place the project. There is the cost of the customer's time and the cost of training the people who use the project.

Variable factors

* Inflation – the costs and revenues may both be higher at the end of a project than at the start
* Raw materials – the price of these may fluctuate. Software will usually go up in price. Hardware continues to drop in unit price.
* Effect of world events – these are unpredictable. For example, the growth in ICT skills in India over the last 10 years has led to running more projects there for use in the UK.
* Environmental considerations – IT project managers need to be aware of any environmental impact of their actions.

Budgets: success or failure

Reasons for success

* Realistic objectives: Submit a realistic bid at the outset, where a company bids for an external contract. It is important to have a realistic business case on costs and benefits.
* Keep within budget.

Reasons for failure

* Resource problems: Lack of resources or expertise.
* Uncontrolled change: For example, escalating costs.
* Scope creep: An unrealistic bid made in the first instance. This is a common ploy to win the business for the project. The project then grows in scope in an attempt to make the project profitable.

HOW SUCCESSFUL IS SUCCESSFUL?

Defining success in project management is key to evaluating a project and learning from your experiences. Think of a well-known project and decide how successful it has been. Was it delivered on time? Was it within budget? How were the messages around the project communicated? Did it meet its objectives?

Functional Skills – Mathematics

You can use mathematical skills to identify and tackle the cost of resources for a project.

Activity 7.1

1 What is a budget?

2 What are costs?

3 Could any variable factors affect your project?

Summary

* Budgets need to include costs for materials, labour and equipment.
* Factors outside the control of the project manager can affect the budget.

Timescale

The time schedule of a project can be critical and is a key factor in its success or failure. Skilled project managers regularly review the project schedule to make sure the deadline will be met.

Deadlines

It is common to read about IT projects that over run their timescale or **deadline** dates. You should complete your project to your tutor's timescale. Deadlines are very important; for example, the facilities for the 2012 Olympic Games need to be ready before the events start, or the bedroom needs redecorating before Aunt Mabel's annual stay with your family. Your project might be part of a much larger project but meeting your deadline could be key to the major project's overall success. You need to know what would happen if a project fails to keep to its time schedule.

Deadlines occur throughout a project and do not just signify the date when everything must be complete. For example, equipment expenditure might be in this year's budget, so all equipment orders might have a timescale of before 31 December. Holidays and business demand might prevent training during the months of June to September. This might mean a timescale of 31 May to complete all training.

Interdependent tasks

Many **tasks** in a project are interdependent. This means that a delay on finishing one task has a knock-on effect in starting the next. If these are on the critical path, then this could delay the whole project. For example, delay in installation of equipment in a training room will probably mean that training cannot start, which in turn might mean that a new system cannot be launched, thereby affecting a company's sales.

Estimating time

For project success it is important to have a realistic project plan. This means that the tasks that make up the project plan should have good estimates of the time they will take and the resources they will use. A good project plan will identify where early delays might occur and allow more time to replan to get the project back on track.

TIMING'S EVERYTHING!

When is a project really complete? Does the project plan cater for everything the client has asked for? In small groups, discuss examples of possible IT projects and list any that you think would be considered a failure if they missed their deadline, for example a computerised timing system for a New Year's Eve firework display.

Deadline
The end date when either a small part of a project or the entire project must be completed. Some interim deadlines are set as milestone dates to monitor the project's progress.

Task
Part of a project that the project manager may plan and control. Some tasks are dependent on other tasks being completed before they can be started.

Activity 7.2

1 What is a task?

2 What is a deadline?

3 Why is it important to have good estimates for how long a task will take? Is your project achievable within the timescale set by your stakeholder? If not, what options are open to you?

4 A website providing help and FAQs for a new and eagerly anticipated software suite ran into some problems in the early stages of production. It's now running two weeks behind schedule. What would be the consequences of the website publishing two weeks after the software it supports is released?

Timescale: success or failure

Reasons for success

* Effective planning: Deliver within time frame. This is best achieved through realistic estimates of the amount of time required for each task.

* Accurate understanding of requirements: Have a clear understanding of client's requirements, especially if the client requires the whole project (or a part of it) delivered by a specific date.

Reasons for failure

* Poor planning or failure to recognise risk: The time frame is not met and the project is not completed within the timescale. This is often caused by unrealistic estimates of time, although variable factors beyond the project manager's control can sometimes cause unexpected delays.

Summary

* Deadlines are key dates in the lifecycle of a project.
* Realistic estimations of the time taken for each task are essential to create an achievable project plan.

Communication and objectives

Communication within a project team is essential to the success of the project. Regular meetings allow the stakeholders to monitor progress and assess whether the objectives of the project are being met.

Communication

Communication between **stakeholders** is essential to the smooth running of a project and it is the project manager's responsibility to make sure this happens. Not all communication needs to go through the project manager, but the project team needs to be aware of progress, issues and risks that may affect interdependent tasks.

Means of communication may be:

* regular meetings
* highlight reports sent to senior management and the client
* emails
* the intranet or Internet

Objectives

Objectives are what the project is trying to do. They are very important to the success of a project. Many stakeholders judge the success of a project on how closely it has met its objectives. Most projects have objectives about time and budget.

A project may also have objectives about the business benefits that the project hopes to achieve. These might be about increased **revenue**, reduced costs or greater efficiency. These may be outside the direct control of the project. The five steps to manage objectives are to:

* identify the client's requirements – unless you know what the client wants, it is impossible to set objectives that will meet the requirements. It may be appropriate for the client to classify them as essential, highly desirable or beneficial
* define the objectives of the project – you should convert what the client wants in business terms into objectives that are a mix of business and IT
* make a clear statement of deliverables at the outset – you should then turn these objectives into the set of deliverables that your project supplies
* review objectives as the project proceeds – this is so that if meeting the objectives starts to look unlikely, timely decisions can be made to bring them back to target or to change the objectives or deliverables
* have a final review on project completion to check all the deliverables are met – this should achieve a common view on how well the project went. It should also give you feedback on what could go better on your next project

Stakeholder
A person or organisation that is actively involved in a project or whose interests the project may affect.

Objective
What the project is trying to do. One, often unstated, objective is that a project should deliver on time. A specific objective may be that the project finishes by July. This statement removes all doubt as to what 'on time' means.

Revenue
How much money the successful project will bring in.

Communication and objectives: success or failure

Reasons for success

* Accurate understanding of requirements: Have a clear understanding of client's requirements and deliverables.

* Good communication: Regular communication between project team and client.

Reasons for failure

* Poor communication: A lack of understanding of client's requirements or the deliverables.

* Scope creep: An unrealistic bid made in the first instance. The project then grows in scope and costs in an attempt to make the project profitable.

* Uncontrolled change: The client changing required deliverables during the project. This can be caused by failure to manage objectives.

* Internal politics: This often involves a clash of priorities or agendas. In some cases a project may fail in order for a different project to succeed.

* Political, cultural and social reasons: These often lie at the heart of assumptions and perceptions that lead to miscommunication. Remember that not everyone attaches the same values and level of importance to the same things.

Functional Skills – English

Communication must be fit for purpose and suitable for the audience. Any reports mentioning delays caused by the client should be neutral and highlight how the project will deal with the delays, not pointing the finger of blame! Changes to requirement often have financial and contractual implications which need to be dealt with professionally.

Activity 7.3

1 What four ways might a project manager use to communicate? Which are suitable for your project?

2 What is an objective?

3 What are the five steps to manage objectives?

Summary

* Projects need to have clearly defined objectives that have been agreed to.
* Regular communication is key to the success of a project.

External factors

External factors affect almost every project. Even if you are the only person working on a project and you have everything you need things happen to delay you.

Impact of external conditions

Here are some examples of external influences, the impact that they may have and what you might do to overcome them. When you plan your project, you should consider what to do about a specific **external factor** if there is a risk it will happen.

Changes in government policy

These may have a limited effect on business projects, but they may have a major impact on a government project. A major policy change often has profound effects on the scope of the project. Here you should re-scope, re-cost and re-plan the project. Treat it as a different project with different timescales. Don't try to meet the original deadlines if the scope is increased.

Financial changes

Changes in interest rates, VAT and tax rates should not affect the build part of a project. A good design allows these items to change easily. However, they may have an impact on the business case for a project.

Bad publicity

High-profile projects that involve public money often come under scrutiny. Poor publicity and public criticism can result in a change in scope or an attempt to complete the project in less time.

Resource problems

Not all unexpected conditions are truly external, although they may be equally beyond the project manager's control.

Staff unavailability

Illness, resignation or reassignment of staff to another project may detrimentally impact your project. They mean your project is short on personnel. At the extreme, for a one-person project, it will mean that all work on the project stops. If the person can be replaced, then their replacement may not have the skills or project knowledge so there will be a delay while they are trained and become effective. They may not be able to deliver at the same rate of work as the original staff member. The usual solution is to re-plan the project based on when the staff member can return to work or how quickly a replacement can be found.

Industrial action

This could be by the project team, by the project's suppliers or by the users. If the project team take industrial action, the project manager

WHAT EXTERNAL FACTORS MIGHT AFFECT MY PROJECT?

Do you rely on using resources that you do not already have? Do you need skilled workers? What would happen if your centre were closed by a natural disaster?

External factors
These are things outside the control of the project manager that affect the on-time, on-budget delivery of the project.

should re-plan the project in the same way as for any other staff unavailability. If a project's supplier takes industrial action, the project manager's action may involve finding another supplier or changing the contract with the supplier. In both cases, the project is likely to need re-planning.

Late or non-delivery of supplies

Unavailability of equipment and materials will potentially delay your project. As with supplier industrial action, the project manager may find another supplier, change the contract and re-plan the project.

Cash flow problems

The plans for many projects aim to deliver at minimum cost within a reasonable timescale. This usually produces the best business case. If an organisation has **cash flow** problems, it may:

* stop those projects that have the worst business case
* reduce costs by slowing the spend on some projects
* re-plan to bring in some benefits earlier. This means that the deadlines for some deliverables change and the project may have more phases. This is often a high-risk approach

> **Cash flow**
> The movement of money into or out of a business.

Environmental changes

This may affect the people working on the project, the equipment that they use or the project site. For people, there may be a contingency plan to have them work from home or from another location with suitable equipment. For an equipment or environment failure, there is often not a suitable alternative. For a small problem, the project manager should work on getting the problem fixed and assign staff to other tasks. For a longer outage, a re-plan is needed.

Activity 7.4

1 What are external factors? If contingency plans are used to mitigate any impact on the success of a project, discuss how the plans themselves might affect the project.

2 What four resource problems may impact a project?

3 What may a project do if there are problems with a supplier?

Summary

* Shortage of staff is a common source of delay in later stages of a project.
* Even with the right number of people, they must have the right skills.
* Be ready to change suppliers if a supplier has problems.

GETTING THE POINT ACROSS

Business cases should present clear arguments to highlight the benefits of proceeding to the next stage of a project. What improvements would you like to see made to your centre's website or intranet? How would you present a case for these changes to be made? What kind of information would you need to show?

Deliverable
Something that the project produces for, or delivers to, one or more of the stakeholders. It may be, for example, equipment, a working part of a system, documentation or training.

Scope
The boundaries of a project, which can be written in the specification, and which outline what the project sets out to achieve.

Specification
A document that will list all the objectives (or deliverables) of the project. The specification will not explain how the project will be achieved.

7.2 Produce a project proposal and plan a small-scale IT project

In this section you will learn how to produce a project proposal and project plan for a small-scale IT project. A small-scale IT project is capable of execution by one person, e.g. a small local area network.

Every project should have a defined aim and purpose. The project initiation stage is all about setting out what the project should achieve. This is also the stage at which a business case is produced.

Project proposal

Project initiation

Project initiation may include recording what the users do now, what the customer wants to happen once the new system is in place and any performance needs. The three main activities of this phase are:

* interviewing the customer to identify the **objectives** – you need to find out both what new features the customer wants in the future and what features of the present system are still required. You should encourage the customer to express needs in business rather than IT terms. For example, 'reduce the time to record a sale by 50 per cent' rather than 'a new transaction to do X and one to do Y'

* analysing the customer's requirements to identify the **deliverables** – you need to record all the things that the new project must do. Remember to include replacing existing systems. For example, a project to install new PCs in an office might also require you to install all the existing software on the new PCs

* agree the **evaluation criteria** with the customer – in order to identify the end point of the project all shareholders need to agree on criteria that can be used to judge the success of the project. These may include timescale, cost or quality – or usually all three. The evaluation criteria should identify the priorities for the project team and so need to be decided carefully

Definition of scope

The plan for the **scope** stage turns the customer's requirements into objectives. The objectives will later form a potential computer solution. The scope stage has just one major activity: produce the **specification**.

For example, the customer has a requirement for a word-processing system. The objectives, among others, might say that:

* new documents must be compatible with existing documents

* documents must be compatible with those within the rest of the organisation

* the new system must be similar to the old system as only a limited amount of effort is available for training

Stakeholders

All projects – no matter how small – will have a number of stakeholder roles. However, on really small projects, more than one of these roles could be held by one person! The stakeholder roles most common to IT projects are:

* **Customers** – the project's client. In IT these are often commercial organisations, or governmental bodies, who define the project's objectives
* **Backers** – sometimes projects have a 'sponsor' role that is separated from the role of the customers. An example of this would be where the project involved improving a government department's IT systems as part of a wider updating project. The department or person overseeing the larger-scale project would be the backer, whereas the department receiving the new IT system would be the customer
* **Suppliers** – most projects will rely on suppliers for certain aspects. Suppliers may provide hardware (for example, cables, connectors and components for a technology system) or expertise (for example, some really specialist coding). From the customer's perspective, the project team will be their suppliers, but the project team may have their own suppliers depending on their resource needs

> **Man-hours**
> The amount of time in hours it would take one person to complete a task.

> **Activity 7.5**
>
> 1 What is a deliverable?
>
> 2 What is the specification from the scope stage?
>
> 3 Why should you interview the customer?

Resource requirements

Once the objectives, scope and evaluation criteria for the project have been agreed between the client and the project manager, the resources required for the project will need to be assessed. The project manager will need to identify the resources required to complete each deliverable. Resources will often be based on:

* **Equipment** – the project manager will need to identify what specialist equipment is required for the project. Hardware may need to be hired to complete a particular task, and the amount of time required for this should be identified at an early stage as this will have an implication for the budget
* **Expertise** – similarly, the project manager will need to identify any tasks within the project that requires expertise beyond the project team. Again, the project manager will need to assess the amount of time required for this kind of a task so the cost of hiring a specialist can be accounted for in the budget
* **People** – sometimes a project may not need a great deal of specialist equipment or expertise, but it may need a lot of **man-hours**. In this case, the timescale of the project may be shortened by increasing the size of the project team. However, this also carries a consequence for the budget, and the client should state whether time or money is their priority

> **Summary**
>
> * Requirements and objectives should be kept in business terms and should be agreed with the client.
> * A business case should present the benefits of the project and the anticipated costs.

Timescale and risk

The timescale of a project is often one of the most important variables. It will often be dictated by the client's needs, but the complexity of the project will always need to be taken into account.

Timescales

At a basic level, the timescale of a project can be measured by its start date and its completion date. However, project managers will need to consider the time required for each step of a project, which will need to work within the overall timescale.

Start dates

A schedule should be created before work on the project starts. This means that it is broken down into manageable tasks in a logical order. It may be possible to begin a project immediately, but more often than not, preparation will need to be completed before work can begin. For example, the project manager will need to make sure that the required resources are in place for the project to start – equipment may need to be hired or bought, experts may need to be hired, etc.

Some project teams cannot start work until something outside their control has happened. This is called an external critical dependency. For example, work on the facilities for the Olympics in 2012 could not be started until London had been formally confirmed as the host – but plans would have been drawn up prior to the announcement as part of the bid.

Deadlines

All projects should have a target end date – even if it's not critical. The end date of a project will often be set by the client, and may be incorporated into their acceptance criteria. Some deadlines are fundamental to the success of the project (for example, the facilities for the 2012 Olympics need to be completed in time for the games).

The project manager will need to work out how the schedule can meet the project deadline. If the project timescale is short, but the project requires a lot of work, the project manager may look at increasing the number of people working on tasks so they can be completed quicker.

However, if the end date is unmanageable, the project manager may need to negotiate a revised date with the client. The client should be aware of the priorities of the project – identified through the project's objectives – and so will be able to decide whether timeliness, cost or quality is most important.

Actual dates

Project managers need to update their schedules on a regular basis to monitor progress against plan. This helps to identify where tasks have taken longer than expected, and where tasks have taken less time than planned to try to catch up.

This approach can help you develop other project plans. For example,

RISKY BUSINESS!

Project managers have to identify risks and resolve issues. What do you think the differences are between risks and issues? Can you think of any examples of risks or issues for your project?

if you're planning to do something similar again, you can make better estimates of the time required for each stage. It may also highlight if there are consistent problems with a supplier that cause delays in the schedule.

Risk

At the outset of a project, the project team should identify the **risks** to a schedule or project plan, and identify ways to minimise these. Once a risk becomes a reality, it becomes an **issue** for the project and needs to be dealt with.

If a risk has been identified early in the project, a contingency plan should have been identified to minimise the effect if it became an issue.

However, it is not always possible – or practical – to predict all risks that could affect a project. For example, during filming for *Gladiator* (2000), Oliver Reed died of a heart attack. This was a risk that had not been identified, and quickly became an issue. To resolve the issue, the production company spent an estimated $3.2 million creating a digital body double for Reed in order to finish his part in the film.

Risk
Something that could happen that would have an effect on the project. For example, falling house prices could be a risk for a builder. This would remain a risk until it happened.

Issue
Something that directly affects the project (often in terms of schedule or budget, but sometimes in terms of quality). For example, a builder would be affected by falling house prices and would need to save money or time in building a new house in order to keep the project on track.

Case Study: Laying cable

It's a gloriously warm July and Sonic's Supafast Broadband is coming to Skegness. They offer an exceptionally wide bandwidth for a very reasonable price. However, before they can start selling broadband packages to their eager customers, they need to install extra thick fibre optic cables through the sewer network.

Skegness Council have contracted local plumbers Mario and Luigi to undertake necessary maintenance of the aging sewerage system. The sewers are prone to flooding, and the plumbers have been asked to try to resolve the problem. Work on the sewers must be completed before Sonic's engineers can install the cables.

Skegness Council have asked Mario and Luigi to complete their work by the end of January. This would mean that the sewer network would be ready for the annual peak of rainfall in March or April, when the town suffers most from flooding. This would leave Sonic and their team roughly a month – February – to install the majority of the fibre optic cable and start testing the system. Sonic aims to connect their first customers in March.

1. What is the timescale for Sonic and their team to install the cable?
2. Sonic can't start work on the installation until the maintenance work in the sewer is completed. What tasks can be – or need to be – completed before work can start in February?
3. What risks can you identify in this case study?
4. What steps would you recommend Sonic takes to try to reduce the chances of the risks becoming issues?

The importance of planning

A good project manager should make sure that a project is planned in great detail before work starts. It can be easy to dismiss risks, assuming you will deal with them when they happen. However, identifying the main risks to a project can save you time if they become issues and you have a contingency plan. In fact, it may be possible to completely avoid some risks once they are identified.

Summary

* Timescales are decided by when the project should start, and when the project should be completed by.
* Risks are problems that haven't happened yet!
* Issues are problems that need to be dealt with.

Planning a project

Turning objectives into deliverables can be a long process that involves many different skilled people. The project manager is responsible for pulling the project together at this stage and making sure everyone knows what they are doing and by when.

Tasks and subtasks

The planning stage of a project should identify what tasks have to be completed, who will undertake each task, when each task should be completed and which tasks are dependent on which other tasks. Once these are all identified, the **critical path** can be drawn.

Start date and end date

In order to plan a project, you need to know when work on the project should start and by when the project should be completed. Some projects may not have a critical end date (e.g. time isn't a critical issue for the client), whereas for others the delivery date will be unmoveable (e.g. facilities for the 2012 Olympics). You also need to consider whether work on the project can start immediately, or will you need to plan each step in detail before work can start?

Tasks to be completed

Each objective (or deliverable) from the project specification may consist of a number of smaller tasks. For example, if the deliverable was a cup of tea, the tasks could be broken down into boil water, put tea bag in mug, pour water into mug, add milk, and remove tea bag.

Who will undertake each task?

At this point the project manager will need to identify tasks that need specialist skills. For example, a network engineer will be required to install a network and a programmer will be required to code an application.

When should each task be completed?

Project managers often measure tasks in man-hours. For example, one person could not complete a task that represented 24 man-hours in one day. With an eight-hour day, four people in one day or one person in four days may complete it. Remember, deadlines should be realistic!

Dependent tasks

Once tasks have been broken down and the timescales of each task have been estimated, **dependent** and **independent tasks** should be identified.

Dependent tasks fall into **chronological** order. Independent tasks can start and finish at the same time as other non-related tasks in the project.

CHICKEN AND EGG

Some tasks can be dealt with independently of each other; others cannot be started until a previous task has been completed. In small groups, create a list of tasks involved in creating this book. Start with writing and end with printing, and put them in the order you expect.

Critical path

The sequence of tasks in a project, taking into account dependencies and durations, that results in the shortest overall project time. Any delay of an activity on the critical path will result in extending the schedule.

Dependent task

A task that depends on the completion of a previous task before it can be started.

Independent task

A task that does not rely on the completion of a previous stage of a project before it can be started.

Chronological

Listed by date or by time, for example a student revision plan which had Monday – Revise Unit 1; Tuesday – Revise Unit 2; Wednesday – Revise Unit 3.

Milestones and interim reviews

The tasks and subtasks of a project can be small and difficult to monitor. In order to successfully and meaningfully track the progress of a project, you need to identify the milestone stages of the schedule. For example, where a sequence of small tasks is allocated to a network engineer in an IT project, it may be more helpful to identify the engineer's last task as a milestone.

Many projects will use a number of interim reviews to assess the quality of the project. This is different from the schedule and budget, which can be easily measured in terms of time or money. In order to assess the project at different stages of its production, evaluation criteria will need to be used. For many IT projects, a prototype stage is built into the schedule.

For example, a video game developer may produce a sample level for play testing or client review. This means that problems can be identified early on and resolved while they are still small scale, saving both time and money.

Evaluation

Following completion, an evaluation phase may follow:

* handover – the customer now 'owns' the product and has responsibility for the use of it. Any supporting (functional or technical) documentation should be handed over with the product. There may be a payment at this point

* final review – the stakeholders, including the customer, review how well the project went and decide on what remains to be done to complete the project

* acceptance tests – although technical tests will have been run in the development stage, the customer must test that the project works in a way that fits their business. After they are happy with the acceptance tests, the customer will start to use the product

> **Personal, Learning and Thinking Skills**
>
> You can demonstrate your independent enquiry skills by identifying the key tasks involved in a particular project and defining the resources required to achieve them.

Activity 7.6

1 What happens at a final review?

2 What are man-hours?

3 Why is it important to have interim reviews?

Summary

* The design stage turns the specification into a detailed project plan.
* Development may involve many different skilled individuals working on different tasks at the same time.
* Implementation is the customer using this IT solution to meet their needs.

Critical paths

Critical path methods identify the shortest time to complete a project, showing which tasks are on the critical path. This lets you, as project manager, set priorities for these tasks to make the project more likely to finish on time.

Critical path analysis (CPA) works on the principle that some tasks cannot start until previous tasks are finished. For example, you cannot test a program until after you have coded it. You must complete these dependent or sequential tasks in a sequence. Often, tasks are not dependent on other tasks starting or finishing. You can do these in parallel (that is, at the same time).

Consider this series of tasks for a computer system.

1 Specify and design system
2 Code program 1
3 Test program 1
4 Code program 2
5 Test program 2
6 Test and implement system

The project manager works out the dependencies and timescales as shown in the diagram. From this you can see that tasks 1, 2, 3 and 6 are on the critical path, with a minimum time of 21 days.

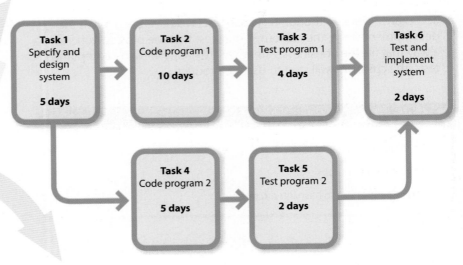

A critical path analysis will show which tasks are dependent on which other tasks, and which tasks can be run in parallel

Many large projects have much more complex dependencies, so it can be a very time-consuming task to recalculate the critical path if any key dates change. A number of software applications are available that will create critical paths and recalculate dates based on dependencies to save the project manager's time.

Activity 7.7

A critical path analysis should highlight the important tasks and dates in a project that must take priority. You can see from the critical path diagram that task 5 is dependent on task 4, but is separate from tasks 1, 2 and 3 and so can run alongside these. However, what happens if one of the tasks takes longer than expected?

1 If coding program 1 takes 12 days rather than the expected 10 days, what is the effect on the critical path?

2 If all tasks take are completed in the expected amount of time, except coding program 2 takes six days rather than five, will the project be completed any sooner than planned?

3 If all tasks are completed in the expected amount of time, except coding program 1 takes eight days rather than 10 days, will the project be completed any sooner than planned?

4 What is the effect on the project timescale if program 1 turns out to be much simpler than expected and takes three days to code and one day to test?

Contingency

It's a fact of life in the project management community that the more complex the project, the lower the chance of everything going exactly as planned. This means that it's essential to build in contingency in case something unexpected happens.

It is important to build contingency into a project's budget. This should be money that you don't plan to spend, but that could be spent without jeopardising the project. If something goes wrong and a stage of the project needs to be repeated, or the cost of hardware rises, contingency should mean that you can complete the work within the agreed budget.

Contingency should also be built into the schedule. This means that any staff absences, power failures or late delivery of essential equipment can be absorbed by the schedule without affecting the agreed deadline.

Activity 7.8

1 How might software help you in project management?

2 Why might you not always want to use the critical path for a project?

Summary

* The critical path defines the fastest way to complete a project.
* You may not always want the critical path: you might want to complete at lowest cost, limited resources or least risk.

7.3 Managing a successful project

Managing a project involves being aware of a number of shifting priorities while making sure that you never lose track of the overall objective. Being organised, efficient and communicating clearly and effectively are all essential traits of successful project managers.

Management

The project manager role requires specific tasks to be completed.

Track progress against plan

A schedule will have been drawn up at the planning stage of the project, listing all the tasks that need to be completed, and what length of time is allocated to each task. The project manager will record the actual date of completion for each task, so any slippage in the schedule can be quickly identified and plans can be put in place to regain time.

Regular meetings are used to track progress with the project team, and to inform of any changes to plan. Regular monitoring of progress can identify any risks to the schedule, and may mean that they can be resolved within the meeting.

Carry out interim reviews

Interim reviews will be planned into the schedule. If the project is to be completed for an external customer, the project manager will **facilitate** the review process.

A review should focus on the customer's acceptance criteria, which will have been established at the outset of the project. This will confirm that the project is on track to delivery on the customer's expectations. However, if any problems are identified as part of this review, they can be resolved at an early stage.

Outcomes of the interim reviews should be recorded. This helps to minute the action points for both the client and the project team, but also formalises the process.

Identify risk and take appropriate action

Many project managers keep logs of risks and issues for each project they are working on. This helps monitor any ongoing issues, record any risks and any contingency plans to minimise or avoid the risk becoming an issue. In small project teams, the project manager may be able to identify and resolve most, or all, of the risks. However, in a large team or a complex project, the project manager will rely on the project team to keep them informed of all risks and all possible alternatives.

If a risk becomes an issue, the project manager need to make sure that appropriate action is taken. For example, if a key supplier suddenly stops trading, the project manager will need to make sure that an alternative supplier is lined up as quickly as possible.

LEFT HAND, MEET RIGHT HAND...

You will need good communication and negotiation skills to be a great project manager – how else are you going to get your team to agree to meet dates, and explain any issues to your customer? Many project teams meet on a weekly or fortnightly basis. Why do you think they need to meet so regularly, if they all know what they're doing?

Facilitate
To help, often without actually being the most important part of the event.

Adjust the project plan as necessary

As well as tracking the progress of the project against plan, the project manager will need to adjust the plan to make up any lost time.

Sometimes a project plan will be too simple and it will become evident that additional tasks need to be included. This may involve an unavoidable extending of the project timescale.

Any changes that affect the end date of a project must be negotiated with the client. After all, it's their money that's funding the project…

Communicate progress and changes

The project manager will be the main point of contact for the client – in fact, some clients will only ever see the project manager. A key part of the role involves communicating progress to the customer on a regular basis.

Any changes in the schedule that affect the client need to be communicated as soon as possible. Depending on the client's success criteria, they may be willing to extend the project deadline to meet the budget. However, for some projects they will be willing to increase the budget in order to meet the original deadline.

The project manager should also communicate any changes in the project plan to the team. This may be through the regular project meetings, or – if requiring urgent action – outside of the meeting.

Summary

* The project manager should monitor progress at all stages and communicate any changes to the plan with the customer and the project team.
* Risks and issues need to be monitored and contingency plans should be put in place as early as possible.

Project management software

Project managers now use powerful project management software to track schedules, set out dependencies and analyse critical paths. In many cases, this software can also check resource allocations and budgets. On large and complex projects, the project plans may be shared on networks so different parts of the team can update them, allowing the project manager to more easily track progress.

Software tools

There are several types of software that you can use to help manage and plan your project. These include:

* specialist project management software – these are the most powerful aid, but they may be too complex for simple projects. They can present projects in a variety of views and will automatically update schedules. Microsoft Project is probably one of the most commonly used project management programs

* spreadsheets – These can be used to present schedules in limited graphical detail and can update date dependencies using formulas. They may be suitable for smaller projects but are too inflexible to use for more complex projects

* word processors – all dates and details will need to be updated manually, but schedules can be presented more graphically than by using spreadsheets. They are suitable only for simple projects without many task dependencies

Project charts

Project schedules are easiest to understand when they are presented graphically – it's the best way to show the dependencies in a project, the timescale and who is involved in each task. The two most common presentation styles are:

* Gantt charts – these present each task as a bar between a start date and an end date. Dependencies are shown by linking the end of one task with the start of the next. These can also include information about who is doing the task and what the task involves. More complex Gantt charts can also include information about how much of each task is completed

* logic networks – also known as project network diagram or PERT (Programme Evaluation and Review Technique) charts. This groups all the logical relationships in a project (so highlights all the dependencies and interdependencies) and presents them in a chronological sequence. This technique can also capture pessimistic, optimistic and most likely timescales for each task

PROS AND CONS

Before project management software became available, project managers had to manually record any changes in dates and update any dependent tasks. What are the advantages of manually altering dates? What are the advantages of a program that will alter dates for you?

For Your Project

You will need to produce a project plan for your project. This should help you track your progress and will help you meet your deadline.

Project management software helps you to manage the administration, planning and scheduling of your project. You can often use the software-charting facilities this software includes to produce graphical versions of your plans.

Project management software allows you to do the following:

* create a task
* store information about a task. This may include who will do it, how long it will take, how it is to be done and how it depends on other tasks
* update task information as your project changes
* generate plans based on the tasks
* publish charts and reports to help you manage the project and to present information to the stakeholders

Functional Skills – ICT

By producing a project plan you can show how you gather, develop and format information to suit its meaning and purpose.

Activity 7.9

1 Write a report on different ways IT can help a project manager plan and manage a project. Include the advantages and disadvantages of each, giving an example of an IT project suited to each type.

2 What are the two most common project charts?

3 List five features of project management software.

Summary

* Use the most appropriate available software for the size and complexity of your project.
* Presenting complex information in a chart can make it much easier to understand.

Schedule charts

Charts are visual methods of presenting complex information. By displaying project information in a chart it is easy to show where dependencies lie and how the project is progressing.

Gantt charts

A Gantt chart presents information as bars and allows the project manager to highlight dependencies and to add information to each task. The chart below shows the dependencies of the tasks within a project.

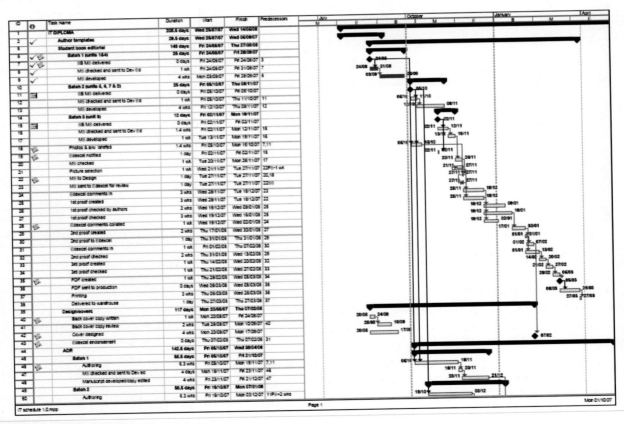

A Gantt chart can show all the dependencies and dates in a project

Gantt charts are:

* good for everyday project management – it is easy to see where dependencies lie and how long each task should take

* sometimes confusing if the project involves a lot of small tasks

Logic networks

Logic networks (PERT charts) include more information in a graphic form than Gantt charts, but tend to be larger and more difficult to use on a day-to-day basis. A logic network would be useful at the start of a project in order to clearly highlight all the dependencies in a project and to show the critical path. A logic network for the same project is shown below.

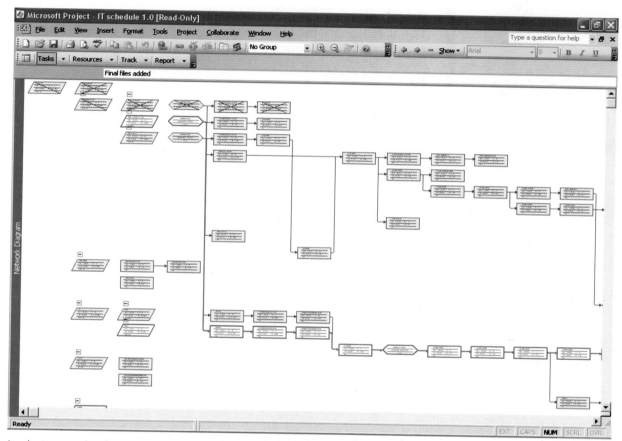

In a logic network, information about each task is included in each box; the critical path is highlighted in red

Logic networks charts are:

* good for starting a project – tasks are clearly broken down, dependencies are clear and a critical path highlights the most important tasks

* not so useful on a day-to-day basis – they don't give so much visual information about the timescale of each task and can be much larger than a Gantt chart

Summary

* Gantt charts are excellent tools for day-to-day project management.
* Logic networks are more useful for project initiation and early planning.
* Logic networks are sometimes referred to as PERT charts or project network diagrams.

7.4 Carry out an end-of-project review

At the end of a project, it is important to complete an end-of-project review process. This is a chance for the client to review the product to make sure that it meets their acceptance criteria. It is also a chance for the whole project team to identify what went well, and what could be improved.

Original objectives

At the start of the project, a number of criteria should have been identified and agreed on between the stakeholders. These will identify the deliverables and the objectives of the project. The obvious measure of how successful, or otherwise, the project has been will be whether the customer is happy with the outcome.

Projects are often judged on the following criteria:

* **Deliverables** – these will have been set out in the project specification (part of the scoping stage). If the client asked the project manager to deliver a network of PCs, printers and install the necessary software, the client will check that PCs, printers and software are in place as requested.

* **Schedule** – the client will often need the deliverables within a certain timescale; again, this will have been specified at the outset of the project. The schedule will have been kept and updated by the project manager, recording the dates at which milestones were reached. This should prove that the dates set out originally were met, but if not, it should identify where and why dates have not been met.

* **Budget** – the budget of the project will have been set based on the original specification. Any changes in the budget as a result of a changing project specification should have been agreed with the client.

* **Quality** – this is often the most difficult aspect of a project to review effectively. Quality can depend greatly on the purpose of the project, and the individuals reviewing it. If necessary, quality criteria should have been identified and agreed on as part of the acceptance criteria.

Views of others

It may be beneficial to seek the views of others to review a project outcome. Many IT projects will rely on extensive user testing before they are released to the public, or to customers. Users may consist of an existing user group (for example, in a company updating its systems the users will be the company employees) or of a likely customer base (for example, casual gamers who might be interested in a video game being developed).

Feedback from others can be gathered in a number of ways:

* **Focus group** – allow the users to test the system (or a prototype of the system) and then encourage them to discuss their experiences. For a focus group to be successful, it needs to be mediated by a neutral person with a number of open questions. Focus groups can be very successful because they establish a majority view, but they do depend on the mix of personality types.

* **Questionnaire** – allow the users to test the system (or a prototype of the system) and then provide them with a questionnaire to complete. Where you are testing with an existing set of users, this can be very successful as you can ensure a good return rate of completed questionnaires. However, if you are relying on a potential user group, the return rate may be much lower. When creating a questionnaire, you need to think carefully about the type of questions you are using – are they **open** or are they **closed**? Are your questions leading your user towards the 'right' answer, or are they neutral?

* **Feedback form** – many websites, or web-based services, will go through an extensive beta phase involving open user testing. This works well when there is likely to be a lot of interest in the website or service in question, but can have poor results if it's not well publicised. For example, both Microsoft and Google make extensive use of beta testing because they have an established customer base, and their users are likely to be interested in future developments.

When seeking the views of others, it is important to remember what you want their views on. For example, if your client has specified that the colour theme of their website needs to be red and burgundy, but that they want the navigation to be user friendly, you won't want to lead your users into discussing the colour scheme.

Closed question

A question that provides a user with a fixed number of answers. At its most basic, this will be 'yes' or 'no', but could be any other multiple choice format. Think about whether you want users to tick one box, or possibly more than one.

Open questions

A question that allows the user to provide an unspecified answer. In a questionnaire, this will involve leaving space for the user to write their answer, and in a focus group this will involve prompting users to explore their experiences.

Summary

* A project is only as successful as the acceptance criteria it meets.
* The success of a project should be defined by more than just your opinion. User testing can help check that the project really does meet the project brief.

Lessons learnt

Checking the outcomes of a project against the client's success criteria is only one measure of a project's success. Project teams will often work on many similar projects and while it's important that they meet the client's brief, it's equally important that they learn from previous mistakes and put their experience to good use.

End-of-project review

At the end of a project, the project team will gather to discuss how things went – in some cases, the customer will also be present to give their view of what it was like to work with the project team. The review should be an open forum for discussing opinions – it's not about attributing blame – and the outcomes should be positive and constructive. The meeting should consider the successful, or otherwise, factors for the project.

Factors that contributed to success or failure

It's important to remember the factors that contributed to the success of a project as these are often the things you will want to do again.

If a project hasn't been successful it doesn't mean that all elements of the project have been a failure. There may be certain aspects that worked very well, but which were ultimately overshadowed by the less successful aspects.

Some of the most important lessons to be learnt from a project concern what doesn't work and, most importantly, why. Even if a project has been a resounding success and the client is satisfied, there are still likely to be areas for improvement. Sometimes the success of a project can hide a variety of failures that it is helpful to identify in order to improve the efficiency of the project team next time round.

Identifying factors

When thinking about factors that contributed to the success or failure of a project, it is helpful to categorise them. Some suggested categories are:

* **Planning** – how accurate and helpful was the planning stage? If the project was well planned and problems were identified and resolved before they arose, what made the planning so successful? If the planning didn't go so well – perhaps the schedule wasn't achievable, or risks weren't identified until they became issues – what could be done to improve it?

* **Process** – how well did the project process work? Was the breakdown of tasks accurate and logical, or should extra stages have been included in the schedule? Were they any tasks that could have been completed at the same time to reduce the schedule? If you had to do this project again, would you do it in the same way?

* **Team** – how well did the team work together? Was there enough communication between the team and the different stakeholders? How effectively were the actions and decisions of meetings minuted

and communicated? If you had to change anything, what would it be? Or pick something that you would do again, what would it be?

* **Budget –** how accurate was the initial budget? Did anything cost more or less than anticipated? Was there sufficient contingency to deal with any changes in the project plan? How well was the budget managed, and how could it be managed better?

* **Timescale –** how accurate was the timescale? How did the actual time for specific tasks compare with the time taken for those tasks? Is there any way that time could have been better planned or allocated?

* **Quality –** what quality tests were built into the project schedule and did they fulfil the project needs? What interim review stages produced the most useful results, and where would you put the review stages next time? How were the quality reviews monitored, recorded and acted on? What could be done more effectively?

Lessons learnt

The project manager should record a list of lessons learnt following the end-of-project review. This will consist of a list of suggestions and recommendations based on the project team's experiences. The lessons learnt will help the project team – or their colleagues – avoid repeating the same mistakes, and will identify good practice that should be repeated.

It is important to remember that lessons learnt should be positive and constructive – this isn't a witch hunt! Comments should be kept **objective** and should focus on evaluating why something worked well, or why something didn't work well.

> **Objective**
> To state something without personal opinion.

> ### Summary
>
> * It's important to assess the success of a project team to identify how things can be improved next time.
> * Remember that comments should be objective – this will help everyone learn from their experiences.

Preparation for assessment

In this unit you will learn how to manage projects. You should explore the factors that influenced the success of a project, and the reasons for failure of a different project. This information should inform the way you plan, manage and evaluate your own small-scale technology-based project.

How you will be assessed

This unit is assessed internally. You will need to collect your evidence in a portfolio. You will be assessed through:

* an investigation of two different IT projects – one that was successful and one that was not
* planning a project proposal for a small-scale IT project, producing a project plan, executing your project plan and completing an end-of-project review.

Your small-scale IT project should be suitable for completion by a single person – i.e. you – within the allotted time. Your project could be anything from installing a small network of computers, developing a website, or a multimedia product.

Assessment tips

When planning a project, or assessing the success of a project, you should always consider what factors define the project's success. For example, the success criteria for a client's network installation may include:

* providing access to the Internet
* sharing a single printer
* providing effective back-up of information
* including a firewall for security

However, if a network installation covers all these within the set budget, but is late on delivery, does this mean that the project was a failure?

When planning and managing a project, remember that things will change. Some tasks will take longer than others, and there will always be some unexpected problems that need to be resolved. Keep a log of all the changes to the project plan so you can evaluate how effectively you responded to change in your end-of-project review.

Useful links

You may find some useful project management information on Spottydog's Project Management Website (www.spottydog-u.net).

You must show that you can:	Guidance	To gain higher marks you must:
7.1 Explain why one IT project was successful, and why another IT project was unsuccessful.	* Think about why the project was successful/unsuccessful * What could have been done to make the project more successful? * How did individual factors contribute to the success of the project?	Explain why following your suggestions would have made the project successful. You should aim to evaluate at least **three** success/failure factors, and tips for encouraging/avoiding these.
7.2 How to produce a clear project proposal and can produce a workable project plan.	* Think about how practical your project plan is – this is something you need to complete within a limited time, so make sure it's manageable. * What milestones can you put into your project plan?	Produce a realistic project plan with clearly identified milestones and review points. To gain higher marks, you should work independently and apply your knowledge of key success factors.
7.3 Use your project plan to track the progress of your project and carry out at least one interim review.	* How can you use the review process to monitor progress? * How can you use the review process to identify risks?	Make regular use of your project plan, updating and reviewing it as necessary and communicate progress through at least three interim reviews.
7.4 Consider the extent to which you have achieved your project objectives and indicate at least one factor that contributed to the outcome.	* Why not ask others to assess whether they think your project meets the project outcomes? * How did you apply your knowledge of key success factors in executing your project?	Reflect on the views of others within your detailed review of your project, and you must draw realistic conclusions.

The Project

As part of your full Higher Diploma course, you will complete a separate Project qualification at Level 2. In this section, we will take a brief look at what you need to do in order to achieve the Project qualification, and how to choose and plan an appropriate project.

Choosing an appropriate project

When choosing a project, you must make sure that it satisfies one or more of the following criteria.

* The Project should support progression in the subject area of the Principal Learning. For example, a learner wanting to progress in the IT sector could complete a project relating to IT in order to satisfy this criterion.

* If, however, the learner wanted to change direction with their studies and pursue a different career, then the project should support progression into this sector. For example, if a learner wanted to progress into a science subject, they could complete a project relating to the sciences in order to satisfy this criterion.

The project must also result in an outcome, and, if necessary, be supported by evidence. The different types of outcome your project could produce are as follows.

* **Written**

  Your project could be investigative, in which case your project outcome could be a report. For example, if you wanted to produce recommendations for a local business as to whether they should start an e-commerce website, you would probably present your findings in a written document.

* **Ephemeral**

  This means something that takes place at a specific place and time, like a presentation. For example, if producing recommendations for a local business, you may want to present your findings rather than produce a report. In this case you should record your presentation and try to include witness statements, you should also keep any slides you produce as part of your portfolio.

* **Artefact**

  Your project may result in a tangible outcome, for example a networked computer system, a website, a multimedia product, etc. You must keep records of your development and research for this kind of project in order to show the processes you went through in order to produce the outcome.

Learning outcomes

The Project at Level 2 is split into four learning outcomes, each representing a percentage of the marks. You will need to keep records throughout your project – meeting minutes, progress reports, etc. – to keep track of your progress.

<aside>
DID YOU KNOW?

Although you will need to work on a project outcome on your own, you can work on a project as part of a group. This means that you can have group, or overall, outcomes (for example, producing a website) but you must have individual outcomes within the group (for example, producing a specific section of the website).
</aside>

Be able to choose, plan and manage a project

Learning outcome 1

20% weighting for final grade.

You should choose an appropriate topic for your project, either individually or as part of a group. Once the topic has been selected, you should identify a question, task or brief and an intended format for the project outcome. Remember that if you are working as a group, each individual *must* have an outcome that they will produce themselves.

Your project should either complement and develop the themes of the Principal Learning of the Diploma, or support progression into a different subject area. You must also make sure that your project has the potential to meet all the assessment objectives. Your project title should be agreed and accepted with your tutor.

It is acceptable to choose a working title – a title that is adapted as the project progresses – but only if your tutor agrees the changes to the title. If you use a working title, you should keep a record of the reasons for this. If your project title changes completely, you will have to start the project again from the beginning.

Assessment: Learning outcome 1

For the assessment of this learning outcome, you must be able to:

* describe why you have chosen the project, and the skills and knowledge you want to improve through the project
* identify objectives for the project
* plan activities and agree deadlines against the project
* identify possible risks and how to overcome them
* keep records of activities undertaken using the original project plan

To gain higher marks, you should:

* work mainly independently
* produce a detailed and clear rationale for choosing the project
* describe a range of skills and/or knowledge you hope to improve
* list all the key activities in an appropriate order and give realistic times required for each of the activities
* describe and justify the key resources required
* identify realistic potential problems and assess how serious these would be; your solutions for these problems should be plausible and convincing

Be able to research information and apply it to a project

Learning outcome 2

20% weighting for final grade.

Your research may have begun at the same time as work was being carried out on learning outcome 1. In fact, your research may carry on throughout the duration of your project. Your research must be more than just obtaining information; you should choose and locate sources for yourself and shouldn't rely too much on your tutor to point you in the right direction.

You should use at least three sources of information, and these must represent different types of information. So, for example, you can't just use three different websites. You may achieve higher marks by using primary sources (e.g. interviewing people); for example, if you are creating an e-commerce website, you could interview potential customers to find out what they like or dislike about other websites.

You must keep records of your sources. If you find information on the Internet, remember to take a note of the URL. If you find information in a publication, take a note of the publisher, the author, the location and the year of publication. If your information comes from interviews or conversations, keep a record of who the conversation was with, summarise the process used to get the information and explain the relevance of the information to the project.

You should also assess how reliable your sources are. For example, information from a personal blog will not necessarily be representative of anyone other than the writer of the blog.

Assessment: Learning outcome 2

For the assessment of this learning outcome, you must be able to:

* research information from a range of sources and different types of sources
* evaluate the reliability of your sources
* keep records of the relevant information obtained

To gain higher marks, you should:

* use information from both secondary (i.e. the Internet and publications) and primary (i.e. interviews, questionnaires, etc.) research where appropriate
* provide an accurate and consistent reference for your sources – this could be a bibliography for websites and publications used, or a detailed description of what you did and where and when you did it
* evaluate the relevance of each source and show a clear awareness of the reliability of your source

Be able to select and apply skills to complete a project

Learning outcome 3

40% weighting for final grade.

For this learning outcome, you should apply the information available to you and complete the objectives that you set in learning outcome 1. This will test your capacity to see a project through to completion. If you have been using a working title for your project, you should finalise the title with your tutor before starting this stage of your project.

Your project must result in some kind of outcome:

* **Ephemeral**

  You must be able to show the stages that you went through to arrive at your final outcome and show how your ideas have developed. For a presentation, you should produce evidence of the research and planning and show how the conclusion of your outcome has developed through the course of the project.

* **Artefact**

  You must show the stages that you have gone through to arrive at your final outcome – these could be sketches, prototypes, diagrams, etc. You should also show how your ideas have developed and how alternative designs have been considered. For example, you may have built a prototype website and tested it with some sample users; the feedback from this testing could have in uenced the final design of the website.

* **Written**

  You must explain what the project is about, what was done to achieve the outcome and give an explanation of your results or conclusion. You must make sure that your writing – and the structure of your writing – is coherent. Does it follow a logical order? Are there clear connections between the different parts of the text? Is the information clearly relevant to the project?

Make sure that you spell check any written work that you produce for your project, and make sure that the language used is appropriate for the report's audience.

Assessment: Learning outcome 3

For the assessment of this learning outcome, you must be able to:

* use a range of skills including appropriate technologies, working with others and problem solving in order to achieve the project's outcome

* demonstrate that you have met the project's objectives (e.g. complete a website, draw conclusions for a report, produce a summary and recommendations for a presentation, etc.)

* share the outcomes with your audience, as a product, a report, a presentation, etc.

To gain higher marks:

* For a written outcome, you must present information relevant to the project in a logical order (you should show evidence of redrafting). There must be few errors in the use of language, your communication must be clear, it must include all relevant features of effective presentation and an appropriate language style and register should be used consistently throughout.

* For an artefact, the outcome must be consistently successful (e.g. complete, rather than with some areas still needing the finishing touches). You must show evidence of careful and well thought out development of ideas and designs and show that alternative approaches have been considered and evaluated. The relevant features of effective presentation should be used consistently and the audience can understand without di culty what has been done well and why.

* For an ephemeral outcome, there should be evidence of thorough and effective preparation, and you should use any appropriate resources (e.g. PowerPoint, props, etc.) with a consistent level of success to realise the outcome. There should be supporting information to show how you developed your ideas and you should describe and evaluate alternative ideas. This information should make it consistently clear to the audience what was done and why.

Be able to review a project and own performance, and analyse the project outcomes

Learning outcome 4

20% weighting for final grade.

You should review the results of the project and your own performance through the course of the project. This can be communicated in writing, a display to your peers or an oral presentation in front of an audience. You should make sure that your review is logical in its ow, appropriate in its language and includes the following topics:

* a review of the project's outcome
* conclusions that you have drawn from the project
* an evaluation of which project objectives (as outlined in your project proposal) were/were not achieved and the reasons for success or lack of success
* what you have learned and the skills that you have used during the project
* how well you performed, which could include feedback from other people
* how you could improve your own learning and performance in the future
* where appropriate, you should include links to other areas of study and/or interest
* you should also consider how you will transfer the skills you learned and used in the project to other areas of your study

Your project outcome may give you scope to incorporate learning outcome 4 (especially if your outcome is written or a presentation). Otherwise, this learning outcome can be achieved as a separate piece of work.

Assessment: Learning outcome 4

For the assessment of this learning outcome, you must be able to:

* analyse results
* draw your own conclusions
* review the results of your project
* review your own performance throughout the project
* share the review and evaluation of your learning and performance

To gain higher marks, you should:

* structure your review clearly and consistently – you should analyse the results and draw your own detailed conclusions
* identify which objectives were not met and give convincing reasons for success (or lack of it) in each objective, describing the range of knowledge and skills involved
* describe in detail how well you performed, incorporating feedback from others and suggest clear and realistic plans for improving your learning
* describe links to other areas of study or interest and suggest clear and realistic ideas for how you would transfer your skills to these areas

Index